Dear reader,

thank you for your trust and for buying this book. I'm always greatly moved when I see someone with a desire to get closer to God, to accept Him as their Lord and Saviour and invite Him into their everyday life, to each and every part of it.

By studying His Word systematically, each and every day is a day we live with Him, we let Him illuminate the path of our lives.

I am glad that together we can walk this wonderful path. I ask each of you to pray for me, and I, for my part, promise to remember each and every one of you in my prayers.

Before every encounter with the Lord in His Word, let us pray to the Holy Spirit, may He guide us, for He is the true author of this Word and, at the same time, He knows us better than anyone else, better even than we know ourselves. May He speak directly to our hearts, our minds. May He enter with His Word into our lives, into all our affairs - the pleasant ones as well as the difficult ones

After praying to the Holy Spirit, let us read a given passage of the Scripture. Let's do this slowly, we may even repeat it several times. The Lord will speak to us sometimes through a whole passage, sometimes through a single sentence or word. Sometimes He speaks immediately, sometimes He speaks subtly, after a long time.

Let's write down what the Lord wants to say through the given passage. His Word will sustain us as we remember it throughout the day, act and live with it, with HIM.

May The Lord in Heaven bless you, dear reader. Amen.

# CONTENTS

## PRINCIPAL CELEBRATIONS OF THE LITURGICAL YEAR 2024

| | |
|---|---|
| First Sunday of Advent | December 3, 2023 |
| Ash Wednesday | February 14, 2024 |
| Easter Sunday | March 31, 2024 |
| The Ascension of the Lord [Thursday] | May 9, 2024 |
| Pentecost Sunday | May 19, 2024 |
| The Most Holy Body and Blood of Christ | June 2, 2024 |
| First Sunday of Advent | December 1, 2024 |

## CYCLES — LECTIONARY FOR MASS

| | | |
|---|---|---|
| Sunday Cycle | YEAR B | December 3, 2023 to November 24, 2024 |
| Weekday Cycle | CYCLE II | January 9 to February 13, 2024<br>May 20 to November 30, 2024 |
| Sunday Cycle | YEAR C | December 1, 2024 to November 23, 2025 |

**First Reading:** Amos 2: 6-10, 13-16

6 Yahweh says:
"For three transgressions of Israel, yes, for four,
I will not turn away its punishment,
because they have sold the righteous for silver,
and the needy for a pair of sandals;
7 They trample the heads of the poor into the dust of the earth
and deny justice to the oppressed.
A man and his father use the same maiden, to profane my holy name.
8 They lay themselves down beside every altar on clothes taken in pledge.
In the house of their God† they drink the wine of those who have been fined.
9 Yet I destroyed the Amorite before them,
whose height was like the height of the cedars,
and he was strong as the oaks;
yet I destroyed his fruit from above,
and his roots from beneath.
10 Also I brought you up out of the land of Egypt
and led you forty years in the wilderness,
to possess the land of the Amorite.
13 Behold,‡ I will crush you in your place,
as a cart crushes that is full of grain.
14 Flight will perish from the swift.
The strong won't strengthen his force.
The mighty won't deliver himself.
15 He who handles the bow won't stand.
He who is swift of foot won't escape.
He who rides the horse won't deliver himself.
16 He who is courageous among the mighty
will flee away naked on that day,"
says Yahweh.

**Responsorial Psalm:** Psalms 50: 16bc-23

16b "What right do you have to declare my statutes,
that you have taken my covenant on your lips,
17 since you hate instruction,
and throw my words behind you?
18 When you saw a thief, you consented with him,
and have participated with adulterers.
19 "You give your mouth to evil.
Your tongue frames deceit.
20 You sit and speak against your brother.
You slander your own mother's son.
21 You have done these things, and I kept silent.
You thought that I was just like you.
I will rebuke you, and accuse you in front of your eyes.
22 "Now consider this, you who forget God,
lest I tear you into pieces, and there be no one to deliver.
23 Whoever offers the sacrifice of thanksgiving glorifies me,
and prepares his way so that I will show God's salvation to him."

## Gospel: Matthew 8: 18-22

18 Now when Jesus saw great multitudes around him, he gave the order to depart to the other side.
19 A scribe came and said to him, "Teacher, I will follow you wherever you go."
20 Jesus said to him, "The foxes have holes and the birds of the sky have nests, but the Son of Man has nowhere to lay his head."
21 Another of his disciples said to him, "Lord, allow me first to go and bury my father."
22 But Jesus said to him, "Follow me, and leave the dead to bury their own dead."

1. Invite the Holy Spirit into this reading, asking the Author of Scripture to speak to you through His Word
2. Read today's passage as many times as you need, take your time
3. Write down (below) what the Lord is saying to you today
4. Live with this Word in your heart through the day

_____

_____

**First Reading:** Amos 3: 1-8; 4: 11-12

1 Hear this word that Yahweh has spoken against you, children of Israel, against the whole family which I brought up out of the land of Egypt, saying:
2 "I have only chosen you of all the families of the earth.
Therefore I will punish you for all of your sins."
3 Do two walk together,
unless they have agreed?
4 Will a lion roar in the thicket,
when he has no prey?
Does a young lion cry out of his den,
if he has caught nothing?
5 Can a bird fall in a trap on the earth,
where no snare is set for him?
Does a snare spring up from the ground,
when there is nothing to catch?
6 Does the trumpet alarm sound in a city,
without the people being afraid?
Does evil happen to a city,
and Yahweh hasn't done it?
7 Surely the Lord Yahweh will do nothing,
unless he reveals his secret to his servants the prophets.
8 The lion has roared.
Who will not fear?
The Lord Yahweh has spoken.
Who can but prophesy?
11 "I have overthrown some of you,
as when God overthrew Sodom and Gomorrah,
and you were like a burning stick plucked out of the fire;
yet you haven't returned to me," says Yahweh.
12 "Therefore I will do this to you, Israel;
because I will do this to you,
prepare to meet your God, Israel.

**Responsorial Psalm:** Psalms 5: 4b-8

4 For you are not a God who has pleasure in wickedness.
Evil can't live with you.
5 The arrogant will not stand in your sight.
You hate all workers of iniquity.
6 You will destroy those who speak lies.
Yahweh abhors the bloodthirsty and deceitful man.
7 But as for me, in the abundance of your loving kindness I will come into your house.
I will bow toward your holy temple in reverence of you.
8 Lead me, Yahweh, in your righteousness because of my enemies.
Make your way straight before my face.

**Gospel: Matthew 8: 23-27**

23 When he got into a boat, his disciples followed him. 24 Behold, a violent storm came up on the sea, so much that the boat was covered with the waves; but he was asleep. 25 The disciples came to him and woke him up, saying, "Save us, Lord! We are dying!"
26 He said to them, "Why are you fearful, O you of little faith?" Then he got up, rebuked the wind and the sea, and there was a great calm.
27 The men marveled, saying, "What kind of man is this, that even the wind and the sea obey him?"

1. Invite the Holy Spirit into this reading, asking the Author of Scripture to speak to you through His Word
2. Read today's passage as many times as you need, take your time
3. Write down (below) what the Lord is saying to you today
4. Live with this Word in your heart through the day

_____

_____

**Wednesday, July 3, 2024**
Saint Thomas, Apostle

**First Reading:** Ephesians 2: 19-22

19 So then you are no longer strangers and foreigners, but you are fellow citizens with the saints and of the household of God, 20 being built on the foundation of the apostles and prophets, Christ Jesus himself being the chief cornerstone; 21 in whom the whole building, fitted together, grows into a holy temple in the Lord; 22 in whom you also are built together for a habitation of God in the Spirit.

**Responsorial Psalm:** Psalms 117: 1bc, 2

1 Praise Yahweh, all you nations!
Extol him, all you peoples!
2 For his loving kindness is great toward us.
Yahweh's faithfulness endures forever.
Praise Yah!

**Gospel: John 20: 24-29**

24 But Thomas, one of the twelve, called Didymus,§ wasn't with them when Jesus came. 25 The other disciples therefore said to him, "We have seen the Lord!"
But he said to them, "Unless I see in his hands the print of the nails, put my finger into the print of the nails, and put my hand into his side, I will not believe."
26 After eight days, again his disciples were inside and Thomas was with them. Jesus came, the doors being locked, and stood in the middle, and said, "Peace be to you." 27 Then he said to Thomas, "Reach here your finger, and see my hands. Reach here your hand, and put it into my side. Don't be unbelieving, but believing."
28 Thomas answered him, "My Lord and my God!"
29 Jesus said to him, "Because you have seen me,† you have believed. Blessed are those who have not seen and have believed."

1. Invite the Holy Spirit into this reading, asking the Author of Scripture to speak to you through His Word
2. Read today's passage as many times as you need, take your time
3. Write down (below) what the Lord is saying to you today
4. Live with this Word in your heart through the day

_____

_____

**First Reading:** Amos 7: 10-17

10 Then Amaziah the priest of Bethel sent to Jeroboam king of Israel, saying, "Amos has conspired against you in the middle of the house of Israel. The land is not able to bear all his words. 11 For Amos says, 'Jeroboam will die by the sword, and Israel shall surely be led away captive out of his land.' "
12 Amaziah also said to Amos, "You seer, go, flee away into the land of Judah, and there eat bread, and prophesy there, 13 but don't prophesy again any more at Bethel; for it is the king's sanctuary, and it is a royal house!"
14 Then Amos answered Amaziah, "I was no prophet, neither was I a prophet's son, but I was a herdsman, and a farmer of sycamore figs; 15 and Yahweh took me from following the flock, and Yahweh said to me, 'Go, prophesy to my people Israel.' 16 Now therefore listen to Yahweh's word: 'You say, Don't prophesy against Israel, and don't preach against the house of Isaac.' 17 Therefore Yahweh says: 'Your wife shall be a prostitute in the city, and your sons and your daughters shall fall by the sword, and your land shall be divided by line; and you yourself shall die in a land that is unclean, and Israel shall surely be led away captive out of his land.' "

**Responsorial Psalm:** Psalms 19: 8- 11

8 Yahweh's precepts are right, rejoicing the heart.
Yahweh's commandment is pure, enlightening the eyes.
9 The fear of Yahweh is clean, enduring forever.
Yahweh's ordinances are true, and righteous altogether.
10 They are more to be desired than gold, yes, than much fine gold,
sweeter also than honey and the extract of the honeycomb.
11 Moreover your servant is warned by them.
In keeping them there is great reward.

**Gospel: Matthew 9: 1-8**

1 He entered into a boat and crossed over, and came into his own city. 2 Behold, they brought to him a man who was paralyzed, lying on a bed. Jesus, seeing their faith, said to the paralytic, "Son, cheer up! Your sins are forgiven you."

3 Behold, some of the scribes said to themselves, "This man blasphemes."
4 Jesus, knowing their thoughts, said, "Why do you think evil in your hearts? 5 For which is easier, to say, 'Your sins are forgiven;' or to say, 'Get up, and walk'? 6 But that you may know that the Son of Man has authority on earth to forgive sins—" (then he said to the paralytic), "Get up, and take up your mat, and go to your house."
7 He arose and departed to his house. 8 But when the multitudes saw it, they marveled and glorified God, who had given such authority to men.

1. Invite the Holy Spirit into this reading, asking the Author of Scripture to speak to you through His Word
2. Read today's passage as many times as you need, take your time
3. Write down (below) what the Lord is saying to you today
4. Live with this Word in your heart through the day

_____

_____


# Friday, July 5, 2024
Saint Anthony Zaccaria, Priest; USA: Saint Elizabeth of Portugal


**First Reading:** Amos 8: 4-6, 9-12

4 Hear this, you who desire to swallow up the needy,
and cause the poor of the land to fail,
5 saying, 'When will the new moon be gone, that we may sell grain?
And the Sabbath, that we may market wheat,
making the ephah† small, and the shekel‡ large,
and dealing falsely with balances of deceit;
6 that we may buy the poor for silver,
and the needy for a pair of sandals,
and sell the sweepings with the wheat?' "
9 It will happen in that day," says the Lord Yahweh,
"that I will cause the sun to go down at noon,
and I will darken the earth in the clear day.
10 I will turn your feasts into mourning,

and all your songs into lamentation;
and I will make you wear sackcloth on all your bodies,
and baldness on every head.
I will make it like the mourning for an only son,
and its end like a bitter day.
11 Behold, the days come," says the Lord Yahweh,
"that I will send a famine in the land,
not a famine of bread,
nor a thirst for water,
but of hearing Yahweh's words.
12 They will wander from sea to sea,
and from the north even to the east;
they will run back and forth to seek Yahweh's word,
and will not find it.

**Responsorial Psalm:** Psalms 119: 2, 10, 20, 30, 40, 131

2 Blessed are those who keep his statutes,
who seek him with their whole heart.
10 With my whole heart I have sought you.
Don't let me wander from your commandments.
20 My soul is consumed with longing for your ordinances at all times.
30 I have chosen the way of truth.
I have set your ordinances before me.
40 Behold, I long for your precepts!
Revive me in your righteousness.
131 I opened my mouth wide and panted,
for I longed for your commandments.

**Gospel: Matthew 9: 9-13**

9 As Jesus passed by from there, he saw a man called Matthew sitting at the tax collection office. He said to him, "Follow me." He got up and followed him. 10 As he sat in the house, behold, many tax collectors and sinners came and sat down with Jesus and his disciples. 11 When the Pharisees saw it, they said to his disciples, "Why does your teacher eat with tax collectors and sinners?"
12 When Jesus heard it, he said to them, "Those who are healthy have no need for a physician, but those who are sick do. 13  But you go and learn what this means: 'I desire

mercy, and not sacrifice,'* for I came not to call the righteous, but sinners to repentance."

1. Invite the Holy Spirit into this reading, asking the Author of Scripture to speak to you through His Word
2. Read today's passage as many times as you need, take your time
3. Write down (below) what the Lord is saying to you today
4. Live with this Word in your heart through the day

---

---

# Saturday, July 6, 2024
## Saint Maria Goretti, Virgin and Martyr; BVM

**First Reading:** Amos 9: 11-15

11 In that day I will raise up the tent of David who is fallen and close up its breaches, and I will raise up its ruins, and I will build it as in the days of old, 12 that they may possess the remnant of Edom and all the nations who are called by my name," says Yahweh who does this.
13 "Behold, the days come," says Yahweh,
"that the plowman shall overtake the reaper,
and the one treading grapes him who sows seed;
and sweet wine will drip from the mountains,
and flow from the hills.
14 I will bring my people Israel back from captivity,
and they will rebuild the ruined cities, and inhabit them;
and they will plant vineyards, and drink wine from them.
They shall also make gardens,
and eat their fruit.
15 I will plant them on their land,
and they will no more be plucked up out of their land which I have given them,"
says Yahweh your God.

**Responsorial Psalm:** Psalms 85: 9ab-13

9 Surely his salvation is near those who fear him,
that glory may dwell in our land.
10 Mercy and truth meet together.
Righteousness and peace have kissed each other.
11 Truth springs out of the earth.
Righteousness has looked down from heaven.
12 Yes, Yahweh will give that which is good.
Our land will yield its increase.
13 Righteousness goes before him,
and prepares the way for his steps.

**Gospel: Matthew 9: 14-17**

14 Then John's disciples came to him, saying, "Why do we and the Pharisees fast often, but your disciples don't fast?"
15 Jesus said to them, "Can the friends of the bridegroom mourn as long as the bridegroom is with them? But the days will come when the bridegroom will be taken away from them, and then they will fast. 16 No one puts a piece of unshrunk cloth on an old garment; for the patch would tear away from the garment, and a worse hole is made. 17 Neither do people put new wine into old wine skins, or else the skins would burst, and the wine be spilled, and the skins ruined. No, they put new wine into fresh wine skins, and both are preserved."

1. Invite the Holy Spirit into this reading, asking the Author of Scripture to speak to you through His Word
2. Read today's passage as many times as you need, take your time
3. Write down (below) what the Lord is saying to you today
4. Live with this Word in your heart through the day

_____

_____

**Sunday, July 7, 2024**
FOURTEENTH SUNDAY IN ORDINARY TIME

**First Reading:** Ezekiel 2: 2-5

2 The Spirit entered into me when he spoke to me, and set me on my feet; and I heard him who spoke to me.

3 He said to me, "Son of man, I send you to the children of Israel, to a nation of rebels who have rebelled against me. They and their fathers have transgressed against me even to this very day. 4 The children are impudent and stiff-hearted. I am sending you to them, and you shall tell them, 'This is what the Lord† Yahweh says.' 5 They, whether they will hear, or whether they will refuse—for they are a rebellious house—yet they will know that there has been a prophet among them.

**Responsorial Psalm:** Psalms 123: 1-4

1 I lift up my eyes to you,
you who sit in the heavens.
2 Behold, as the eyes of servants look to the hand of their master,
as the eyes of a maid to the hand of her mistress,
so our eyes look to Yahweh, our God,
until he has mercy on us.
3 Have mercy on us, Yahweh, have mercy on us,
for we have endured much contempt.
4 Our soul is exceedingly filled with the scoffing of those who are at ease,
with the contempt of the proud.

**Second Reading:** Second Corinthians 12: 7-10

7 By reason of the exceeding greatness of the revelations, that I should not be exalted excessively, a thorn in the flesh was given to me: a messenger of Satan to torment me, that I should not be exalted excessively. 8 Concerning this thing, I begged the Lord three times that it might depart from me. 9 He has said to me, "My grace is sufficient for you, for my power is made perfect in weakness." Most gladly therefore I will rather glory in my weaknesses, that the power of Christ may rest on me.

10 Therefore I take pleasure in weaknesses, in injuries, in necessities, in persecutions, and in distresses, for Christ's sake. For when I am weak, then am I strong.

**Gospel: Mark 6: 1-6**

1 He went out from there. He came into his own country, and his disciples followed him. 2 When the Sabbath had come, he began to teach in the synagogue, and many hearing him were astonished, saying, "Where did this man get these things?" and, "What is the wisdom that is given to this man, that such mighty works come about by his hands? 3 Isn't this the carpenter, the son of Mary and brother of James, Joses, Judah, and Simon? Aren't his sisters here with us?" So they were offended at him. 4 Jesus said to them, "A prophet is not without honor, except in his own country, and among his own relatives, and in his own house." 5 He could do no mighty work there, except that he laid his hands on a few sick people and healed them. 6 He marveled because of their unbelief.

1. Invite the Holy Spirit into this reading, asking the Author of Scripture to speak to you through His Word
2. Read today's passage as many times as you need, take your time
3. Write down (below) what the Lord is saying to you today
4. Live with this Word in your heart through the day

_____

_____

## Monday, July 8, 2024

**First Reading:** Hosea 2: 16-18, 21-22

16 It will be in that day," says Yahweh,
"that you will call me 'my husband,'
and no longer call me 'my master.'
17 For I will take away the names of the Baals out of her mouth,
and they will no longer be mentioned by name.
18 In that day I will make a covenant for them with the animals of the field,
and with the birds of the sky,
and with the creeping things of the ground.
I will break the bow, the sword, and the battle out of the land,
and will make them lie down safely.
21 It will happen in that day, that I will respond," says Yahweh.

"I will respond to the heavens,
and they will respond to the earth;
22 and the earth will respond to the grain, and the new wine, and the oil;
and they will respond to Jezreel.

**Responsorial Psalm:** Psalms 145: 2-9

2 Every day I will praise you.
I will extol your name forever and ever.
3 Great is Yahweh, and greatly to be praised!
His greatness is unsearchable.
4 One generation will commend your works to another,
and will declare your mighty acts.
5 I will meditate on the glorious majesty of your honor,
on your wondrous works.
6 Men will speak of the might of your awesome acts.
I will declare your greatness.
7 They will utter the memory of your great goodness,
and will sing of your righteousness.
8 Yahweh is gracious, merciful,
slow to anger, and of great loving kindness.
9 Yahweh is good to all.
His tender mercies are over all his works.

**Gospel: Matthew 9: 18-26**

18 While he told these things to them, behold, a ruler came and worshiped him, saying, "My daughter has just died, but come and lay your hand on her, and she will live."
19 Jesus got up and followed him, as did his disciples. 20 Behold, a woman who had a discharge of blood for twelve years came behind him, and touched the fringe‡ of his garment; 21 for she said within herself, "If I just touch his garment, I will be made well."
22 But Jesus, turning around and seeing her, said, "Daughter, cheer up! Your faith has made you well." And the woman was made well from that hour.
23 When Jesus came into the ruler's house and saw the flute players and the crowd in noisy disorder, 24 he said to them, "Make room, because the girl isn't dead, but sleeping."

They were ridiculing him. 25 But when the crowd was sent out, he entered in, took her by the hand, and the girl arose. 26 The report of this went out into all that land.

1. Invite the Holy Spirit into this reading, asking the Author of Scripture to speak to you through His Word
2. Read today's passage as many times as you need, take your time
3. Write down (below) what the Lord is saying to you today
4. Live with this Word in your heart through the day

_____

_____

## Tuesday, July 9, 2024
### Saint Augustine Zhao Rong, Priest, and Companions, Martyrs

**First Reading:** Hosea 8: 4-7, 11-13

4 They have set up kings, but not by me.
They have made princes, and I didn't approve.
Of their silver and their gold they have made themselves idols,
that they may be cut off.
5 Let Samaria throw out his calf idol!
My anger burns against them!
How long will it be until they are capable of purity?
6 For this is even from Israel!
The workman made it, and it is no God;
indeed, the calf of Samaria shall be broken in pieces.
7 For they sow the wind,
and they will reap the whirlwind.
He has no standing grain.
The stalk will yield no head.
If it does yield, strangers will swallow it up.
11 Because Ephraim has multiplied altars for sinning,
they became for him altars for sinning.
12 I wrote for him the many things of my law,

but they were regarded as a strange thing.
13 As for the sacrifices of my offerings,
they sacrifice meat and eat it,
but Yahweh doesn't accept them.
Now he will remember their iniquity,
and punish their sins.
They will return to Egypt.

**Responsorial Psalm:** Psalms 115: 3-10

3 But our God is in the heavens.
He does whatever he pleases.
4 Their idols are silver and gold,
the work of men's hands.
5 They have mouths, but they don't speak.
They have eyes, but they don't see.
6 They have ears, but they don't hear.
They have noses, but they don't smell.
7 They have hands, but they don't feel.
They have feet, but they don't walk,
neither do they speak through their throat.
8 Those who make them will be like them;
yes, everyone who trusts in them.
9 Israel, trust in Yahweh!
He is their help and their shield.
10 House of Aaron, trust in Yahweh!
He is their help and their shield.

**Gospel: Matthew 9: 32-38**

32 As they went out, behold, a mute man who was demon possessed was brought to him. 33 When the demon was cast out, the mute man spoke. The multitudes marveled, saying, "Nothing like this has ever been seen in Israel!"
34 But the Pharisees said, "By the prince of the demons, he casts out demons."
35 Jesus went about all the cities and the villages, teaching in their synagogues and preaching the Good News of the Kingdom, and healing every disease and every sickness among the people. 36 But when he saw the multitudes, he was moved with compassion for them because they were harassed§ and scattered, like sheep without a shepherd.

37 Then he said to his disciples, "The harvest indeed is plentiful, but the laborers are few. 38 Pray therefore that the Lord of the harvest will send out laborers into his harvest."

1. Invite the Holy Spirit into this reading, asking the Author of Scripture to speak to you through His Word
2. Read today's passage as many times as you need, take your time
3. Write down (below) what the Lord is saying to you today
4. Live with this Word in your heart through the day

_____

_____

## Wednesday, July 10, 2024

**First Reading:** Hosea 10: 1-3, 7-8, 12

1 Israel is a luxuriant vine that produces his fruit.
According to the abundance of his fruit he has multiplied his altars.
As their land has prospered, they have adorned their sacred stones.
2 Their heart is divided.
Now they will be found guilty.
He will demolish their altars.
He will destroy their sacred stones.
3 Surely now they will say, "We have no king; for we don't fear Yahweh;
and the king, what can he do for us?"
7 Samaria and her king float away
like a twig on the water.
8 The high places also of Aven, the sin of Israel, will be destroyed.
The thorn and the thistle will come up on their altars.
They will tell the mountains, "Cover us!" and the hills, "Fall on us!"
12 Sow to yourselves in righteousness,
reap according to kindness.
Break up your fallow ground,
for it is time to seek Yahweh,

until he comes and rains righteousness on you.

**Responsorial Psalm:** Psalms 105: 2-7

2 Sing to him, sing praises to him!
Tell of all his marvelous works.
3 Glory in his holy name.
Let the heart of those who seek Yahweh rejoice.
4 Seek Yahweh and his strength.
Seek his face forever more.
5 Remember his marvelous works that he has done:
his wonders, and the judgments of his mouth,
6 you offspring of Abraham, his servant,
you children of Jacob, his chosen ones.
7 He is Yahweh, our God.
His judgments are in all the earth.

**Gospel: Matthew 10: 1-7**

1 He called to himself his twelve disciples, and gave them authority over unclean spirits, to cast them out, and to heal every disease and every sickness. 2 Now the names of the twelve apostles are these. The first, Simon, who is called Peter; Andrew, his brother; James the son of Zebedee; John, his brother; 3 Philip; Bartholomew; Thomas; Matthew the tax collector; James the son of Alphaeus; Lebbaeus, who was also called† Thaddaeus; 4 Simon the Zealot; and Judas Iscariot, who also betrayed him.
5 Jesus sent these twelve out and commanded them, saying, "Don't go among the Gentiles, and don't enter into any city of the Samaritans. 6 Rather, go to the lost sheep of the house of Israel. 7 As you go, preach, saying, 'The Kingdom of Heaven is at hand!'

1. Invite the Holy Spirit into this reading, asking the Author of Scripture to speak to you through His Word
2. Read today's passage as many times as you need, take your time
3. Write down (below) what the Lord is saying to you today
4. Live with this Word in your heart through the day

_____

_____

# Thursday, July 11, 2024
Saint Benedict, Abbot

**First Reading:** Hosea 11: 1-4, 8c-9

1 "When Israel was a child, then I loved him,
and called my son out of Egypt.
2 They called to them, so they went from them.
They sacrificed to the Baals,
and burned incense to engraved images.
3 Yet I taught Ephraim to walk.
I took them by their arms,
but they didn't know that I healed them.
4 I drew them with cords of a man, with ties of love;
and I was to them like those who lift up the yoke on their necks;
and I bent down to him and I fed him.
8c How can I make you like Admah?
How can I make you like Zeboiim?
My heart is turned within me,
my compassion is aroused.
9 I will not execute the fierceness of my anger.
I will not return to destroy Ephraim,
for I am God, and not man—the Holy One among you.
I will not come in wrath.

**Responsorial Psalm:** Psalms 80: 2ac and 3b, 15-16

2 Before Ephraim, Benjamin, and Manasseh, stir up your might!
Come to save us!
3 Turn us again, God.
Cause your face to shine,
and we will be saved.
15 the stock which your right hand planted,
the branch that you made strong for yourself.
16 It's burned with fire.
It's cut down.
They perish at your rebuke.

## Gospel: Matthew 10: 7-15

7  As you go, preach, saying, 'The Kingdom of Heaven is at hand!' 8  Heal the sick, cleanse the lepers,‡ and cast out demons. Freely you received, so freely give. 9  Don't take any gold, silver, or brass in your money belts. 10  Take no bag for your journey, neither two coats, nor sandals, nor staff: for the laborer is worthy of his food. 11  Into whatever city or village you enter, find out who in it is worthy, and stay there until you go on. 12  As you enter into the household, greet it. 13  If the household is worthy, let your peace come on it, but if it isn't worthy, let your peace return to you. 14  Whoever doesn't receive you or hear your words, as you go out of that house or that city, shake the dust off your feet. 15  Most certainly I tell you, it will be more tolerable for the land of Sodom and Gomorrah in the day of judgment than for that city.

1. Invite the Holy Spirit into this reading, asking the Author of Scripture to speak to you through His Word
2. Read today's passage as many times as you need, take your time
3. Write down (below) what the Lord is saying to you today
4. Live with this Word in your heart through the day

_____

_____

## Friday, July 12, 2024

**First Reading:** Hosea 14: 2-9

2 Take words with you, and return to Yahweh.
Tell him, "Forgive all our sins,
and accept that which is good;
so we offer bulls as we vowed of our lips.
3 Assyria can't save us.
We won't ride on horses;
neither will we say any more to the work of our hands, 'Our gods!'
for in you the fatherless finds mercy."
4 "I will heal their waywardness.

I will love them freely;
for my anger is turned away from them.
5 I will be like the dew to Israel.
He will blossom like the lily,
and send down his roots like Lebanon.
6 His branches will spread,
and his beauty will be like the olive tree,
and his fragrance like Lebanon.
7 Men will dwell in his shade.
They will revive like the grain,
and blossom like the vine.
Their fragrance will be like the wine of Lebanon.
8 Ephraim, what have I to do any more with idols?
I answer, and will take care of him.
I am like a green cypress tree;
from me your fruit is found."
9 Who is wise, that he may understand these things?
Who is prudent, that he may know them?
For the ways of Yahweh are right,
and the righteous walk in them,
but the rebellious stumble in them.

**Responsorial Psalm:** Psalms 51: 3-4, 8-9, 12-14 and 17

3 For I know my transgressions.
My sin is constantly before me.
4 Against you, and you only, I have sinned,
and done that which is evil in your sight,
so you may be proved right when you speak,
and justified when you judge.
8 Let me hear joy and gladness,
that the bones which you have broken may rejoice.
9 Hide your face from my sins,
and blot out all of my iniquities.
12 Restore to me the joy of your salvation.
Uphold me with a willing spirit.
13 Then I will teach transgressors your ways.
Sinners will be converted to you.

14 Deliver me from the guilt of bloodshed, O God, the God of my salvation. My tongue will sing aloud of your righteousness.
17 The sacrifices of God are a broken spirit.
O God, you will not despise a broken and contrite heart.

**Gospel: Matthew 10: 16-23**

16 "Behold, I send you out as sheep among wolves. Therefore be wise as serpents and harmless as doves. 17 But beware of men, for they will deliver you up to councils, and in their synagogues they will scourge you. 18 Yes, and you will be brought before governors and kings for my sake, for a testimony to them and to the nations. 19 But when they deliver you up, don't be anxious how or what you will say, for it will be given you in that hour what you will say. 20 For it is not you who speak, but the Spirit of your Father who speaks in you.
21 "Brother will deliver up brother to death, and the father his child. Children will rise up against parents and cause them to be put to death. 22 You will be hated by all men for my name's sake, but he who endures to the end will be saved. 23 But when they persecute you in this city, flee into the next, for most certainly I tell you, you will not have gone through the cities of Israel until the Son of Man has come.

1. Invite the Holy Spirit into this reading, asking the Author of Scripture to speak to you through His Word
2. Read today's passage as many times as you need, take your time
3. Write down (below) what the Lord is saying to you today
4. Live with this Word in your heart through the day

_____

_____

**Saturday, July 13, 2024**
Saint Henry; BVM

**First Reading:** Isaiah 6: 1-8

1 In the year that King Uzziah died, I saw the Lord sitting on a throne, high and lifted up; and his train filled the temple. 2 Above him stood the seraphim. Each one had six wings. With two he covered his face. With two he covered his feet. With two he flew. 3 One called to another, and said,

"Holy, holy, holy, is Yahweh of Armies!
The whole earth is full of his glory!"

4 The foundations of the thresholds shook at the voice of him who called, and the house was filled with smoke. 5 Then I said, "Woe is me! For I am undone, because I am a man of unclean lips and I live among a people of unclean lips, for my eyes have seen the King, Yahweh of Armies!"

6 Then one of the seraphim flew to me, having a live coal in his hand, which he had taken with the tongs from off the altar. 7 He touched my mouth with it, and said, "Behold, this has touched your lips; and your iniquity is taken away, and your sin forgiven."

8 I heard the Lord's voice, saying, "Whom shall I send, and who will go for us?"
Then I said, "Here I am. Send me!"

**Responsorial Psalm:** Psalms 93: 1- 5

1 Yahweh reigns!
He is clothed with majesty!
Yahweh is armed with strength.
The world also is established.
It can't be moved.
2 Your throne is established from long ago.
You are from everlasting.
3 The floods have lifted up, Yahweh,
the floods have lifted up their voice.
The floods lift up their waves.
4 Above the voices of many waters,
the mighty breakers of the sea,
Yahweh on high is mighty.
5 Your statutes stand firm.
Holiness adorns your house,
Yahweh, forever more.

**Gospel: Matthew 10: 24-33**

24 "A disciple is not above his teacher, nor a servant above his lord. 25 It is enough for the disciple that he be like his teacher, and the servant like his lord. If they have called the master of the house Beelzebul,§ how much more those of his household! 26 Therefore don't be afraid of them, for there is nothing covered that will not be revealed, or hidden that will not be known. 27 What I tell you in the darkness, speak in the light; and what you hear whispered in the ear, proclaim on the housetops. 28 Don't be afraid of those who kill the body, but are not able to kill the soul. Rather, fear him who is able to destroy both soul and body in Gehenna.†

29 "Aren't two sparrows sold for an assarion coin?‡ Not one of them falls to the ground apart from your Father's will. 30 But the very hairs of your head are all numbered. 31 Therefore don't be afraid. You are of more value than many sparrows. 32 Everyone therefore who confesses me before men, I will also confess him before my Father who is in heaven. 33 But whoever denies me before men, I will also deny him before my Father who is in heaven.

1. Invite the Holy Spirit into this reading, asking the Author of Scripture to speak to you through His Word
2. Read today's passage as many times as you need, take your time
3. Write down (below) what the Lord is saying to you today
4. Live with this Word in your heart through the day

_____

_____

## Sunday, July 14, 2024
### FIFTEENTH SUNDAY IN ORDINARY TIME

**First Reading:** Amos 7: 12-15

12 Amaziah also said to Amos, "You seer, go, flee away into the land of Judah, and there eat bread, and prophesy there, 13 but don't prophesy again any more at Bethel; for it is the king's sanctuary, and it is a royal house!"

14 Then Amos answered Amaziah, "I was no prophet, neither was I a prophet's son, but I was a herdsman, and a farmer of sycamore figs; 15 and Yahweh took me from following the flock, and Yahweh said to me, 'Go, prophesy to my people Israel.'

**Responsorial Psalm:** Psalms 85: 9-13

9 Surely his salvation is near those who fear him,
that glory may dwell in our land.
10 Mercy and truth meet together.
Righteousness and peace have kissed each other.
11 Truth springs out of the earth.
Righteousness has looked down from heaven.
12 Yes, Yahweh will give that which is good.
Our land will yield its increase.
13 Righteousness goes before him,
and prepares the way for his steps.

**Second Reading:** Ephesians 1: 3-14

3 Blessed be the God and Father of our Lord Jesus Christ, who has blessed us with every spiritual blessing in the heavenly places in Christ, 4 even as he chose us in him before the foundation of the world, that we would be holy and without defect before him in love, 5 having predestined us for adoption as children through Jesus Christ to himself, according to the good pleasure of his desire, 6 to the praise of the glory of his grace, by which he freely gave us favor in the Beloved. 7 In him we have our redemption through his blood, the forgiveness of our trespasses, according to the riches of his grace 8 which he made to abound toward us in all wisdom and prudence, 9 making known to us the mystery of his will, according to his good pleasure which he purposed in him 10 to an administration of the fullness of the times, to sum up all things in Christ, the things in the heavens and the things on the earth, in him. 11 We were also assigned an inheritance in him, having been foreordained according to the purpose of him who does all things after the counsel of his will, 12 to the end that we should be to the praise of his glory, we who had before hoped in Christ. 13 In him you also, having heard the word of the truth, the Good News of your salvation—in whom, having also believed, you were sealed with the promised Holy Spirit, 14 who is a pledge of our inheritance, to the redemption of God's own possession, to the praise of his glory.

**Gospel: Mark 6: 7-13**

7 He called to himself the twelve, and began to send them out two by two; and he gave them authority over the unclean spirits. 8 He commanded them that they should take

nothing for their journey, except a staff only: no bread, no wallet, no money in their purse, 9 but to wear sandals, and not put on two tunics. 10 He said to them, "Wherever you enter into a house, stay there until you depart from there. 11 Whoever will not receive you nor hear you, as you depart from there, shake off the dust that is under your feet for a testimony against them. Assuredly, I tell you, it will be more tolerable for Sodom and Gomorrah in the day of judgment than for that city!"

12 They went out and preached that people should repent. 13 They cast out many demons, and anointed many with oil who were sick and healed them.

1. Invite the Holy Spirit into this reading, asking the Author of Scripture to speak to you through His Word
2. Read today's passage as many times as you need, take your time
3. Write down (below) what the Lord is saying to you today
4. Live with this Word in your heart through the day

---

---

## Monday, July 15, 2024
### Saint Bonaventure, Bishop and Doctor of the Church

**First Reading:** Isaiah 1: 10-17

10 Hear Yahweh's word, you rulers of Sodom!
Listen to the law of our God,§ you people of Gomorrah!
11 "What are the multitude of your sacrifices to me?", says Yahweh.
"I have had enough of the burnt offerings of rams
and the fat of fed animals.
I don't delight in the blood of bulls,
or of lambs,
or of male goats.
12 When you come to appear before me,
who has required this at your hand, to trample my courts?
13 Bring no more vain offerings.
Incense is an abomination to me.

New moons, Sabbaths, and convocations—
I can't stand evil assemblies.
14 My soul hates your New Moons and your appointed feasts.
They are a burden to me.
I am weary of bearing them.
15 When you spread out your hands, I will hide my eyes from you.
Yes, when you make many prayers, I will not hear.
Your hands are full of blood.
16 Wash yourselves. Make yourself clean.
Put away the evil of your doings from before my eyes.
Cease to do evil.
17 Learn to do well.
Seek justice.
Relieve the oppressed.
Defend the fatherless.
Plead for the widow."

**Responsorial Psalm:** Psalms 50: 8-9, 16bc-17, 21 and 23

8 I don't rebuke you for your sacrifices.
Your burnt offerings are continually before me.
9 I have no need for a bull from your stall,
nor male goats from your pens.
16 But to the wicked God says,
"What right do you have to declare my statutes,
that you have taken my covenant on your lips,
17 since you hate instruction,
and throw my words behind you?
21 You have done these things, and I kept silent.
You thought that I was just like you.
I will rebuke you, and accuse you in front of your eyes.
23 Whoever offers the sacrifice of thanksgiving glorifies me,
and prepares his way so that I will show God's salvation to him."

**Gospel: Matthew 10: 34 – 11: 1**

34 "Don't think that I came to send peace on the earth. I didn't come to send peace, but a sword. 35 For I came to set a man at odds against his father, and a daughter

against her mother, and a daughter-in-law against her mother-in-law. 36 A man's foes will be those of his own household.* 37 He who loves father or mother more than me is not worthy of me; and he who loves son or daughter more than me isn't worthy of me. 38 He who doesn't take his cross and follow after me isn't worthy of me. 39 He who seeks his life will lose it; and he who loses his life for my sake will find it.

40 "He who receives you receives me, and he who receives me receives him who sent me. 41 He who receives a prophet in the name of a prophet will receive a prophet's reward. He who receives a righteous man in the name of a righteous man will receive a righteous man's reward. 42 Whoever gives one of these little ones just a cup of cold water to drink in the name of a disciple, most certainly I tell you, he will in no way lose his reward."

1 When Jesus had finished directing his twelve disciples, he departed from there to teach and preach in their cities.

1. Invite the Holy Spirit into this reading, asking the Author of Scripture to speak to you through His Word
2. Read today's passage as many times as you need, take your time
3. Write down (below) what the Lord is saying to you today
4. Live with this Word in your heart through the day

_____

_____

### Tuesday, July 16, 2024
Our Lady of Mount Carmel

**First Reading:** Isaiah 7: 1-9

1 In the days of Ahaz the son of Jotham, the son of Uzziah, king of Judah, Rezin the king of Syria and Pekah the son of Remaliah, king of Israel, went up to Jerusalem to war against it, but could not prevail against it. 2 David's house was told, "Syria is allied with Ephraim." His heart trembled, and the heart of his people, as the trees of the forest tremble with the wind.

3 Then Yahweh said to Isaiah, "Go out now to meet Ahaz, you, and Shearjashub your son, at the end of the conduit of the upper pool, on the highway of the fuller's field. 4

Tell him, 'Be careful, and keep calm. Don't be afraid, neither let your heart be faint because of these two tails of smoking torches, for the fierce anger of Rezin and Syria, and of the son of Remaliah. 5 Because Syria, Ephraim, and the son of Remaliah, have plotted evil against you, saying, 6 "Let's go up against Judah, and tear it apart, and let's divide it among ourselves, and set up a king within it, even the son of Tabeel." 7 This is what the Lord Yahweh says: "It shall not stand, neither shall it happen." 8 For the head of Syria is Damascus, and the head of Damascus is Rezin. Within sixty-five years Ephraim shall be broken in pieces, so that it shall not be a people. 9 The head of Ephraim is Samaria, and the head of Samaria is Remaliah's son. If you will not believe, surely you shall not be established.' "

**Responsorial Psalm:** Psalms 48: 2-8

2 Beautiful in elevation, the joy of the whole earth,
is Mount Zion, on the north sides,
the city of the great King.
3 God has shown himself in her citadels as a refuge.
4 For, behold, the kings assembled themselves,
they passed by together.
5 They saw it, then they were amazed.
They were dismayed.
They hurried away.
6 Trembling took hold of them there,
pain, as of a woman in travail.
7 With the east wind, you break the ships of Tarshish.
8 As we have heard, so we have seen,
in the city of Yahweh of Armies, in the city of our God.
God will establish it forever.

**Gospel: Matthew 11: 20-24**

20 Then he began to denounce the cities in which most of his mighty works had been done, because they didn't repent. 21 "Woe to you, Chorazin! Woe to you, Bethsaida! For if the mighty works had been done in Tyre and Sidon which were done in you, they would have repented long ago in sackcloth and ashes. 22 But I tell you, it will be more tolerable for Tyre and Sidon on the day of judgment than for you. 23 You, Capernaum, who are exalted to heaven, you will go down to Hades. § For if the mighty works had been done in Sodom which were done in you, it would have remained until today. 24

But I tell you that it will be more tolerable for the land of Sodom on the day of judgment, than for you."

---

---

## Wednesday, July 17, 2024

**First Reading:** Isaiah 10: 5-7, 13b-16

5 Alas Assyrian, the rod of my anger, the staff in whose hand is my indignation! 6 I will send him against a profane nation, and against the people who anger me I will give him a command to take the plunder and to take the prey, and to tread them down like the mire of the streets. 7 However, he doesn't mean so, neither does his heart think so; but it is in his heart to destroy, and to cut off not a few nations.

13 For he has said, "By the strength of my hand I have done it, and by my wisdom, for I have understanding. I have removed the boundaries of the peoples, and have robbed their treasures. Like a valiant man I have brought down their rulers. 14 My hand has found the riches of the peoples like a nest, and like one gathers eggs that are abandoned, I have gathered all the earth. There was no one who moved their wing, or that opened their mouth, or chirped."

15 Should an ax brag against him who chops with it? Should a saw exalt itself above him who saws with it? As if a rod should lift those who lift it up, or as if a staff should lift up someone who is not wood. 16 Therefore the Lord, Yahweh of Armies, will send among his fat ones leanness; and under his glory a burning will be kindled like the burning of fire.

**Responsorial Psalm:** Psalms 94: 5-10, 14-15

5 They break your people in pieces, Yahweh,
and afflict your heritage.
6 They kill the widow and the alien,
and murder the fatherless.
7 They say, "Yah will not see,
neither will Jacob's God consider."
8 Consider, you senseless among the people;
you fools, when will you be wise?
9 He who implanted the ear, won't he hear?
He who formed the eye, won't he see?
10 He who disciplines the nations, won't he punish?
He who teaches man knows.
14 For Yahweh won't reject his people,
neither will he forsake his inheritance.
15 For judgment will return to righteousness.
All the upright in heart shall follow it.

## Gospel: Matthew 11: 25-27

25 At that time, Jesus answered, "I thank you, Father, Lord of heaven and earth, that you hid these things from the wise and understanding, and revealed them to infants. 26 Yes, Father, for so it was well-pleasing in your sight. 27 All things have been delivered to me by my Father. No one knows the Son, except the Father; neither does anyone know the Father, except the Son and he to whom the Son desires to reveal him.

1. Invite the Holy Spirit into this reading, asking the Author of Scripture to speak to you through His Word
2. Read today's passage as many times as you need, take your time
3. Write down (below) what the Lord is saying to you today
4. Live with this Word in your heart through the day

_____

_____

**Thursday, July 18, 2024**
USA: Saint Camillus de Lellis, Priest

**First Reading:** Isaiah 26: 7-9, 11, 16-19

7 The way of the just is uprightness.
You who are upright make the path of the righteous level.
8 Yes, in the way of your judgments, Yahweh, we have waited for you.
Your name and your renown are the desire of our soul.
9 With my soul I have desired you in the night.
Yes, with my spirit within me I will seek you earnestly;
for when your judgments are in the earth, the inhabitants of the world learn righteousness.
11 Yahweh, your hand is lifted up, yet they don't see;
but they will see your zeal for the people and be disappointed.
Yes, fire will consume your adversaries.
16 Yahweh, in trouble they have visited you.
They poured out a prayer when your chastening was on them.
17 Just as a woman with child, who draws near the time of her delivery,
is in pain and cries out in her pangs,
so we have been before you, Yahweh.
18 We have been with child.
We have been in pain.
We gave birth, it seems, only to wind.
We have not worked any deliverance in the earth;
neither have the inhabitants of the world fallen.
19 Your dead shall live.
Their dead bodies shall arise.
Awake and sing, you who dwell in the dust;
for your dew is like the dew of herbs,
and the earth will cast out the departed spirits.

**Responsorial Psalm:** Psalms 102: 13-21

13 You will arise and have mercy on Zion,
for it is time to have pity on her.
Yes, the set time has come.
14 For your servants take pleasure in her stones,
and have pity on her dust.

15 So the nations will fear Yahweh's name,
all the kings of the earth your glory.
16 For Yahweh has built up Zion.
He has appeared in his glory.
17 He has responded to the prayer of the destitute,
and has not despised their prayer.
18 This will be written for the generation to come.
A people which will be created will praise Yah,
19 for he has looked down from the height of his sanctuary.
From heaven, Yahweh saw the earth,
20 to hear the groans of the prisoner,
to free those who are condemned to death,
21 that men may declare Yahweh's name in Zion,
and his praise in Jerusalem,

### Gospel: Matthew 11: 28-30

28 "Come to me, all you who labor and are heavily burdened, and I will give you rest.
29 Take my yoke upon you and learn from me, for I am gentle and humble in heart;
and you will find rest for your souls. 30 For my yoke is easy, and my burden is light."

1. Invite the Holy Spirit into this reading, asking the Author of Scripture to speak to you through His Word
2. Read today's passage as many times as you need, take your time
3. Write down (below) what the Lord is saying to you today
4. Live with this Word in your heart through the day

_____

_____

### Friday, July 19, 2024

**First Reading:** Isaiah 38: 1-6, 21-22, 7-8

1 In those days Hezekiah was sick and near death. Isaiah the prophet, the son of Amoz, came to him, and said to him, "Yahweh says, 'Set your house in order, for you will die, and not live.' "

2 Then Hezekiah turned his face to the wall and prayed to Yahweh, 3 and said, "Remember now, Yahweh, I beg you, how I have walked before you in truth and with a perfect heart, and have done that which is good in your sight." Then Hezekiah wept bitterly.

4 Then Yahweh's word came to Isaiah, saying, 5 "Go, and tell Hezekiah, 'Yahweh, the God of David your father, says, "I have heard your prayer. I have seen your tears. Behold, I will add fifteen years to your life. 6 I will deliver you and this city out of the hand of the king of Assyria, and I will defend this city.

21 Now Isaiah had said, "Let them take a cake of figs, and lay it for a poultice on the boil, and he shall recover." 22 Hezekiah also had said, "What is the sign that I will go up to Yahweh's house?"

7 This shall be the sign to you from Yahweh, that Yahweh will do this thing that he has spoken. 8 Behold, I will cause the shadow on the sundial, which has gone down on the sundial of Ahaz with the sun, to return backward ten steps." ' " So the sun returned ten steps on the sundial on which it had gone down.

**Responsorial Psalm:** Isaiah 38: 10, 11, 12abcd, 16

10 I said, "In the middle of my life I go into the gates of Sheol.†
I am deprived of the residue of my years."
11 I said, "I won't see Yah,
Yah in the land of the living.
I will see man no more with the inhabitants of the world.
12 My dwelling is removed,
and is carried away from me like a shepherd's tent.
I have rolled up my life like a weaver.
He will cut me off from the loom.
From day even to night you will make an end of me.
16 Lord, men live by these things;
and my spirit finds life in all of them.
You restore me, and cause me to live.

**Gospel: Matthew 12: 1-8**

1 At that time, Jesus went on the Sabbath day through the grain fields. His disciples were hungry and began to pluck heads of grain and to eat. 2 But the Pharisees, when they saw it, said to him, "Behold, your disciples do what is not lawful to do on the Sabbath."

3 But he said to them, "Haven't you read what David did when he was hungry, and those who were with him: 4 how he entered into God's house and ate the show bread, which was not lawful for him to eat, nor for those who were with him, but only for the priests?* 5 Or have you not read in the law that on the Sabbath day the priests in the temple profane the Sabbath and are guiltless? 6 But I tell you that one greater than the temple is here. 7 But if you had known what this means, 'I desire mercy, and not sacrifice,'* you wouldn't have condemned the guiltless. 8 For the Son of Man is Lord of the Sabbath."

1. Invite the Holy Spirit into this reading, asking the Author of Scripture to speak to you through His Word
2. Read today's passage as many times as you need, take your time
3. Write down (below) what the Lord is saying to you today
4. Live with this Word in your heart through the day

_____

_____

# Saturday, July 20, 2024
### Saint Apollinaris, Bishop and Martyr; BVM

**First Reading:** Micah 2: 1-5

1 Woe to those who devise iniquity
and work evil on their beds!
When the morning is light, they practice it,
because it is in the power of their hand.
2 They covet fields and seize them,
and houses, then take them away.
They oppress a man and his house,
even a man and his heritage.

3 Therefore Yahweh says:
"Behold, I am planning against these people a disaster,
from which you will not remove your necks,
neither will you walk haughtily,
for it is an evil time.
4 In that day they will take up a parable against you,
and lament with a doleful lamentation, saying,
'We are utterly ruined!
My people's possession is divided up.
Indeed he takes it from me and assigns our fields to traitors!' "
5 Therefore you will have no one who divides the land by lot in Yahweh's assembly.

**Responsorial Psalm:** Psalms 10: 1-4, 7-8, 14

1 Why do you stand far off, Yahweh?
Why do you hide yourself in times of trouble?
2 In arrogance, the wicked hunt down the weak.
They are caught in the schemes that they devise.
3 For the wicked boasts of his heart's cravings.
He blesses the greedy and condemns Yahweh.
4 The wicked, in the pride of his face,
has no room in his thoughts for God.
7 His mouth is full of cursing, deceit, and oppression.
Under his tongue is mischief and iniquity.
8 He lies in wait near the villages.
From ambushes, he murders the innocent.
His eyes are secretly set against the helpless.
14 But you do see trouble and grief.
You consider it to take it into your hand.
You help the victim and the fatherless.

**Gospel: Matthew 12: 14-21**

14 But the Pharisees went out and conspired against him, how they might destroy him.
15 Jesus, perceiving that, withdrew from there. Great multitudes followed him; and he
healed them all, 16 and commanded them that they should not make him known, 17
that it might be fulfilled which was spoken through Isaiah the prophet, saying,
18 "Behold, my servant whom I have chosen,

my beloved in whom my soul is well pleased.
I will put my Spirit on him.
He will proclaim justice to the nations.
19 He will not strive, nor shout,
neither will anyone hear his voice in the streets.
20 He won't break a bruised reed.
He won't quench a smoking flax,
until he leads justice to victory.
21 In his name, the nations will hope."

1. Invite the Holy Spirit into this reading, asking the Author of Scripture to speak to you through His Word
2. Read today's passage as many times as you need, take your time
3. Write down (below) what the Lord is saying to you today
4. Live with this Word in your heart through the day

---

---

## Sunday, July 21, 2024
### SIXTEENTH SUNDAY IN ORDINARY TIME

**First Reading:** Jeremiah 23: 1-6

1 "Woe to the shepherds who destroy and scatter the sheep of my pasture!" says Yahweh. 2 Therefore Yahweh, the God of Israel, says against the shepherds who feed my people: "You have scattered my flock, driven them away, and have not visited them. Behold, I will visit on you the evil of your doings," says Yahweh. 3 "I will gather the remnant of my flock out of all the countries where I have driven them, and will bring them again to their folds; and they will be fruitful and multiply. 4 I will set up shepherds over them who will feed them. They will no longer be afraid or dismayed, neither will any be lacking," says Yahweh.
5 "Behold, the days come," says Yahweh,
"that I will raise to David a righteous Branch;
and he will reign as king and deal wisely,

and will execute justice and righteousness in the land.
6 In his days Judah will be saved,
and Israel will dwell safely.
This is his name by which he will be called:
Yahweh our righteousness.

**Responsorial Psalm:** Psalms 23: 1-6

1 Yahweh is my shepherd;
I shall lack nothing.
2 He makes me lie down in green pastures.
He leads me beside still waters.
3 He restores my soul.
He guides me in the paths of righteousness for his name's sake.
4 Even though I walk through the valley of the shadow of death,
I will fear no evil, for you are with me.
Your rod and your staff,
they comfort me.
5 You prepare a table before me
in the presence of my enemies.
You anoint my head with oil.
My cup runs over.
6 Surely goodness and loving kindness shall follow me all the days of my life,
and I will dwell in Yahweh's house forever.

**Second Reading:** Ephesians 2: 13-18

13 But now in Christ Jesus you who once were far off are made near in the blood of Christ. 14 For he is our peace, who made both one, and broke down the middle wall of separation, 15 having abolished in his flesh the hostility, the law of commandments contained in ordinances, that he might create in himself one new man of the two, making peace, 16 and might reconcile them both in one body to God through the cross, having killed the hostility through it. 17 He came and preached peace to you who were far off and to those who were near. 18 For through him we both have our access in one Spirit to the Father.

**Gospel: Mark 6: 30-34**

30 The apostles gathered themselves together to Jesus, and they told him all things, whatever they had done, and whatever they had taught. 31 He said to them, "Come away into a deserted place, and rest awhile." For there were many coming and going, and they had no leisure so much as to eat. 32 They went away in the boat to a deserted place by themselves. 33 They† saw them going, and many recognized him and ran there on foot from all the cities. They arrived before them and came together to him. 34 Jesus came out, saw a great multitude, and he had compassion on them because they were like sheep without a shepherd; and he began to teach them many things.

1. Invite the Holy Spirit into this reading, asking the Author of Scripture to speak to you through His Word
2. Read today's passage as many times as you need, take your time
3. Write down (below) what the Lord is saying to you today
4. Live with this Word in your heart through the day

_____

_____

### Monday, July 22, 2024
Saint Mary Magdalene

**First Reading:** Second Corinthians 5: 14-17

14 For the love of Christ compels us; because we judge thus: that one died for all, therefore all died. 15 He died for all, that those who live should no longer live to themselves, but to him who for their sakes died and rose again.
16 Therefore we know no one according to the flesh from now on. Even though we have known Christ according to the flesh, yet now we know him so no more. 17 Therefore if anyone is in Christ, he is a new creation. The old things have passed away. Behold,† all things have become new.

**Responsorial Psalm:** Psalms 63: 2-6, 8-9

2 So I have seen you in the sanctuary,
watching your power and your glory.
3 Because your loving kindness is better than life,

my lips shall praise you.

4 So I will bless you while I live.

I will lift up my hands in your name.

5 My soul shall be satisfied as with the richest food.

My mouth shall praise you with joyful lips,

6 when I remember you on my bed,

and think about you in the night watches.

8 My soul stays close to you.

Your right hand holds me up.

9 But those who seek my soul to destroy it

shall go into the lower parts of the earth.

**Gospel: John 20: 1-2, 11-18**

1 Now on the first day of the week, Mary Magdalene went early, while it was still dark, to the tomb, and saw that the stone had been taken away from the tomb. 2 Therefore she ran and came to Simon Peter and to the other disciple whom Jesus loved, and said to them, "They have taken away the Lord out of the tomb, and we don't know where they have laid him!"

11 But Mary was standing outside at the tomb weeping. So as she wept, she stooped and looked into the tomb, 12 and she saw two angels in white sitting, one at the head and one at the feet, where the body of Jesus had lain. 13 They asked her, "Woman, why are you weeping?"

She said to them, "Because they have taken away my Lord, and I don't know where they have laid him." 14 When she had said this, she turned around and saw Jesus standing, and didn't know that it was Jesus.

15 Jesus said to her, "Woman, why are you weeping? Who are you looking for?"

She, supposing him to be the gardener, said to him, "Sir, if you have carried him away, tell me where you have laid him, and I will take him away."

16 Jesus said to her, "Mary."

She turned and said to him, "Rabboni!"† which is to say, "Teacher!"‡

17 Jesus said to her, "Don't hold me, for I haven't yet ascended to my Father; but go to my brothers and tell them, 'I am ascending to my Father and your Father, to my God and your God.'"

18 Mary Magdalene came and told the disciples that she had seen the Lord, and that he had said these things to her.

1. Invite the Holy Spirit into this reading, asking the Author of Scripture to speak to you through His Word
2. Read today's passage as many times as you need, take your time
3. Write down (below) what the Lord is saying to you today
4. Live with this Word in your heart through the day

_____

_____

## Tuesday, July 23, 2024
### Saint Bridget, Religious

**First Reading:** Micah 7: 14-15, 18-20

14 Shepherd your people with your staff,
the flock of your heritage,
who dwell by themselves in a forest.
Let them feed in the middle of fertile pasture land,
in Bashan and Gilead, as in the days of old.
15 "As in the days of your coming out of the land of Egypt,
I will show them marvelous things."
18 Who is a God like you, who pardons iniquity,
and passes over the disobedience of the remnant of his heritage?
He doesn't retain his anger forever,
because he delights in loving kindness.
19 He will again have compassion on us.
He will tread our iniquities under foot.
You will cast all their sins into the depths of the sea.
20 You will give truth to Jacob,
and mercy to Abraham,
as you have sworn to our fathers from the days of old.

**Responsorial Psalm:** Psalms 85: 2-8

2 You have forgiven the iniquity of your people.

You have covered all their sin.

3 You have taken away all your wrath.

You have turned from the fierceness of your anger.

4 Turn us, God of our salvation,

and cause your indignation toward us to cease.

5 Will you be angry with us forever?

Will you draw out your anger to all generations?

6 Won't you revive us again,

that your people may rejoice in you?

7 Show us your loving kindness, Yahweh.

Grant us your salvation.

8 I will hear what God, Yahweh, will speak,

for he will speak peace to his people, his saints;

but let them not turn again to folly.

**Gospel: Matthew 12: 46-50**

46 While he was yet speaking to the multitudes, behold, his mother and his brothers stood outside, seeking to speak to him. 47 One said to him, "Behold, your mother and your brothers stand outside, seeking to speak to you."

48 But he answered him who spoke to him, "Who is my mother? Who are my brothers?" 49 He stretched out his hand toward his disciples, and said, "Behold, my mother and my brothers! 50  For whoever does the will of my Father who is in heaven, he is my brother, and sister, and mother."

1. Invite the Holy Spirit into this reading, asking the Author of Scripture to speak to you through His Word
2. Read today's passage as many times as you need, take your time
3. Write down (below) what the Lord is saying to you today
4. Live with this Word in your heart through the day

_____

_____

**Wedneday, July 24, 2024**
Saint Sharbel Makhlūf, Priest

**First Reading:** Jeremiah 1: 1, 4-10

1 The words of Jeremiah the son of Hilkiah, one of the priests who were in Anathoth in the land of Benjamin.

4 Now Yahweh's word came to me, saying,

5 "Before I formed you in the womb, I knew you.
Before you were born, I sanctified you.
I have appointed you a prophet to the nations."

6 Then I said, "Ah, Lord‡ Yahweh! Behold,§ I don't know how to speak; for I am a child."

7 But Yahweh said to me, "Don't say, 'I am a child;' for you must go to whomever I send you, and you must say whatever I command you. 8 Don't be afraid because of them, for I am with you to rescue you," says Yahweh.

9 Then Yahweh stretched out his hand and touched my mouth. Then Yahweh said to me, "Behold, I have put my words in your mouth. 10 Behold, I have today set you over the nations and over the kingdoms, to uproot and to tear down, to destroy and to overthrow, to build and to plant."

**Responsorial Psalm:** Psalms 71: 1-2, 3-4a, 5-6ab, 15 and 17

1 In you, Yahweh, I take refuge.
Never let me be disappointed.
2 Deliver me in your righteousness, and rescue me.
Turn your ear to me, and save me.
3 Be to me a rock of refuge to which I may always go.
Give the command to save me,
for you are my rock and my fortress.
4 Rescue me, my God, from the hand of the wicked,
from the hand of the unrighteous and cruel man.
5 For you are my hope, Lord Yahweh,
my confidence from my youth.
6 I have relied on you from the womb.
You are he who took me out of my mother's womb.
15 My mouth will tell about your righteousness,
and of your salvation all day,
though I don't know its full measure.

17 God, you have taught me from my youth.
Until now, I have declared your wondrous works.

**Gospel: Matthew 13: 1-9**

1 On that day Jesus went out of the house and sat by the seaside. 2 Great multitudes gathered to him, so that he entered into a boat and sat; and all the multitude stood on the beach. 3 He spoke to them many things in parables, saying, "Behold, a farmer went out to sow. 4 As he sowed, some seeds fell by the roadside, and the birds came and devoured them. 5 Others fell on rocky ground, where they didn't have much soil, and immediately they sprang up, because they had no depth of earth. 6 When the sun had risen, they were scorched. Because they had no root, they withered away. 7 Others fell among thorns. The thorns grew up and choked them. 8 Others fell on good soil and yielded fruit: some one hundred times as much, some sixty, and some thirty. 9 He who has ears to hear, let him hear."

1. Invite the Holy Spirit into this reading, asking the Author of Scripture to speak to you through His Word
2. Read today's passage as many times as you need, take your time
3. Write down (below) what the Lord is saying to you today
4. Live with this Word in your heart through the day

_____

_____

## Thursday, July 25, 2024
Saint James, Apostle

**First Reading:** Second Corinthians 4: 7-15

7 But we have this treasure in clay vessels, that the exceeding greatness of the power may be of God and not from ourselves. 8 We are pressed on every side, yet not crushed; perplexed, yet not to despair; 9 pursued, yet not forsaken; struck down, yet not destroyed; 10 always carrying in the body the putting to death of the Lord Jesus, that the life of Jesus may also be revealed in our body. 11 For we who live are always

delivered to death for Jesus' sake, that the life also of Jesus may be revealed in our mortal flesh. 12 So then death works in us, but life in you.

13 But having the same spirit of faith, according to that which is written, "I believed, and therefore I spoke."* We also believe, and therefore we also speak, 14 knowing that he who raised the Lord Jesus will raise us also with Jesus, and will present us with you. 15 For all things are for your sakes, that the grace, being multiplied through the many, may cause the thanksgiving to abound to the glory of God.

**Responsorial Psalm:** Psalms 126: 1bc-6

1 When Yahweh brought back those who returned to Zion,
we were like those who dream.
2 Then our mouth was filled with laughter,
and our tongue with singing.
Then they said among the nations,
"Yahweh has done great things for them."
3 Yahweh has done great things for us,
and we are glad.
4 Restore our fortunes again, Yahweh,
like the streams in the Negev.
5 Those who sow in tears will reap in joy.
6 He who goes out weeping, carrying seed for sowing,
will certainly come again with joy, carrying his sheaves.

**Gospel: Matthew 20: 20-28**

20 Then the mother of the sons of Zebedee came to him with her sons, kneeling and asking a certain thing of him. 21 He said to her, "What do you want?"
She said to him, "Command that these, my two sons, may sit, one on your right hand and one on your left hand, in your Kingdom."
22 But Jesus answered, "You don't know what you are asking. Are you able to drink the cup that I am about to drink, and be baptized with the baptism that I am baptized with?"
They said to him, "We are able."
23 He said to them, "You will indeed drink my cup, and be baptized with the baptism that I am baptized with; but to sit on my right hand and on my left hand is not mine to give, but it is for whom it has been prepared by my Father."
24 When the ten heard it, they were indignant with the two brothers.

25 But Jesus summoned them, and said, "You know that the rulers of the nations lord it over them, and their great ones exercise authority over them. 26 It shall not be so among you; but whoever desires to become great among you shall be‡ your servant. 27 Whoever desires to be first among you shall be your bondservant, 28 even as the Son of Man came not to be served, but to serve, and to give his life as a ransom for many."

1. Invite the Holy Spirit into this reading, asking the Author of Scripture to speak to you through His Word
2. Read today's passage as many times as you need, take your time
3. Write down (below) what the Lord is saying to you today
4. Live with this Word in your heart through the day

_____

_____

### Friday, July 26, 2024
Saints Joachim and Anne, Parents of the Blessed Virgin Mary

**First Reading:** Jeremiah 3: 14-17

14 "Return, backsliding children," says Yahweh, "for I am a husband to you. I will take one of you from a city, and two from a family, and I will bring you to Zion. 15 I will give you shepherds according to my heart, who will feed you with knowledge and understanding. 16 It will come to pass, when you are multiplied and increased in the land in those days," says Yahweh, "they will no longer say, 'the ark of Yahweh's covenant!' It will not come to mind. They won't remember it. They won't miss it, nor will another be made. 17 At that time they will call Jerusalem 'Yahweh's Throne;' and all the nations will be gathered to it, to Yahweh's name, to Jerusalem. They will no longer walk after the stubbornness of their evil heart.

**Responsorial Psalm:** Jeremiah 31: 10, 11-12abcd, 13

10 "Hear Yahweh's word, you nations,
and declare it in the distant islands. Say,
'He who scattered Israel will gather him,

and keep him, as a shepherd does his flock.'
11 For Yahweh has ransomed Jacob,
and redeemed him from the hand of him who was stronger than he.
12 They will come and sing in the height of Zion,
and will flow to the goodness of Yahweh,
to the grain, to the new wine, to the oil,
and to the young of the flock and of the herd.
Their soul will be as a watered garden.
They will not sorrow any more at all.
13 Then the virgin will rejoice in the dance,
the young men and the old together;
for I will turn their mourning into joy,
and will comfort them, and make them rejoice from their sorrow.

**Gospel: Matthew 13: 18-23**

18 "Hear, then, the parable of the farmer. 19 When anyone hears the word of the Kingdom and doesn't understand it, the evil one comes and snatches away that which has been sown in his heart. This is what was sown by the roadside. 20 What was sown on the rocky places, this is he who hears the word and immediately with joy receives it; 21 yet he has no root in himself, but endures for a while. When oppression or persecution arises because of the word, immediately he stumbles. 22 What was sown among the thorns, this is he who hears the word, but the cares of this age and the deceitfulness of riches choke the word, and he becomes unfruitful. 23 What was sown on the good ground, this is he who hears the word and understands it, who most certainly bears fruit and produces, some one hundred times as much, some sixty, and some thirty."

1. Invite the Holy Spirit into this reading, asking the Author of Scripture to speak to you through His Word
2. Read today's passage as many times as you need, take your time
3. Write down (below) what the Lord is saying to you today
4. Live with this Word in your heart through the day

_____

_____

**First Reading:** Jeremiah 7: 1-11

1 The word that came to Jeremiah from Yahweh, saying, 2 "Stand in the gate of Yahweh's house, and proclaim this word there, and say, 'Hear Yahweh's word, all you of Judah, who enter in at these gates to worship Yahweh.'"
3 Yahweh of Armies, the God of Israel says, "Amend your ways and your doings, and I will cause you to dwell in this place. 4 Don't trust in lying words, saying, 'Yahweh's temple, Yahweh's temple, Yahweh's temple, are these.' 5 For if you thoroughly amend your ways and your doings, if you thoroughly execute justice between a man and his neighbor; 6 if you don't oppress the foreigner, the fatherless, and the widow, and don't shed innocent blood in this place, and don't walk after other gods to your own hurt, 7 then I will cause you to dwell in this place, in the land that I gave to your fathers, from of old even forever more. 8 Behold, you trust in lying words that can't profit. 9 Will you steal, murder, commit adultery, swear falsely, burn incense to Baal, and walk after other gods that you have not known, 10 then come and stand before me in this house, which is called by my name, and say, 'We are delivered,' that you may do all these abominations? 11 Has this house, which is called by my name, become a den of robbers in your eyes? Behold, I myself have seen it," says Yahweh.

**Responsorial Psalm:** Psalms 84: 3, 4, 5-6a and 8a, 11

3 Yes, the sparrow has found a home,
and the swallow a nest for herself, where she may have her young,
near your altars, Yahweh of Armies, my King, and my God.
4 Blessed are those who dwell in your house.
They are always praising you.
Selah.
5 Blessed are those whose strength is in you,
who have set their hearts on a pilgrimage.
6 Passing through the valley of Weeping, they make it a place of springs.
8 Yahweh, God of Armies, hear my prayer.
11 For Yahweh God is a sun and a shield.
Yahweh will give grace and glory.
He withholds no good thing from those who walk blamelessly.

**Gospel: Matthew 13: 24-30**

24 He set another parable before them, saying, "The Kingdom of Heaven is like a man who sowed good seed in his field, 25 but while people slept, his enemy came and sowed darnel weeds† also among the wheat, and went away. 26 But when the blade sprang up and produced grain, then the darnel weeds appeared also. 27 The servants of the householder came and said to him, 'Sir, didn't you sow good seed in your field? Where did these darnel weeds come from?'
28 "He said to them, 'An enemy has done this.'
"The servants asked him, 'Do you want us to go and gather them up?'
29 "But he said, 'No, lest perhaps while you gather up the darnel weeds, you root up the wheat with them. 30 Let both grow together until the harvest, and in the harvest time I will tell the reapers, "First, gather up the darnel weeds, and bind them in bundles to burn them; but gather the wheat into my barn." ' "

1. Invite the Holy Spirit into this reading, asking the Author of Scripture to speak to you through His Word
2. Read today's passage as many times as you need, take your time
3. Write down (below) what the Lord is saying to you today
4. Live with this Word in your heart through the day

_____

_____

### Sunday, July 28, 2024
SEVENTEENTH SUNDAY IN ORDINARY TIME

**First Reading:** Second Kings 4: 42-44

42 A man from Baal Shalishah came, and brought the man of God some bread of the first fruits: twenty loaves of barley and fresh ears of grain in his sack. Elisha said, "Give to the people, that they may eat."
43 His servant said, "What, should I set this before a hundred men?"
But he said, "Give it to the people, that they may eat; for Yahweh says, 'They will eat, and will have some left over.' "

44 So he set it before them and they ate and had some left over, according to Yahweh's word.

**Responsorial Psalm:** Psalms 145: 10-11, 15-18

10 All your works will give thanks to you, Yahweh.
Your saints will extol you.
11 They will speak of the glory of your kingdom,
and talk about your power,
15 The eyes of all wait for you.
You give them their food in due season.
16 You open your hand,
and satisfy the desire of every living thing.
17 Yahweh is righteous in all his ways,
and gracious in all his works.
18 Yahweh is near to all those who call on him,
to all who call on him in truth.

**Second Reading:** Ephesians 4: 1-6

1 I therefore, the prisoner in the Lord, beg you to walk worthily of the calling with which you were called, 2 with all lowliness and humility, with patience, bearing with one another in love, 3 being eager to keep the unity of the Spirit in the bond of peace. 4 There is one body and one Spirit, even as you also were called in one hope of your calling, 5 one Lord, one faith, one baptism, 6 one God and Father of all, who is over all and through all and in us all.

**Gospel: John 6: 1-15**

1 After these things, Jesus went away to the other side of the sea of Galilee, which is also called the Sea of Tiberias. 2 A great multitude followed him, because they saw his signs which he did on those who were sick. 3 Jesus went up into the mountain, and he sat there with his disciples. 4 Now the Passover, the feast of the Jews, was at hand. 5 Jesus therefore, lifting up his eyes and seeing that a great multitude was coming to him, said to Philip, "Where are we to buy bread, that these may eat?" 6 He said this to test him, for he himself knew what he would do.
7 Philip answered him, "Two hundred denarii† worth of bread is not sufficient for them, that every one of them may receive a little."

8 One of his disciples, Andrew, Simon Peter's brother, said to him, 9 "There is a boy here who has five barley loaves and two fish, but what are these among so many?"

10 Jesus said, "Have the people sit down." Now there was much grass in that place. So the men sat down, in number about five thousand. 11 Jesus took the loaves, and having given thanks, he distributed to the disciples, and the disciples to those who were sitting down, likewise also of the fish as much as they desired. 12 When they were filled, he said to his disciples, "Gather up the broken pieces which are left over, that nothing be lost." 13 So they gathered them up, and filled twelve baskets with broken pieces from the five barley loaves, which were left over by those who had eaten. 14 When therefore the people saw the sign which Jesus did, they said, "This is truly the prophet who comes into the world." 15 Jesus therefore, perceiving that they were about to come and take him by force to make him king, withdrew again to the mountain by himself.

1. Invite the Holy Spirit into this reading, asking the Author of Scripture to speak to you through His Word
2. Read today's passage as many times as you need, take your time
3. Write down (below) what the Lord is saying to you today
4. Live with this Word in your heart through the day

_____

_____

## Monday, July 29, 2024
### Saints Martha, Mary and Lazarus

**First Reading:** Jeremiah 13: 1-11

1 Yahweh said to me, "Go, and buy yourself a linen belt, and put it on your waist, and don't put it in water."

2 So I bought a belt according to Yahweh's word, and put it on my waist.

3 Yahweh's word came to me the second time, saying, 4 "Take the belt that you have bought, which is on your waist, and arise, go to the Euphrates, and hide it there in a cleft of the rock."

5 So I went and hid it by the Euphrates, as Yahweh commanded me.

6 After many days, Yahweh said to me, "Arise, go to the Euphrates, and take the belt from there, which I commanded you to hide there."

7 Then I went to the Euphrates, and dug, and took the belt from the place where I had hidden it; and behold, the belt was ruined. It was profitable for nothing.

8 Then Yahweh's word came to me, saying, 9 "Yahweh says, 'In this way I will ruin the pride of Judah, and the great pride of Jerusalem. 10 This evil people, who refuse to hear my words, who walk in the stubbornness of their heart, and have gone after other gods to serve them and to worship them, will even be as this belt, which is profitable for nothing. 11 For as the belt clings to the waist of a man, so I have caused the whole house of Israel and the whole house of Judah to cling to me,' says Yahweh; 'that they may be to me for a people, for a name, for praise, and for glory; but they would not hear.'

**Responsorial Psalm:** Deuteronomy 32: 18-21

18 Of the Rock who became your father, you are unmindful,
and have forgotten God who gave you birth.
19 Yahweh saw and abhorred,
because of the provocation of his sons and his daughters.
20 He said, "I will hide my face from them.
I will see what their end will be;
for they are a very perverse generation,
children in whom is no faithfulness.
21 They have moved me to jealousy with that which is not God.
They have provoked me to anger with their vanities.
I will move them to jealousy with those who are not a people.
I will provoke them to anger with a foolish nation.

**Gospel: John 11: 19-27**

19 Many of the Jews had joined the women around Martha and Mary, to console them concerning their brother. 20 Then when Martha heard that Jesus was coming, she went and met him, but Mary stayed in the house. 21 Therefore Martha said to Jesus, "Lord, if you would have been here, my brother wouldn't have died. 22 Even now I know that whatever you ask of God, God will give you."

23 Jesus said to her, "Your brother will rise again."

24 Martha said to him, "I know that he will rise again in the resurrection at the last day."

25 Jesus said to her, "I am the resurrection and the life. He who believes in me will still live, even if he dies. 26 Whoever lives and believes in me will never die. Do you believe this?"

27 She said to him, "Yes, Lord. I have come to believe that you are the Christ, God's Son, he who comes into the world."

1. Invite the Holy Spirit into this reading, asking the Author of Scripture to speak to you through His Word
2. Read today's passage as many times as you need, take your time
3. Write down (below) what the Lord is saying to you today
4. Live with this Word in your heart through the day

---

---

## Tuesday, July 30, 2024
### Saint Peter Chrysologus, Bishop and Doctor of the Church

**First Reading:** Jeremiah 14: 17-22

17 "You shall say this word to them:
" 'Let my eyes run down with tears night and day,
and let them not cease;
for the virgin daughter of my people is broken with a great breach,
with a very grievous wound.
18 If I go out into the field,
then behold, the slain with the sword!
If I enter into the city,
then behold, those who are sick with famine!
For both the prophet and the priest go about in the land,
and have no knowledge.' "
19 Have you utterly rejected Judah?
Has your soul loathed Zion?
Why have you struck us, and there is no healing for us?
We looked for peace, but no good came;
and for a time of healing, and behold, dismay!

20 We acknowledge, Yahweh, our wickedness,
and the iniquity of our fathers;
for we have sinned against you.
21 Do not abhor us, for your name's sake.
Do not disgrace the throne of your glory.
Remember, and don't break your covenant with us.
22 Are there any among the vanities of the nations that can cause rain?
Or can the sky give showers?
Aren't you he, Yahweh our God?
Therefore we will wait for you;
for you have made all these things.

**Responsorial Psalm:** Psalms 79: 8, 9, 11 and 13

8 Don't hold the iniquities of our forefathers against us.
Let your tender mercies speedily meet us,
for we are in desperate need.
9 Help us, God of our salvation, for the glory of your name.
Deliver us, and forgive our sins, for your name's sake.
11 Let the sighing of the prisoner come before you.
According to the greatness of your power, preserve those who are sentenced to death.
13 So we, your people and sheep of your pasture,
will give you thanks forever.
We will praise you forever, to all generations.

**Gospel: Matthew 13: 36-43**

36 Then Jesus sent the multitudes away, and went into the house. His disciples came to him, saying, "Explain to us the parable of the darnel weeds of the field."
37 He answered them, "He who sows the good seed is the Son of Man, 38 the field is the world, the good seeds are the children of the Kingdom, and the darnel weeds are the children of the evil one. 39 The enemy who sowed them is the devil. The harvest is the end of the age, and the reapers are angels. 40 As therefore the darnel weeds are gathered up and burned with fire; so will it be at the end of this age. 41 The Son of Man will send out his angels, and they will gather out of his Kingdom all things that cause stumbling and those who do iniquity, 42 and will cast them into the furnace of fire. There will be weeping and gnashing of teeth. 43 Then the righteous will shine like the sun in the Kingdom of their Father. He who has ears to hear, let him hear.

1. Invite the Holy Spirit into this reading, asking the Author of Scripture to speak to you through His Word
2. Read today's passage as many times as you need, take your time
3. Write down (below) what the Lord is saying to you today
4. Live with this Word in your heart through the day

---

---

## Wednesday, July 31, 2024
### Saint Ignatius of Loyola, Priest

**First Reading:** Jeremiah 15: 10, 16-21

10 Woe is me, my mother, that you have borne me, a man of strife,
and a man of contention to the whole earth!
I have not lent, neither have men lent to me;
yet every one of them curses me.
16 Your words were found,
and I ate them.
Your words were to me a joy and the rejoicing of my heart,
for I am called by your name, Yahweh, God of Armies.
17 I didn't sit in the assembly of those who make merry and rejoice.
I sat alone because of your hand,
for you have filled me with indignation.
18 Why is my pain perpetual,
and my wound incurable,
which refuses to be healed?
Will you indeed be to me as a deceitful brook,
like waters that fail?
19 Therefore Yahweh says,
"If you return, then I will bring you again,
that you may stand before me;
and if you take out the precious from the vile,

you will be as my mouth.
They will return to you,
but you will not return to them.
20 I will make you to this people a fortified bronze wall.
They will fight against you,
but they will not prevail against you;
for I am with you to save you
and to deliver you," says Yahweh.
21 "I will deliver you out of the hand of the wicked,
and I will redeem you out of the hand of the terrible."

**Responsorial Psalm:** Psalms 59: 2-4, 10-11, 17

2 Deliver me from the workers of iniquity.
Save me from the bloodthirsty men.
3 For, behold, they lie in wait for my soul.
The mighty gather themselves together against me,
not for my disobedience, nor for my sin, Yahweh.
4 I have done no wrong, yet they are ready to attack me.
Rise up, behold, and help me!
10 My God will go before me with his loving kindness.
God will let me look at my enemies in triumph.
11 Don't kill them, or my people may forget.
Scatter them by your power, and bring them down, Lord our shield.
17 To you, my strength, I will sing praises.
For God is my high tower, the God of my mercy.

**Gospel: Matthew 13: 44-46**

44 "Again, the Kingdom of Heaven is like treasure hidden in the field, which a man found and hid. In his joy, he goes and sells all that he has and buys that field.
45 "Again, the Kingdom of Heaven is like a man who is a merchant seeking fine pearls,
46 who having found one pearl of great price, he went and sold all that he had and bought it.

1. Invite the Holy Spirit into this reading, asking the Author of Scripture to speak to you through His Word
2. Read today's passage as many times as you need, take your time

3. Write down (below) what the Lord is saying to you today
4. Live with this Word in your heart through the day

_____

_____

## Thursday, August 1, 2024
### Saint Alphonsus Liguori, Bishop and Doctor of the Church

**First Reading:** Jeremiah 18: 1-6

1 The word which came to Jeremiah from Yahweh, saying, 2 "Arise, and go down to the potter's house, and there I will cause you to hear my words."
3 Then I went down to the potter's house, and behold, he was making something on the wheels. 4 When the vessel that he made of the clay was marred in the hand of the potter, he made it again another vessel, as seemed good to the potter to make it.
5 Then Yahweh's word came to me, saying, 6 "House of Israel, can't I do with you as this potter?" says Yahweh. "Behold, as the clay in the potter's hand, so are you in my hand, house of Israel.

**Responsorial Psalm:** Psalms 146: 1b-6ab

1b Praise Yahweh, my soul.
2 While I live, I will praise Yahweh.
I will sing praises to my God as long as I exist.
3 Don't put your trust in princes,
in a son of man in whom there is no help.
4 His spirit departs, and he returns to the earth.
In that very day, his thoughts perish.
5 Happy is he who has the God of Jacob for his help,
whose hope is in Yahweh, his God,
6 who made heaven and earth,
the sea, and all that is in them;
who keeps truth forever;

## Gospel: Matthew 13: 47-53

47 "Again, the Kingdom of Heaven is like a dragnet that was cast into the sea and gathered some fish of every kind, 48 which, when it was filled, fishermen drew up on the beach. They sat down and gathered the good into containers, but the bad they threw away. 49 So it will be in the end of the world.§ The angels will come and separate the wicked from among the righteous, 50 and will cast them into the furnace of fire. There will be weeping and gnashing of teeth." 51 Jesus said to them, "Have you understood all these things?"

They answered him, "Yes, Lord."

52 He said to them, "Therefore every scribe who has been made a disciple in the Kingdom of Heaven is like a man who is a householder, who brings out of his treasure new and old things."

53 When Jesus had finished these parables, he departed from there.

1. Invite the Holy Spirit into this reading, asking the Author of Scripture to speak to you through His Word
2. Read today's passage as many times as you need, take your time
3. Write down (below) what the Lord is saying to you today
4. Live with this Word in your heart through the day

---

---

### Friday, August 2, 2024
Saint Eusebius of Vercelli, Bishop; Saint Peter Julian Eymard, Priest

**First Reading:** Jeremiah 26: 1-9

1 In the beginning of the reign of Jehoiakim the son of Josiah, king of Judah, this word came from Yahweh: 2 "Yahweh says: 'Stand in the court of Yahweh's house, and speak to all the cities of Judah which come to worship in Yahweh's house, all the words that I command you to speak to them. Don't omit a word. 3 It may be they will listen, and every man turn from his evil way, that I may relent from the evil which I intend to do to them because of the evil of their doings.' " 4 You shall tell them, "Yahweh says: 'If

you will not listen to me, to walk in my law which I have set before you, 5 to listen to the words of my servants the prophets whom I send to you, even rising up early and sending them—but you have not listened— 6 then I will make this house like Shiloh, and will make this city a curse to all the nations of the earth.' "

7 The priests and the prophets and all the people heard Jeremiah speaking these words in Yahweh's house. 8 When Jeremiah had finished speaking all that Yahweh had commanded him to speak to all the people, the priests and the prophets and all the people seized him, saying, "You shall surely die! 9 Why have you prophesied in Yahweh's name, saying, 'This house will be like Shiloh, and this city will be desolate, without inhabitant'?" All the people were crowded around Jeremiah in Yahweh's house.

**Responsorial Psalm:** Psalms 69: 5, 8-10, 14

5 God, you know my foolishness.
My sins aren't hidden from you.
8 I have become a stranger to my brothers,
an alien to my mother's children.
9 For the zeal of your house consumes me.
The reproaches of those who reproach you have fallen on me.
10 When I wept and I fasted,
that was to my reproach.
14 Deliver me out of the mire, and don't let me sink.
Let me be delivered from those who hate me, and out of the deep waters.

**Gospel: Matthew 13: 54-58**

54 Coming into his own country, he taught them in their synagogue, so that they were astonished and said, "Where did this man get this wisdom and these mighty works? 55 Isn't this the carpenter's son? Isn't his mother called Mary, and his brothers James, Joses, Simon, and Judas?† 56 Aren't all of his sisters with us? Where then did this man get all of these things?" 57 They were offended by him.
But Jesus said to them, "A prophet is not without honor, except in his own country and in his own house." 58 He didn't do many mighty works there because of their unbelief.

1. Invite the Holy Spirit into this reading, asking the Author of Scripture to speak to you through His Word
2. Read today's passage as many times as you need, take your time

---

---

## Saturday, August 3, 2024

**First Reading:** Jeremiah 26: 11-16, 24

11 Then the priests and the prophets spoke to the princes and to all the people, saying, "This man is worthy of death, for he has prophesied against this city, as you have heard with your ears."
12 Then Jeremiah spoke to all the princes and to all the people, saying, "Yahweh sent me to prophesy against this house and against this city all the words that you have heard. 13 Now therefore amend your ways and your doings, and obey Yahweh your God's voice; then Yahweh will relent from the evil that he has pronounced against you. 14 But as for me, behold, I am in your hand. Do with me what is good and right in your eyes. 15 Only know for certain that if you put me to death, you will bring innocent blood on yourselves, on this city, and on its inhabitants; for in truth Yahweh has sent me to you to speak all these words in your ears."
16 Then the princes and all the people said to the priests and to the prophets: "This man is not worthy of death; for he has spoken to us in the name of Yahweh our God."
24 But the hand of Ahikam the son of Shaphan was with Jeremiah, so that they didn't give him into the hand of the people to put him to death.

**Responsorial Psalm:** Psalms 69: 15-16, 30-31, 33-34

15 Don't let the flood waters overwhelm me,
neither let the deep swallow me up.
Don't let the pit shut its mouth on me.
16 Answer me, Yahweh, for your loving kindness is good.
According to the multitude of your tender mercies, turn to me.
30 I will praise the name of God with a song,
and will magnify him with thanksgiving.
31 It will please Yahweh better than an ox,

or a bull that has horns and hoofs.
33 For Yahweh hears the needy,
and doesn't despise his captive people.
34 Let heaven and earth praise him;
the seas, and everything that moves therein!

**Gospel: Matthew 14: 1-12**

1 At that time, Herod the tetrarch heard the report concerning Jesus, 2 and said to his servants, "This is John the Baptizer. He is risen from the dead. That is why these powers work in him." 3 For Herod had arrested John, bound him, and put him in prison for the sake of Herodias, his brother Philip's wife. 4 For John said to him, "It is not lawful for you to have her." 5 When he would have put him to death, he feared the multitude, because they counted him as a prophet. 6 But when Herod's birthday came, the daughter of Herodias danced among them and pleased Herod. 7 Therefore he promised with an oath to give her whatever she should ask. 8 She, being prompted by her mother, said, "Give me here on a platter the head of John the Baptizer."
9 The king was grieved, but for the sake of his oaths and of those who sat at the table with him, he commanded it to be given, 10 and he sent and beheaded John in the prison. 11 His head was brought on a platter and given to the young lady; and she brought it to her mother. 12 His disciples came, took the body, and buried it. Then they went and told Jesus.

1. Invite the Holy Spirit into this reading, asking the Author of Scripture to speak to you through His Word
2. Read today's passage as many times as you need, take your time
3. Write down (below) what the Lord is saying to you today
4. Live with this Word in your heart through the day

_____

_____

**Sunday, August 4, 2024**
EIGHTEENTH SUNDAY IN ORDINARY TIME

**First Reading:** Exodus 16: 2-4, 12-15

2 The whole congregation of the children of Israel murmured against Moses and against Aaron in the wilderness; 3 and the children of Israel said to them, "We wish that we had died by Yahweh's hand in the land of Egypt, when we sat by the meat pots, when we ate our fill of bread, for you have brought us out into this wilderness to kill this whole assembly with hunger."

4 Then Yahweh said to Moses, "Behold, I will rain bread from the sky for you, and the people shall go out and gather a day's portion every day, that I may test them, whether they will walk in my law or not.

12 "I have heard the murmurings of the children of Israel. Speak to them, saying, 'At evening you shall eat meat, and in the morning you shall be filled with bread. Then you will know that I am Yahweh your God.'"

13 In the evening, quail came up and covered the camp; and in the morning the dew lay around the camp. 14 When the dew that lay had gone, behold, on the surface of the wilderness was a small round thing, small as the frost on the ground. 15 When the children of Israel saw it, they said to one another, "What is it?" For they didn't know what it was. Moses said to them, "It is the bread which Yahweh has given you to eat.

**Responsorial Psalm:** Psalms 78: 3-4, 23-25, 54

3 which we have heard and known,
and our fathers have told us.
4 We will not hide them from their children,
telling to the generation to come the praises of Yahweh,
his strength, and his wondrous deeds that he has done.
23 Yet he commanded the skies above,
and opened the doors of heaven.
24 He rained down manna on them to eat,
and gave them food from the sky.
25 Man ate the bread of angels.
He sent them food to the full.
54 He brought them to the border of his sanctuary,
to this mountain, which his right hand had taken.

**Second Reading:** Ephesians 4: 17, 20-24

17 This I say therefore, and testify in the Lord, that you no longer walk as the rest of the Gentiles also walk, in the futility of their mind,

20 But you didn't learn Christ that way, 21 if indeed you heard him and were taught in him, even as truth is in Jesus: 22 that you put away, as concerning your former way of life, the old man that grows corrupt after the lusts of deceit, 23 and that you be renewed in the spirit of your mind, 24 and put on the new man, who in the likeness of God has been created in righteousness and holiness of truth.

## Gospel: John 6: 24-35

24 When the multitude therefore saw that Jesus wasn't there, nor his disciples, they themselves got into the boats and came to Capernaum, seeking Jesus. 25 When they found him on the other side of the sea, they asked him, "Rabbi, when did you come here?"

26 Jesus answered them, "Most certainly I tell you, you seek me, not because you saw signs, but because you ate of the loaves and were filled. 27 Don't work for the food which perishes, but for the food which remains to eternal life, which the Son of Man will give to you. For God the Father has sealed him."

28 They said therefore to him, "What must we do, that we may work the works of God?"

29 Jesus answered them, "This is the work of God, that you believe in him whom he has sent."

30 They said therefore to him, "What then do you do for a sign, that we may see and believe you? What work do you do? 31 Our fathers ate the manna in the wilderness. As it is written, 'He gave them bread out of heaven† to eat.' "*

32 Jesus therefore said to them, "Most certainly, I tell you, it wasn't Moses who gave you the bread out of heaven, but my Father gives you the true bread out of heaven. 33 For the bread of God is that which comes down out of heaven and gives life to the world."

34 They said therefore to him, "Lord, always give us this bread."

35 Jesus said to them, "I am the bread of life. Whoever comes to me will not be hungry, and whoever believes in me will never be thirsty.

1. Invite the Holy Spirit into this reading, asking the Author of Scripture to speak to you through His Word
2. Read today's passage as many times as you need, take your time
3. Write down (below) what the Lord is saying to you today
4. Live with this Word in your heart through the day

_____

_____

**First Reading:** Jeremiah 28: 1-17

1 That same year, in the beginning of the reign of Zedekiah king of Judah, in the fourth year, in the fifth month, Hananiah the son of Azzur, the prophet, who was of Gibeon, spoke to me in Yahweh's house, in the presence of the priests and of all the people, saying, 2 "Yahweh of Armies, the God of Israel, says, 'I have broken the yoke of the king of Babylon. 3 Within two full years I will bring again into this place all the vessels of Yahweh's house that Nebuchadnezzar king of Babylon took away from this place and carried to Babylon. 4 I will bring again to this place Jeconiah the son of Jehoiakim, king of Judah, with all the captives of Judah, who went to Babylon,' says Yahweh; 'for I will break the yoke of the king of Babylon.' "

5 Then the prophet Jeremiah said to the prophet Hananiah in the presence of the priests, and in the presence of all the people who stood in Yahweh's house, 6 even the prophet Jeremiah said, "Amen! May Yahweh do so. May Yahweh perform your words which you have prophesied, to bring again the vessels of Yahweh's house, and all those who are captives, from Babylon to this place. 7 Nevertheless listen now to this word that I speak in your ears, and in the ears of all the people: 8 The prophets who have been before me and before you of old prophesied against many countries, and against great kingdoms, of war, of evil, and of pestilence. 9 As for the prophet who prophesies of peace, when the word of the prophet happens, then the prophet will be known, that Yahweh has truly sent him."

10 Then Hananiah the prophet took the bar from off the prophet Jeremiah's neck, and broke it. 11 Hananiah spoke in the presence of all the people, saying, "Yahweh says: 'Even so I will break the yoke of Nebuchadnezzar king of Babylon from off the neck of all the nations within two full years.' " Then the prophet Jeremiah went his way.

12 Then Yahweh's word came to Jeremiah, after Hananiah the prophet had broken the bar from off the neck of the prophet Jeremiah, saying, 13 "Go, and tell Hananiah, saying, 'Yahweh says, "You have broken the bars of wood, but you have made in their place bars of iron." 14 For Yahweh of Armies, the God of Israel says, "I have put a yoke of iron on the neck of all these nations, that they may serve Nebuchadnezzar king of Babylon; and they will serve him. I have also given him the animals of the field." ' "

15 Then the prophet Jeremiah said to Hananiah the prophet, "Listen, Hananiah! Yahweh has not sent you, but you make this people trust in a lie. 16 Therefore Yahweh

says, 'Behold, I will send you away from off the surface of the earth. This year you will die, because you have spoken rebellion against Yahweh.' "

17 So Hananiah the prophet died the same year in the seventh month.

**Responsorial Psalm:** Psalms 119: 29, 43, 79, 80, 95, 102

29 Keep me from the way of deceit.
Grant me your law graciously!
43 Don't snatch the word of truth out of my mouth,
for I put my hope in your ordinances.
79 Let those who fear you turn to me.
They will know your statutes.
80 Let my heart be blameless toward your decrees,
that I may not be disappointed.
95 The wicked have waited for me, to destroy me.
I will consider your statutes.
102 I have not turned away from your ordinances,
for you have taught me.

**Gospel: Matthew 14: 13-21**

13 Now when Jesus heard this, he withdrew from there in a boat to a deserted place apart. When the multitudes heard it, they followed him on foot from the cities.
14 Jesus went out, and he saw a great multitude. He had compassion on them and healed their sick. 15 When evening had come, his disciples came to him, saying, "This place is deserted, and the hour is already late. Send the multitudes away, that they may go into the villages, and buy themselves food."
16 But Jesus said to them, "They don't need to go away. You give them something to eat."
17 They told him, "We only have here five loaves and two fish."
18 He said, "Bring them here to me." 19 He commanded the multitudes to sit down on the grass; and he took the five loaves and the two fish, and looking up to heaven, he blessed, broke and gave the loaves to the disciples; and the disciples gave to the multitudes. 20 They all ate and were filled. They took up twelve baskets full of that which remained left over from the broken pieces. 21 Those who ate were about five thousand men, in addition to women and children.

1. Invite the Holy Spirit into this reading, asking the Author of Scripture to speak to you through His Word
2. Read today's passage as many times as you need, take your time
3. Write down (below) what the Lord is saying to you today
4. Live with this Word in your heart through the day

---

---

## Tuesday, August 6, 2024
### The Transfiguration of the Lord

**First Reading:** Daniel 7: 9-10, 13-14

9 "I watched until thrones were placed,
and one who was ancient of days sat.
His clothing was white as snow,
and the hair of his head like pure wool.
His throne was fiery flames,
and its wheels burning fire.
10 A fiery stream issued and came out from before him.
Thousands of thousands ministered to him.
Ten thousand times ten thousand stood before him.
The judgment was set.
The books were opened.
13 "I saw in the night visions, and behold, there came with the clouds of the sky one like a son of man, and he came even to the Ancient of Days, and they brought him near before him. 14 Dominion was given him, and glory, and a kingdom, that all the peoples, nations, and languages should serve him. His dominion is an everlasting dominion, which will not pass away, and his kingdom one that will not be destroyed.

**Responsorial Psalm:** Psalms 97: 1-2, 5-6, 9

1 Yahweh reigns!
Let the earth rejoice!

Let the multitude of islands be glad!
2 Clouds and darkness are around him.
Righteousness and justice are the foundation of his throne.
5 The mountains melt like wax at the presence of Yahweh,
at the presence of the Lord of the whole earth.
6 The heavens declare his righteousness.
All the peoples have seen his glory.
9 For you, Yahweh, are most high above all the earth.
You are exalted far above all gods.

**Second Reading:** Second Peter 1: 16-19

16 For we didn't follow cunningly devised fables when we made known to you the power and coming of our Lord Jesus Christ, but we were eyewitnesses of his majesty. 17 For he received from God the Father honor and glory when the voice came to him from the Majestic Glory, "This is my beloved Son, in whom I am well pleased."* 18 We heard this voice come out of heaven when we were with him on the holy mountain.
19 We have the more sure word of prophecy; and you do well that you heed it as to a lamp shining in a dark place, until the day dawns and the morning star arises in your hearts,

**Gospel: Mark 9: 2-10**

2 After six days Jesus took with him Peter, James, and John, and brought them up onto a high mountain privately by themselves, and he was changed into another form in front of them. 3 His clothing became glistening, exceedingly white, like snow, such as no launderer on earth can whiten them. 4 Elijah and Moses appeared to them, and they were talking with Jesus.
5 Peter answered Jesus, "Rabbi, it is good for us to be here. Let's make three tents: one for you, one for Moses, and one for Elijah." 6 For he didn't know what to say, for they were very afraid.
7 A cloud came, overshadowing them, and a voice came out of the cloud, "This is my beloved Son. Listen to him."
8 Suddenly looking around, they saw no one with them any more, except Jesus only.
9 As they were coming down from the mountain, he commanded them that they should tell no one what things they had seen, until after the Son of Man had risen from the dead. 10 They kept this saying to themselves, questioning what the "rising from the dead" meant.

1. Invite the Holy Spirit into this reading, asking the Author of Scripture to speak to you through His Word
2. Read today's passage as many times as you need, take your time
3. Write down (below) what the Lord is saying to you today
4. Live with this Word in your heart through the day

---

---

## Wednesday, August 7, 2024
### Saint Sixtus II, Pope, and Companions, Martyrs; Saint Cajetan, Priest

**First Reading:** Jeremiah 31: 1-7

1 "At that time," says Yahweh, "I will be the God of all the families of Israel, and they will be my people."
2 Yahweh says, "The people who survive the sword found favor in the wilderness; even Israel, when I went to cause him to rest."
3 Yahweh appeared of old to me, saying,
"Yes, I have loved you with an everlasting love.
Therefore I have drawn you with loving kindness.
4 I will build you again,
and you will be built, O virgin of Israel.
You will again be adorned with your tambourines,
and will go out in the dances of those who make merry.
5 Again you will plant vineyards on the mountains of Samaria.
The planters will plant,
and will enjoy its fruit.
6 For there will be a day that the watchmen on the hills of Ephraim cry,
'Arise! Let's go up to Zion to Yahweh our God.' "
7 For Yahweh says,
"Sing with gladness for Jacob,
and shout for the chief of the nations.
Publish, praise, and say,
'Yahweh, save your people,

the remnant of Israel!'

**Responsorial Psalm:** Jeremiah 31: 10- 13

10 "Hear Yahweh's word, you nations,
and declare it in the distant islands. Say,
'He who scattered Israel will gather him,
and keep him, as a shepherd does his flock.'
11 For Yahweh has ransomed Jacob,
and redeemed him from the hand of him who was stronger than he.
12 They will come and sing in the height of Zion,
and will flow to the goodness of Yahweh,
to the grain, to the new wine, to the oil,
and to the young of the flock and of the herd.
Their soul will be as a watered garden.
They will not sorrow any more at all.
13 Then the virgin will rejoice in the dance,
the young men and the old together;
for I will turn their mourning into joy,
and will comfort them, and make them rejoice from their sorrow.

**Gospel: Matthew 15: 21-28**

21 Jesus went out from there and withdrew into the region of Tyre and Sidon. 22 Behold, a Canaanite woman came out from those borders and cried, saying, "Have mercy on me, Lord, you son of David! My daughter is severely possessed by a demon!" 23 But he answered her not a word.

His disciples came and begged him, saying, "Send her away; for she cries after us."
24 But he answered, "I wasn't sent to anyone but the lost sheep of the house of Israel."
25 But she came and worshiped him, saying, "Lord, help me."
26 But he answered, "It is not appropriate to take the children's bread and throw it to the dogs."
27 But she said, "Yes, Lord, but even the dogs eat the crumbs which fall from their masters' table."
28 Then Jesus answered her, "Woman, great is your faith! Be it done to you even as you desire." And her daughter was healed from that hour.

1. Invite the Holy Spirit into this reading, asking the Author of Scripture to speak to you through His Word
2. Read today's passage as many times as you need, take your time
3. Write down (below) what the Lord is saying to you today
4. Live with this Word in your heart through the day

_____

_____

## Thursday, August 8, 2024
### Saint Dominic, Priest

**First Reading:** Jeremiah 31: 31-34

31 "Behold, the days come," says Yahweh, "that I will make a new covenant with the house of Israel, and with the house of Judah, 32 not according to the covenant that I made with their fathers in the day that I took them by the hand to bring them out of the land of Egypt, which covenant of mine they broke, although I was a husband to them," says Yahweh. 33 "But this is the covenant that I will make with the house of Israel after those days," says Yahweh:
"I will put my law in their inward parts,
and I will write it in their heart.
I will be their God,
and they shall be my people.
34 They will no longer each teach his neighbor,
and every man teach his brother, saying, 'Know Yahweh;'
for they will all know me,
from their least to their greatest," says Yahweh,
"for I will forgive their iniquity,
and I will remember their sin no more."

**Responsorial Psalm:** Psalms 51: 12-15, 18-19

12 Restore to me the joy of your salvation.
Uphold me with a willing spirit.

13 Then I will teach transgressors your ways.

Sinners will be converted to you.

14 Deliver me from the guilt of bloodshed, O God, the God of my salvation.

My tongue will sing aloud of your righteousness.

15 Lord, open my lips.

My mouth will declare your praise.

18 Do well in your good pleasure to Zion.

Build the walls of Jerusalem.

19 Then you will delight in the sacrifices of righteousness,

in burnt offerings and in whole burnt offerings.

Then they will offer bulls on your altar.

## Gospel: Matthew 16: 13-23

13 Now when Jesus came into the parts of Caesarea Philippi, he asked his disciples, saying, "Who do men say that I, the Son of Man, am?"

14 They said, "Some say John the Baptizer, some, Elijah, and others, Jeremiah or one of the prophets."

15 He said to them, "But who do you say that I am?"

16 Simon Peter answered, "You are the Christ, the Son of the living God."

17 Jesus answered him, "Blessed are you, Simon Bar Jonah, for flesh and blood has not revealed this to you, but my Father who is in heaven. 18  I also tell you that you are Peter,† and on this rock ‡ I will build my assembly, and the gates of Hades§ will not prevail against it. 19  I will give to you the keys of the Kingdom of Heaven, and whatever you bind on earth will have been bound in heaven; and whatever you release on earth will have been released in heaven." 20 Then he commanded the disciples that they should tell no one that he was Jesus the Christ.

21 From that time, Jesus began to show his disciples that he must go to Jerusalem and suffer many things from the elders, chief priests, and scribes, and be killed, and the third day be raised up.

22 Peter took him aside and began to rebuke him, saying, "Far be it from you, Lord! This will never be done to you."

23 But he turned and said to Peter, "Get behind me, Satan! You are a stumbling block to me, for you are not setting your mind on the things of God, but on the things of men."

1. Invite the Holy Spirit into this reading, asking the Author of Scripture to speak to you through His Word

2. Read today's passage as many times as you need, take your time

3. Write down (below) what the Lord is saying to you today
4. Live with this Word in your heart through the day

_____

_____

## Friday, August 9, 2024
### Saint Teresa Benedicta of the Cross, Virgin and Martyr

**First Reading:** Nahum 2: 1, 3; 3: 1-3, 6-7

1 He who dashes in pieces has come up against you. Keep the fortress! Watch the way! Strengthen your waist! Fortify your power mightily!
3 The shield of his mighty men is made red. The valiant men are in scarlet. The chariots flash with steel in the day of his preparation, and the pine spears are brandished.
1 Woe to the bloody city! It is all full of lies and robbery—no end to the prey. 2 The noise of the whip, the noise of the rattling of wheels, prancing horses, and bounding chariots, 3 the horseman charging, and the flashing sword, the glittering spear, and a multitude of slain, and a great heap of corpses, and there is no end of the bodies. They stumble on their bodies
6 I will throw abominable filth on you and make you vile, and will make you a spectacle.
7 It will happen that all those who look at you will flee from you, and say, 'Nineveh is laid waste! Who will mourn for her?' Where will I seek comforters for you?"

**Responsorial Psalm:** Deuteronomy 32: 35cd-36ab, 39abcd, 41

35 Vengeance is mine, and recompense,
at the time when their foot slides,
for the day of their calamity is at hand.
Their doom rushes at them."
36 For Yahweh will judge his people,
and have compassion on his servants,
when he sees that their power is gone,
that there is no one remaining, shut up or left at large.
39 "See now that I myself am he.

There is no god with me.
I kill and I make alive.
I wound and I heal.
There is no one who can deliver out of my hand.
41 if I sharpen my glittering sword,
my hand grasps it in judgment;
I will take vengeance on my adversaries,
and will repay those who hate me.

**Gospel: Matthew 16: 24-28**

24 Then Jesus said to his disciples, "If anyone desires to come after me, let him deny himself, take up his cross, and follow me. 25 For whoever desires to save his life will lose it, and whoever will lose his life for my sake will find it. 26 For what will it profit a man if he gains the whole world and forfeits his life? Or what will a man give in exchange for his life? 27 For the Son of Man will come in the glory of his Father with his angels, and then he will render to everyone according to his deeds. 28 Most certainly I tell you, there are some standing here who will in no way taste of death until they see the Son of Man coming in his Kingdom."

1. Invite the Holy Spirit into this reading, asking the Author of Scripture to speak to you through His Word
2. Read today's passage as many times as you need, take your time
3. Write down (below) what the Lord is saying to you today
4. Live with this Word in your heart through the day

_____

_____

### Saturday, August 10, 2024
Saint Lawrence, Deacon and Martyr

**First Reading:** Second Corinthians 9: 6-10

6 Remember this: he who sows sparingly will also reap sparingly. He who sows bountifully will also reap bountifully. 7 Let each man give according as he has determined in his heart, not grudgingly or under compulsion, for God loves a cheerful giver. 8 And God is able to make all grace abound to you, that you, always having all sufficiency in everything, may abound to every good work. 9 As it is written,
"He has scattered abroad. He has given to the poor.
His righteousness remains forever."*
10 Now may he who supplies seed to the sower and bread for food, supply and multiply your seed for sowing, and increase the fruits of your righteousness,

**Responsorial Psalm:** Psalms 112: 1-2, 5-9

1 Praise Yah!†
Blessed is the man who fears Yahweh,
who delights greatly in his commandments.
2 His offspring will be mighty in the land.
The generation of the upright will be blessed.
5 It is well with the man who deals graciously and lends.
He will maintain his cause in judgment.
6 For he will never be shaken.
The righteous will be remembered forever.
7 He will not be afraid of evil news.
His heart is steadfast, trusting in Yahweh.
8 His heart is established.
He will not be afraid in the end when he sees his adversaries.
9 He has dispersed, he has given to the poor.
His righteousness endures forever.
His horn will be exalted with honor.

**Gospel: John 12: 24-26**

24 Most certainly I tell you, unless a grain of wheat falls into the earth and dies, it remains by itself alone. But if it dies, it bears much fruit. 25 He who loves his life will lose it. He who hates his life in this world will keep it to eternal life. 26 If anyone serves me, let him follow me. Where I am, there my servant will also be. If anyone serves me, the Father will honor him.

1. Invite the Holy Spirit into this reading, asking the Author of Scripture to speak to you through His Word
2. Read today's passage as many times as you need, take your time
3. Write down (below) what the Lord is saying to you today
4. Live with this Word in your heart through the day

_____

_____

## Sunday, August 11, 2024
### NINETEENTH SUNDAY IN ORDINARY TIME

**First Reading:** First Kings 19: 4-8

4 But he himself went a day's journey into the wilderness, and came and sat down under a juniper tree. Then he requested for himself that he might die, and said, "It is enough. Now, O Yahweh, take away my life; for I am not better than my fathers."
5 He lay down and slept under a juniper tree; and behold, an angel touched him, and said to him, "Arise and eat!"
6 He looked, and behold, there was at his head a cake baked on the coals, and a jar of water. He ate and drank, and lay down again. 7 Yahweh's angel came again the second time, and touched him, and said, "Arise and eat, because the journey is too great for you."
8 He arose, and ate and drank, and went in the strength of that food forty days and forty nights to Horeb, God's Mountain.

**Responsorial Psalm:** Psalms 34: 2-9

2 My soul shall boast in Yahweh.
The humble shall hear of it and be glad.
3 Oh magnify Yahweh with me.
Let's exalt his name together.
4 I sought Yahweh, and he answered me,
and delivered me from all my fears.
5 They looked to him, and were radiant.

Their faces shall never be covered with shame.
6 This poor man cried, and Yahweh heard him,
and saved him out of all his troubles.
7 Yahweh's angel encamps around those who fear him,
and delivers them.
8 Oh taste and see that Yahweh is good.
Blessed is the man who takes refuge in him.
9 Oh fear Yahweh, you his saints,
for there is no lack with those who fear him.

**Second Reading**: Ephesians 4: 30 – 5: 2

30 Don't grieve the Holy Spirit of God, in whom you were sealed for the day of redemption. 31 Let all bitterness, wrath, anger, outcry, and slander be put away from you, with all malice. 32 And be kind to one another, tender hearted, forgiving each other, just as God also in Christ forgave you.
1 Be therefore imitators of God, as beloved children. 2 Walk in love, even as Christ also loved us and gave himself up for us, an offering and a sacrifice to God for a sweet-smelling fragrance.

**Gospel: John 6: 41-51**

41 The Jews therefore murmured concerning him, because he said, "I am the bread which came down out of heaven." 42 They said, "Isn't this Jesus, the son of Joseph, whose father and mother we know? How then does he say, 'I have come down out of heaven'?"
43 Therefore Jesus answered them, "Don't murmur among yourselves. 44 No one can come to me unless the Father who sent me draws him; and I will raise him up in the last day. 45 It is written in the prophets, 'They will all be taught by God.' * Therefore everyone who hears from the Father and has learned, comes to me. 46 Not that anyone has seen the Father, except he who is from God. He has seen the Father. 47 Most certainly, I tell you, he who believes in me has eternal life. 48 I am the bread of life. 49 Your fathers ate the manna in the wilderness and they died. 50 This is the bread which comes down out of heaven, that anyone may eat of it and not die. 51 I am the living bread which came down out of heaven. If anyone eats of this bread, he will live forever. Yes, the bread which I will give for the life of the world is my flesh."

1. Invite the Holy Spirit into this reading, asking the Author of Scripture to speak to you through His Word
2. Read today's passage as many times as you need, take your time
3. Write down (below) what the Lord is saying to you today
4. Live with this Word in your heart through the day

_____

_____

## Monday, August 12, 2024
### Saint Jane Frances de Chantal, Religious

**First Reading:** Ezekiel 1: 2-5, 24-28c

2 In the fifth of the month, which was the fifth year of King Jehoiachin's captivity, 3 Yahweh's‡ word came to Ezekiel the priest, the son of Buzi, in the land of the Chaldeans by the river Chebar; and Yahweh's hand was there on him.

4 I looked, and behold,§ a stormy wind came out of the north: a great cloud, with flashing lightning, and a brightness around it, and out of the middle of it as it were glowing metal, out of the middle of the fire. 5 Out of its center came the likeness of four living creatures. This was their appearance: They had the likeness of a man.

24 When they went, I heard the noise of their wings like the noise of great waters, like the voice of the Almighty, a noise of tumult like the noise of an army. When they stood, they let down their wings.

25 There was a voice above the expanse that was over their heads. When they stood, they let down their wings. 26 Above the expanse that was over their heads was the likeness of a throne, as the appearance of a sapphire† stone. On the likeness of the throne was a likeness as the appearance of a man on it above. 27 I saw as it were glowing metal, as the appearance of fire within it all around, from the appearance of his waist and upward; and from the appearance of his waist and downward I saw as it were the appearance of fire, and there was brightness around him. 28 As the appearance of the rainbow that is in the cloud in the day of rain, so was the appearance of the brightness all around.

This was the appearance of the likeness of Yahweh's glory. When I saw it, I fell on my face, and I heard a voice of one that spoke.

**Responsorial Psalm:** Psalms 148: 1-2, 11-14

1 Praise Yah!
Praise Yahweh from the heavens!
Praise him in the heights!
2 Praise him, all his angels!
Praise him, all his army!
11 kings of the earth and all peoples,
princes and all judges of the earth,
12 both young men and maidens,
old men and children.
13 Let them praise Yahweh's name,
for his name alone is exalted.
His glory is above the earth and the heavens.
14 He has lifted up the horn of his people,
the praise of all his saints,
even of the children of Israel, a people near to him.
Praise Yah!

**Gospel: Matthew 17: 22-27**

22 While they were staying in Galilee, Jesus said to them, "The Son of Man is about to be delivered up into the hands of men, 23 and they will kill him, and the third day he will be raised up."
They were exceedingly sorry.
24 When they had come to Capernaum, those who collected the didrachma coins§ came to Peter, and said, "Doesn't your teacher pay the didrachma?" 25 He said, "Yes." When he came into the house, Jesus anticipated him, saying, "What do you think, Simon? From whom do the kings of the earth receive toll or tribute? From their children, or from strangers?"
26 Peter said to him, "From strangers."
Jesus said to him, "Therefore the children are exempt. 27 But, lest we cause them to stumble, go to the sea, cast a hook, and take up the first fish that comes up. When you have opened its mouth, you will find a stater coin.† Take that, and give it to them for me and you."

1. Invite the Holy Spirit into this reading, asking the Author of Scripture to speak to you through His Word
2. Read today's passage as many times as you need, take your time
3. Write down (below) what the Lord is saying to you today
4. Live with this Word in your heart through the day

_____

_____

## Tuesday, August 13, 2024
### Saints Pontian, Pope, and Hippolytus, Priest, Martyrs

**First Reading:** Ezekiel 2: 8 – 3: 4

8 But you, son of man, hear what I tell you. Don't be rebellious like that rebellious house. Open your mouth, and eat that which I give you."
9 When I looked, behold, a hand was stretched out to me; and behold, a scroll of a book was in it. 10 He spread it before me. It was written within and without; and lamentations, mourning, and woe were written in it.
1 He said to me, "Son of man, eat what you find. Eat this scroll, and go, speak to the house of Israel."
2 So I opened my mouth, and he caused me to eat the scroll.
3 He said to me, "Son of man, eat this scroll that I give you and fill your belly and your bowels with it."
Then I ate it. It was as sweet as honey in my mouth.
4 He said to me, "Son of man, go to the house of Israel, and speak my words to them.

**Responsorial Psalm:** Psalms 119: 14, 24, 72, 103, 111, 131

14 I have rejoiced in the way of your testimonies,
as much as in all riches.
24 Indeed your statutes are my delight,
and my counselors.
72 The law of your mouth is better to me than thousands of pieces of gold and silver.
103 How sweet are your promises to my taste,

more than honey to my mouth!
111 I have taken your testimonies as a heritage forever,
for they are the joy of my heart.
131 I opened my mouth wide and panted,
for I longed for your commandments.

### Gospel: Matthew 18: 1-5, 10, 12-14

1 In that hour the disciples came to Jesus, saying, "Who then is greatest in the Kingdom of Heaven?"
2 Jesus called a little child to himself, and set him in the middle of them 3 and said, "Most certainly I tell you, unless you turn and become as little children, you will in no way enter into the Kingdom of Heaven. 4 Whoever therefore humbles himself as this little child is the greatest in the Kingdom of Heaven. 5 Whoever receives one such little child in my name receives me,
10 See that you don't despise one of these little ones, for I tell you that in heaven their angels always see the face of my Father who is in heaven.
12 "What do you think? If a man has one hundred sheep, and one of them goes astray, doesn't he leave the ninety-nine, go to the mountains, and seek that which has gone astray? 13 If he finds it, most certainly I tell you, he rejoices over it more than over the ninety-nine which have not gone astray. 14 Even so it is not the will of your Father who is in heaven that one of these little ones should perish.


1. Invite the Holy Spirit into this reading, asking the Author of Scripture to speak to you through His Word
2. Read today's passage as many times as you need, take your time
3. Write down (below) what the Lord is saying to you today
4. Live with this Word in your heart through the day

_____

_____


**Wednesday, August 14, 2024**
Saint Maximilian Kolbe, Priest and Martyr

**First Reading:** Ezekiel 9: 1-7; 10: 18-22

1 Then he cried in my ears with a loud voice, saying, "Cause those who are in charge of the city to draw near, each man with his destroying weapon in his hand." 2 Behold, six men came from the way of the upper gate, which lies toward the north, every man with his slaughter weapon in his hand. One man in the middle of them was clothed in linen, with a writer's inkhorn by his side. They went in, and stood beside the bronze altar.

3 The glory of the God of Israel went up from the cherub, whereupon it was, to the threshold of the house; and he called to the man clothed in linen, who had the writer's inkhorn by his side. 4 Yahweh said to him, "Go through the middle of the city, through the middle of Jerusalem, and set a mark on the foreheads of the men that sigh and that cry over all the abominations that are done within it."

5 To the others he said in my hearing, "Go through the city after him, and strike. Don't let your eye spare, neither have pity. 6 Kill utterly the old man, the young man, the virgin, little children and women; but don't come near any man on whom is the mark. Begin at my sanctuary."

Then they began at the old men who were before the house.

7 He said to them, "Defile the house, and fill the courts with the slain. Go out!"

They went out, and struck in the city.

18 Yahweh's glory went out from over the threshold of the house and stood over the cherubim. 19 The cherubim lifted up their wings and mounted up from the earth in my sight when they went out, with the wheels beside them. Then they stood at the door of the east gate of Yahweh's house; and the glory of the God of Israel was over them above. 20 This is the living creature that I saw under the God of Israel by the river Chebar; and I knew that they were cherubim. 21 Every one had four faces, and every one four wings. The likeness of the hands of a man was under their wings. 22 As for the likeness of their faces, they were the faces which I saw by the river Chebar, their appearances and themselves. They each went straight forward.

**Responsorial Psalm:** Psalms 113: 1-6

1 Praise Yah!
Praise, you servants of Yahweh,
praise Yahweh's name.
2 Blessed be Yahweh's name,
from this time forward and forever more.
3 From the rising of the sun to its going down,
Yahweh's name is to be praised.

4 Yahweh is high above all nations,
his glory above the heavens.
5 Who is like Yahweh, our God,
who has his seat on high,
6 who stoops down to see in heaven and in the earth?

## Gospel: Matthew 18: 15-20

15 "If your brother sins against you, go, show him his fault between you and him alone. If he listens to you, you have gained back your brother. 16 But if he doesn't listen, take one or two more with you, that at the mouth of two or three witnesses every word may be established.* 17 If he refuses to listen to them, tell it to the assembly. If he refuses to hear the assembly also, let him be to you as a Gentile or a tax collector. 18 Most certainly I tell you, whatever things you bind on earth will have been bound in heaven, and whatever things you release on earth will have been released in heaven. 19 Again, assuredly I tell you, that if two of you will agree on earth concerning anything that they will ask, it will be done for them by my Father who is in heaven. 20 For where two or three are gathered together in my name, there I am in the middle of them."

1. Invite the Holy Spirit into this reading, asking the Author of Scripture to speak to you through His Word
2. Read today's passage as many times as you need, take your time
3. Write down (below) what the Lord is saying to you today
4. Live with this Word in your heart through the day

_____

_____

## Thursday, August 15, 2024
### THE ASSUMPTION OF THE BLESSED VIRGIN MARY

**First Reading:** Revelation 11: 19a; 12: 1-6a, 10ab

19 God's temple that is in heaven was opened, and the ark of the Lord's covenant was seen in his temple.

1 A great sign was seen in heaven: a woman clothed with the sun, and the moon under her feet, and on her head a crown of twelve stars. 2 She was with child. She cried out in pain, laboring to give birth.

3 Another sign was seen in heaven. Behold, a great red dragon, having seven heads and ten horns, and on his heads seven crowns. 4 His tail drew one third of the stars of the sky, and threw them to the earth. The dragon stood before the woman who was about to give birth, so that when she gave birth he might devour her child. 5 She gave birth to a son, a male child, who is to rule all the nations with a rod of iron. Her child was caught up to God and to his throne. 6 The woman fled into the wilderness, where she has a place prepared by God, that there they may nourish her one thousand two hundred sixty days.

10 I heard a loud voice in heaven, saying, "Now the salvation, the power, and the Kingdom of our God, and the authority of his Christ has come; for the accuser of our brothers has been thrown down, who accuses them before our God day and night.

**Responsorial Psalm:** Psalms 45: 10, 11, 12, 16

10 Listen, daughter, consider, and turn your ear.
Forget your own people, and also your father's house.
11 So the king will desire your beauty,
honor him, for he is your lord.
12 The daughter of Tyre comes with a gift.
The rich among the people entreat your favor.
16 Your sons will take the place of your fathers.
You shall make them princes in all the earth.

**Second Reading:** First Corinthians 15: 20-27

20 But now Christ has been raised from the dead. He became the first fruit of those who are asleep. 21 For since death came by man, the resurrection of the dead also came by man. 22 For as in Adam all die, so also in Christ all will be made alive. 23 But each in his own order: Christ the first fruits, then those who are Christ's at his coming. 24 Then the end comes, when he will deliver up the Kingdom to God the Father, when he will have abolished all rule and all authority and power. 25 For he must reign until he has put all his enemies under his feet. 26 The last enemy that will be abolished is death. 27 For, "He put all things in subjection under his feet."* But when he says, "All things are put in subjection", it is evident that he is excepted who subjected all things to him.

## Gospel: Luke 1: 39-56

39 Mary arose in those days and went into the hill country with haste, into a city of Judah, 40 and entered into the house of Zacharias and greeted Elizabeth. 41 When Elizabeth heard Mary's greeting, the baby leaped in her womb; and Elizabeth was filled with the Holy Spirit. 42 She called out with a loud voice and said, "Blessed are you among women, and blessed is the fruit of your womb! 43 Why am I so favored, that the mother of my Lord should come to me? 44 For behold, when the voice of your greeting came into my ears, the baby leaped in my womb for joy! 45 Blessed is she who believed, for there will be a fulfillment of the things which have been spoken to her from the Lord!"

46 Mary said,

"My soul magnifies the Lord.

47 My spirit has rejoiced in God my Savior,

48 for he has looked at the humble state of his servant.

For behold, from now on, all generations will call me blessed.

49 For he who is mighty has done great things for me.

Holy is his name.

50 His mercy is for generations and generations on those who fear him.

51 He has shown strength with his arm.

He has scattered the proud in the imagination of their hearts.

52 He has put down princes from their thrones,

and has exalted the lowly.

53 He has filled the hungry with good things.

He has sent the rich away empty.

54 He has given help to Israel, his servant, that he might remember mercy,

55 as he spoke to our fathers,

to Abraham and his offspring§ forever."

56 Mary stayed with her about three months, and then returned to her house.

1. Invite the Holy Spirit into this reading, asking the Author of Scripture to speak to you through His Word

2. Read today's passage as many times as you need, take your time

3. Write down (below) what the Lord is saying to you today

4. Live with this Word in your heart through the day

_____

_____

## Friday, August 16, 2024
### Saint Stephen of Hungary

**First Reading:** Ezekiel 16: 59-63

59 " 'For the Lord Yahweh says: "I will also deal with you as you have done, who have despised the oath in breaking the covenant. 60 Nevertheless I will remember my covenant with you in the days of your youth, and I will establish an everlasting covenant with you. 61 Then you will remember your ways and be ashamed when you receive your sisters, your elder sisters and your younger; and I will give them to you for daughters, but not by your covenant. 62 I will establish my covenant with you. Then you will know that I am Yahweh; 63 that you may remember, and be confounded, and never open your mouth any more because of your shame, when I have forgiven you all that you have done," says the Lord Yahweh.' "

**Responsorial Psalm:** Isaiah 12: 2-6

2 Behold, God is my salvation. I will trust, and will not be afraid; for Yah, Yahweh, is my strength and song; and he has become my salvation." 3 Therefore with joy you will draw water out of the wells of salvation. 4 In that day you will say, "Give thanks to Yahweh! Call on his name! Declare his doings among the peoples! Proclaim that his name is exalted! 5 Sing to Yahweh, for he has done excellent things! Let this be known in all the earth! 6 Cry aloud and shout, you inhabitant of Zion, for the Holy One of Israel is great among you!"

**Gospel: Matthew 19: 3-12**

3 Pharisees came to him, testing him and saying, "Is it lawful for a man to divorce his wife for any reason?"
4 He answered, "Haven't you read that he who made them from the beginning made them male and female,* 5  and said, 'For this cause a man shall leave his father and mother, and shall be joined to his wife; and the two shall become one flesh'?* 6 So that they are no more two, but one flesh. What therefore God has joined together, don't let man tear apart."
7 They asked him, "Why then did Moses command us to give her a certificate of divorce and divorce her?"

8 He said to them, "Moses, because of the hardness of your hearts, allowed you to divorce your wives, but from the beginning it has not been so. 9 I tell you that whoever divorces his wife, except for sexual immorality, and marries another, commits adultery; and he who marries her when she is divorced commits adultery."

10 His disciples said to him, "If this is the case of the man with his wife, it is not expedient to marry."

11 But he said to them, "Not all men can receive this saying, but those to whom it is given. 12 For there are eunuchs who were born that way from their mother's womb, and there are eunuchs who were made eunuchs by men; and there are eunuchs who made themselves eunuchs for the Kingdom of Heaven's sake. He who is able to receive it, let him receive it."

1. Invite the Holy Spirit into this reading, asking the Author of Scripture to speak to you through His Word
2. Read today's passage as many times as you need, take your time
3. Write down (below) what the Lord is saying to you today
4. Live with this Word in your heart through the day

_____

_____

## Saturday, August 17, 2024
### Saint Stephen of Hungary

**First Reading:** Ezekiel 18: 1-10, 13b, 30-32

1 Yahweh's word came to me again, saying, 2 "What do you mean, that you use this proverb concerning the land of Israel, saying,
'The fathers have eaten sour grapes,
and the children's teeth are set on edge'?
3 "As I live," says the Lord Yahweh, "you shall not use this proverb any more in Israel.
4 Behold, all souls are mine; as the soul of the father, so also the soul of the son is mine. The soul who sins, he shall die.
5 "But if a man is just,
and does that which is lawful and right,
6 and has not eaten on the mountains,

hasn't lifted up his eyes to the idols of the house of Israel,

hasn't defiled his neighbor's wife,

hasn't come near a woman in her impurity,

7 and has not wronged any,

but has restored to the debtor his pledge,

has taken nothing by robbery,

has given his bread to the hungry,

and has covered the naked with a garment;

8 he who hasn't lent to them with interest,

hasn't taken any increase from them,

who has withdrawn his hand from iniquity,

has executed true justice between man and man,

9 has walked in my statutes,

and has kept my ordinances,

to deal truly;

he is just,

he shall surely live," says the Lord Yahweh.

10 "If he fathers a son who is a robber who sheds blood, and who does any one of these things,

13 has lent with interest,

and has taken increase from the poor,

shall he then live? He shall not live. He has done all these abominations. He shall surely die. His blood will be on him.

30 "Therefore I will judge you, house of Israel, everyone according to his ways," says the Lord Yahweh. "Return, and turn yourselves from all your transgressions, so iniquity will not be your ruin. 31 Cast away from you all your transgressions in which you have transgressed; and make yourself a new heart and a new spirit. For why will you die, house of Israel? 32 For I have no pleasure in the death of him who dies," says the Lord Yahweh. "Therefore turn yourselves, and live!

**Responsorial Psalm:** Psalms 51: 12-15, 18-19

12 Restore to me the joy of your salvation.

Uphold me with a willing spirit.

13 Then I will teach transgressors your ways.

Sinners will be converted to you.

14 Deliver me from the guilt of bloodshed, O God, the God of my salvation.

My tongue will sing aloud of your righteousness.

15 Lord, open my lips.
My mouth will declare your praise.
18 Do well in your good pleasure to Zion.
Build the walls of Jerusalem.
19 Then you will delight in the sacrifices of righteousness,
in burnt offerings and in whole burnt offerings.
Then they will offer bulls on your altar.

## Gospel: Matthew 19: 13-15

13 Then little children were brought to him that he should lay his hands on them and pray; and the disciples rebuked them. 14 But Jesus said, "Allow the little children, and don't forbid them to come to me; for the Kingdom of Heaven belongs to ones like these." 15 He laid his hands on them, and departed from there.

1. Invite the Holy Spirit into this reading, asking the Author of Scripture to speak to you through His Word
2. Read today's passage as many times as you need, take your time
3. Write down (below) what the Lord is saying to you today
4. Live with this Word in your heart through the day

_____

_____

## Sunday, August 18, 2024
### TWENTIETH SUNDAY IN ORDINARY TIME

**First Reading:** Proverbs 9: 1-6

1 Wisdom has built her house.
She has carved out her seven pillars.
2 She has prepared her meat.
She has mixed her wine.
She has also set her table.
3 She has sent out her maidens.

She cries from the highest places of the city:
4 "Whoever is simple, let him turn in here!"
As for him who is void of understanding, she says to him,
5 "Come, eat some of my bread,
Drink some of the wine which I have mixed!
6 Leave your simple ways, and live.
Walk in the way of understanding."

**Responsorial Psalm:** Psalms 34: 2-3, 10-15

2 My soul shall boast in Yahweh.
The humble shall hear of it and be glad.
3 Oh magnify Yahweh with me.
Let's exalt his name together.
10 The young lions do lack, and suffer hunger,
but those who seek Yahweh shall not lack any good thing.
11 Come, you children, listen to me.
I will teach you the fear of Yahweh.
12 Who is someone who desires life,
and loves many days, that he may see good?
13 Keep your tongue from evil,
and your lips from speaking lies.
14 Depart from evil, and do good.
Seek peace, and pursue it.
15 Yahweh's eyes are toward the righteous.
His ears listen to their cry.

**Second Reading:** Ephesians 5: 15-20

15 Therefore watch carefully how you walk, not as unwise, but as wise, 16 redeeming the time, because the days are evil. 17 Therefore, don't be foolish, but understand what the will of the Lord is. 18 Don't be drunken with wine, in which is dissipation, but be filled with the Spirit, 19 speaking to one another in psalms, hymns, and spiritual songs; singing and making melody in your heart to the Lord; 20 giving thanks always concerning all things in the name of our Lord Jesus Christ to God, even the Father;

**Gospel: John 6: 51-58**

51 I am the living bread which came down out of heaven. If anyone eats of this bread, he will live forever. Yes, the bread which I will give for the life of the world is my flesh."
52 The Jews therefore contended with one another, saying, "How can this man give us his flesh to eat?"
53 Jesus therefore said to them, "Most certainly I tell you, unless you eat the flesh of the Son of Man and drink his blood, you don't have life in yourselves. 54 He who eats my flesh and drinks my blood has eternal life, and I will raise him up at the last day. 55 For my flesh is food indeed, and my blood is drink indeed. 56 He who eats my flesh and drinks my blood lives in me, and I in him. 57 As the living Father sent me, and I live because of the Father, so he who feeds on me will also live because of me. 58 This is the bread which came down out of heaven—not as our fathers ate the manna and died. He who eats this bread will live forever."

1. Invite the Holy Spirit into this reading, asking the Author of Scripture to speak to you through His Word
2. Read today's passage as many times as you need, take your time
3. Write down (below) what the Lord is saying to you today
4. Live with this Word in your heart through the day

---

---

## Monday, August 19, 2024
### Saint John Eudes, Priest

**First Reading:** Ezekiel 24: 15-23

15 Also Yahweh's word came to me, saying, 16 "Son of man, behold, I will take away from you the desire of your eyes with one stroke; yet you shall neither mourn nor weep, neither shall your tears run down. 17 Sigh, but not aloud. Make no mourning for the dead. Bind your headdress on you, and put your sandals on your feet. Don't cover your lips, and don't eat mourner's bread."
18 So I spoke to the people in the morning, and at evening my wife died. So I did in the morning as I was commanded.
19 The people asked me, "Won't you tell us what these things mean to us, that you act like this?"

20 Then I said to them, "Yahweh's word came to me, saying, 21 'Speak to the house of Israel, "The Lord Yahweh says: 'Behold, I will profane my sanctuary, the pride of your power, the desire of your eyes, and that which your soul pities; and your sons and your daughters whom you have left behind will fall by the sword. 22 You will do as I have done. You won't cover your lips or eat mourner's bread. 23 Your turbans will be on your heads, and your sandals on your feet. You won't mourn or weep; but you will pine away in your iniquities, and moan one toward another.

**Responsorial Psalm:** Deuteronomy 32: 18-19, 20, 21

18 Of the Rock who became your father, you are unmindful,
and have forgotten God who gave you birth.
19 Yahweh saw and abhorred,
because of the provocation of his sons and his daughters.
20 He said, "I will hide my face from them.
I will see what their end will be;
for they are a very perverse generation,
children in whom is no faithfulness.
21 They have moved me to jealousy with that which is not God.
They have provoked me to anger with their vanities.
I will move them to jealousy with those who are not a people.
I will provoke them to anger with a foolish nation.

**Gospel: Matthew 19: 16-22**

16 Behold, one came to him and said, "Good teacher, what good thing shall I do, that I may have eternal life?"
17 He said to him, "Why do you call me good?† No one is good but one, that is, God. But if you want to enter into life, keep the commandments."
18 He said to him, "Which ones?"
Jesus said, " 'You shall not murder.' 'You shall not commit adultery.' 'You shall not steal.' 'You shall not offer false testimony.' 19 'Honor your father and your mother.'* And, 'You shall love your neighbor as yourself.' "*
20 The young man said to him, "All these things I have observed from my youth. What do I still lack?"
21 Jesus said to him, "If you want to be perfect, go, sell what you have, and give to the poor, and you will have treasure in heaven; and come, follow me." 22 But when the young man heard this, he went away sad, for he was one who had great possessions.

1. Invite the Holy Spirit into this reading, asking the Author of Scripture to speak to you through His Word
2. Read today's passage as many times as you need, take your time
3. Write down (below) what the Lord is saying to you today
4. Live with this Word in your heart through the day

---

---

# Tuesday, August 20, 2024
## Saint Bernard, Abbot and Doctor of the Church

**First Reading:** Ezekiel 28: 1-10

1 Yahweh's word came again to me, saying, 2 "Son of man, tell the prince of Tyre, 'The Lord Yahweh says:
"Because your heart is lifted up,
and you have said, 'I am a god,
I sit in the seat of God,
in the middle of the seas;'
yet you are man,
and no god,
though you set your heart as the heart of a god—
3 behold, you are wiser than Daniel.
There is no secret that is hidden from you.
4 By your wisdom and by your understanding you have gotten yourself riches,
and have gotten gold and silver into your treasuries.
5 By your great wisdom
and by your trading you have increased your riches,
and your heart is lifted up because of your riches—"
6 " 'therefore the Lord Yahweh says:
"Because you have set your heart as the heart of God,
7 therefore, behold, I will bring strangers on you,
the terrible of the nations.

They will draw their swords against the beauty of your wisdom.
They will defile your brightness.
8 They will bring you down to the pit.
You will die the death of those who are slain
in the heart of the seas.
9 Will you yet say before him who kills you, 'I am God'?
But you are man, and not God,
in the hand of him who wounds you.
10 You will die the death of the uncircumcised
by the hand of strangers;
for I have spoken it," says the Lord Yahweh.' "

**Responsorial Psalm:** Deuteronomy 32: 26-28, 30, 35cd-36ab

26 I said that I would scatter them afar.
I would make their memory to cease from among men;
27 were it not that I feared the provocation of the enemy,
lest their adversaries should judge wrongly,
lest they should say, 'Our hand is exalted;
Yahweh has not done all this.' "
28 For they are a nation void of counsel.
There is no understanding in them.
30 How could one chase a thousand,
and two put ten thousand to flight,
unless their Rock had sold them,
and Yahweh had delivered them up?
35 Vengeance is mine, and recompense,
at the time when their foot slides,
for the day of their calamity is at hand.
Their doom rushes at them."
36 For Yahweh will judge his people,
and have compassion on his servants,
when he sees that their power is gone,
that there is no one remaining, shut up or left at large.

**Gospel: Matthew 19: 23-30**

23 Jesus said to his disciples, "Most certainly I say to you, a rich man will enter into the Kingdom of Heaven with difficulty. 24 Again I tell you, it is easier for a camel to go through a needle's eye than for a rich man to enter into God's Kingdom."

25 When the disciples heard it, they were exceedingly astonished, saying, "Who then can be saved?"

26 Looking at them, Jesus said, "With men this is impossible, but with God all things are possible."

27 Then Peter answered, "Behold, we have left everything and followed you. What then will we have?"

28 Jesus said to them, "Most certainly I tell you that you who have followed me, in the regeneration when the Son of Man will sit on the throne of his glory, you also will sit on twelve thrones, judging the twelve tribes of Israel. 29 Everyone who has left houses, or brothers, or sisters, or father, or mother, or wife, or children, or lands, for my name's sake, will receive one hundred times, and will inherit eternal life. 30 But many will be last who are first, and first who are last.

1. Invite the Holy Spirit into this reading, asking the Author of Scripture to speak to you through His Word
2. Read today's passage as many times as you need, take your time
3. Write down (below) what the Lord is saying to you today
4. Live with this Word in your heart through the day

_____

_____

## Wednesday, August 21, 2024
### Saint Pius X, Pope

**First Reading:** Ezekiel 34: 1-11

1 Yahweh's word came to me, saying, 2 "Son of man, prophesy against the shepherds of Israel. Prophesy, and tell them, even the shepherds, 'The Lord Yahweh says: "Woe to the shepherds of Israel who feed themselves! Shouldn't the shepherds feed the sheep? 3 You eat the fat. You clothe yourself with the wool. You kill the fatlings, but you don't feed the sheep. 4 You haven't strengthened the diseased. You haven't healed that which was sick. You haven't bound up that which was broken. You haven't brought

back that which was driven away. You haven't sought that which was lost, but you have ruled over them with force and with rigor. 5 They were scattered, because there was no shepherd. They became food to all the animals of the field, and were scattered. 6 My sheep wandered through all the mountains and on every high hill. Yes, my sheep were scattered on all the surface of the earth. There was no one who searched or sought."

7 " 'Therefore, you shepherds, hear Yahweh's word: 8 "As I live," says the Lord Yahweh, "surely because my sheep became a prey, and my sheep became food to all the animals of the field, because there was no shepherd, and my shepherds didn't search for my sheep, but the shepherds fed themselves, and didn't feed my sheep, 9 therefore, you shepherds, hear Yahweh's word!" 10 The Lord Yahweh says: "Behold, I am against the shepherds. I will require my sheep at their hand, and cause them to cease from feeding the sheep. The shepherds won't feed themselves any more. I will deliver my sheep from their mouth, that they may not be food for them."

11 " 'For the Lord Yahweh says: "Behold, I myself, even I, will search for my sheep, and will seek them out

**Responsorial Psalm:** Psalms 23: 1-6

1 Yahweh is my shepherd;
I shall lack nothing.
2 He makes me lie down in green pastures.
He leads me beside still waters.
3 He restores my soul.
He guides me in the paths of righteousness for his name's sake.
4 Even though I walk through the valley of the shadow of death,
I will fear no evil, for you are with me.
Your rod and your staff,
they comfort me.
5 You prepare a table before me
in the presence of my enemies.
You anoint my head with oil.
My cup runs over.
6 Surely goodness and loving kindness shall follow me all the days of my life,
and I will dwell in Yahweh's house forever.

**Gospel: Matthew 20: 1-16**

1 "For the Kingdom of Heaven is like a man who was the master of a household, who went out early in the morning to hire laborers for his vineyard. 2 When he had agreed with the laborers for a denarius† a day, he sent them into his vineyard. 3 He went out about the third hour,‡ and saw others standing idle in the marketplace. 4 He said to them, 'You also go into the vineyard, and whatever is right I will give you.' So they went their way. 5 Again he went out about the sixth and the ninth hour,§ and did likewise. 6 About the eleventh hour† he went out and found others standing idle. He said to them, 'Why do you stand here all day idle?'

7 "They said to him, 'Because no one has hired us.'

"He said to them, 'You also go into the vineyard, and you will receive whatever is right.' 8 "When evening had come, the lord of the vineyard said to his manager, 'Call the laborers and pay them their wages, beginning from the last to the first.' 9 "When those who were hired at about the eleventh hour came, they each received a denarius. 10 When the first came, they supposed that they would receive more; and they likewise each received a denarius. 11 When they received it, they murmured against the master of the household, 12 saying, 'These last have spent one hour, and you have made them equal to us who have borne the burden of the day and the scorching heat!'

13 "But he answered one of them, 'Friend, I am doing you no wrong. Didn't you agree with me for a denarius? 14 Take that which is yours, and go your way. It is my desire to give to this last just as much as to you. 15 Isn't it lawful for me to do what I want to with what I own? Or is your eye evil, because I am good?' 16 So the last will be first, and the first last. For many are called, but few are chosen."

1. Invite the Holy Spirit into this reading, asking the Author of Scripture to speak to you through His Word
2. Read today's passage as many times as you need, take your time
3. Write down (below) what the Lord is saying to you today
4. Live with this Word in your heart through the day

_____

_____

**Thursday, August 22, 2024**
The Queenship of the Blessed Virgin Mary

**First Reading:** Ezekiel 36: 23-28

23 I will sanctify my great name, which has been profaned among the nations, which you have profaned among them. Then the nations will know that I am Yahweh," says the Lord Yahweh, "when I am proven holy in you before their eyes.
24 " ' "For I will take you from among the nations and gather you out of all the countries, and will bring you into your own land. 25 I will sprinkle clean water on you, and you will be clean. I will cleanse you from all your filthiness and from all your idols. 26 I will also give you a new heart, and I will put a new spirit within you. I will take away the stony heart out of your flesh, and I will give you a heart of flesh. 27 I will put my Spirit within you, and cause you to walk in my statutes. You will keep my ordinances and do them. 28 You will dwell in the land that I gave to your fathers. You will be my people, and I will be your God.

**Responsorial Psalm:** Psalms 51: 12-15, 18-19

12 Restore to me the joy of your salvation.
Uphold me with a willing spirit.
13 Then I will teach transgressors your ways.
Sinners will be converted to you.
14 Deliver me from the guilt of bloodshed, O God, the God of my salvation.
My tongue will sing aloud of your righteousness.
15 Lord, open my lips.
My mouth will declare your praise.
18 Do well in your good pleasure to Zion.
Build the walls of Jerusalem.
19 Then you will delight in the sacrifices of righteousness,
in burnt offerings and in whole burnt offerings.
Then they will offer bulls on your altar.

**Gospel: Matthew 22: 1-14**

1 Jesus answered and spoke to them again in parables, saying, 2 "The Kingdom of Heaven is like a certain king, who made a wedding feast for his son, 3 and sent out his servants to call those who were invited to the wedding feast, but they would not come. 4 Again he sent out other servants, saying, 'Tell those who are invited, "Behold, I have prepared my dinner. My cattle and my fatlings are killed, and all things are ready. Come to the wedding feast!" ' 5 But they made light of it, and went their ways, one to

his own farm, another to his merchandise; 6 and the rest grabbed his servants, treated them shamefully, and killed them. 7 When the king heard that, he was angry, and sent his armies, destroyed those murderers, and burned their city.

8 "Then he said to his servants, 'The wedding is ready, but those who were invited weren't worthy. 9 Go therefore to the intersections of the highways, and as many as you may find, invite to the wedding feast.' 10 Those servants went out into the highways and gathered together as many as they found, both bad and good. The wedding was filled with guests.

11 "But when the king came in to see the guests, he saw there a man who didn't have on wedding clothing, 12 and he said to him, 'Friend, how did you come in here not wearing wedding clothing?' He was speechless. 13 Then the king said to the servants, 'Bind him hand and foot, take him away, and throw him into the outer darkness. That is where the weeping and grinding of teeth will be.' 14 For many are called, but few chosen."

1. Invite the Holy Spirit into this reading, asking the Author of Scripture to speak to you through His Word
2. Read today's passage as many times as you need, take your time
3. Write down (below) what the Lord is saying to you today
4. Live with this Word in your heart through the day

_____

_____

## Friday, August 23, 2024
### Saint Rose of Lima, Virgin

**First Reading:** Ezekiel 37: 1-14

1 Yahweh's hand was on me, and he brought me out in Yahweh's Spirit, and set me down in the middle of the valley; and it was full of bones. 2 He caused me to pass by them all around; and behold, there were very many in the open valley, and behold, they were very dry. 3 He said to me, "Son of man, can these bones live?"
I answered, "Lord Yahweh, you know."

4 Again he said to me, "Prophesy over these bones, and tell them, 'You dry bones, hear Yahweh's word. 5 The Lord Yahweh says to these bones: "Behold, I will cause breath to enter into you, and you will live. 6 I will lay sinews on you, and will bring up flesh on you, and cover you with skin, and put breath in you, and you will live. Then you will know that I am Yahweh."'"

7 So I prophesied as I was commanded. As I prophesied, there was a noise, and behold, there was an earthquake. Then the bones came together, bone to its bone. 8 I saw, and, behold, there were sinews on them, and flesh came up, and skin covered them above; but there was no breath in them.

9 Then he said to me, "Prophesy to the wind, prophesy, son of man, and tell the wind, 'The Lord Yahweh says: "Come from the four winds, breath, and breathe on these slain, that they may live."'"

10 So I prophesied as he commanded me, and the breath came into them, and they lived, and stood up on their feet, an exceedingly great army.

11 Then he said to me, "Son of man, these bones are the whole house of Israel. Behold, they say, 'Our bones are dried up, and our hope is lost. We are completely cut off.' 12 Therefore prophesy, and tell them, 'The Lord Yahweh says: "Behold, I will open your graves, and cause you to come up out of your graves, my people; and I will bring you into the land of Israel. 13 You will know that I am Yahweh, when I have opened your graves and caused you to come up out of your graves, my people. 14 I will put my Spirit in you, and you will live. Then I will place you in your own land; and you will know that I, Yahweh, have spoken it and performed it," says Yahweh.'"

**Responsorial Psalm:** Psalms 107: 2-9

2 Let the redeemed by Yahweh say so,
whom he has redeemed from the hand of the adversary,
3 and gathered out of the lands,
from the east and from the west,
from the north and from the south.
4 They wandered in the wilderness in a desert way.
They found no city to live in.
5 Hungry and thirsty,
their soul fainted in them.
6 Then they cried to Yahweh in their trouble,
and he delivered them out of their distresses.
7 He led them also by a straight way,
that they might go to a city to live in.

8 Let them praise Yahweh for his loving kindness,
for his wonderful deeds to the children of men!
9 For he satisfies the longing soul.
He fills the hungry soul with good.

## Gospel: Matthew 22: 34-40

34 But the Pharisees, when they heard that he had silenced the Sadducees, gathered themselves together. 35 One of them, a lawyer, asked him a question, testing him. 36 "Teacher, which is the greatest commandment in the law?"
37 Jesus said to him, " 'You shall love the Lord your God with all your heart, with all your soul, and with all your mind.'* 38  This is the first and great commandment. 39 A second likewise is this, 'You shall love your neighbor as yourself.'* 40  The whole law and the prophets depend on these two commandments."

1. Invite the Holy Spirit into this reading, asking the Author of Scripture to speak to you through His Word
2. Read today's passage as many times as you need, take your time
3. Write down (below) what the Lord is saying to you today
4. Live with this Word in your heart through the day

_____

_____

## Saturday, August 24, 2024
### Saint Bartholomew, Apostle

**First Reading:** Revelation 21: 9b-14

9 One of the seven angels who had the seven bowls which were loaded with the seven last plagues came, and he spoke with me, saying, "Come here. I will show you the bride, the Lamb's wife." 10 He carried me away in the Spirit to a great and high mountain, and showed me the holy city, Jerusalem, coming down out of heaven from God, 11 having the glory of God. Her light was like a most precious stone, like a jasper stone,

clear as crystal; 12 having a great and high wall with twelve gates, and at the gates twelve angels, and names written on them, which are the names of the twelve tribes of the children of Israel. 13 On the east were three gates, and on the north three gates, and on the south three gates, and on the west three gates. 14 The wall of the city had twelve foundations, and on them twelve names of the twelve Apostles of the Lamb.

**Responsorial Psalm:** Psalms 145: 10-13, 17-18

10 All your works will give thanks to you, Yahweh.
Your saints will extol you.
11 They will speak of the glory of your kingdom,
and talk about your power,
12 to make known to the sons of men his mighty acts,
the glory of the majesty of his kingdom.
13 Your kingdom is an everlasting kingdom.
Your dominion endures throughout all generations.
Yahweh is faithful in all his words,
and loving in all his deeds.‡
17 Yahweh is righteous in all his ways,
and gracious in all his works.
18 Yahweh is near to all those who call on him,
to all who call on him in truth.

**Gospel: John 1: 45-51**

45 Philip found Nathanael, and said to him, "We have found him of whom Moses in the law and also the prophets, wrote: Jesus of Nazareth, the son of Joseph."
46 Nathanael said to him, "Can any good thing come out of Nazareth?"
Philip said to him, "Come and see."
47 Jesus saw Nathanael coming to him, and said about him, "Behold, an Israelite indeed, in whom is no deceit!"
48 Nathanael said to him, "How do you know me?"
Jesus answered him, "Before Philip called you, when you were under the fig tree, I saw you."
49 Nathanael answered him, "Rabbi, you are the Son of God! You are King of Israel!"
50 Jesus answered him, "Because I told you, 'I saw you underneath the fig tree,' do you believe? You will see greater things than these!" 51 He said to him, "Most certainly, I tell you all, hereafter you will see heaven opened, and the angels of God ascending and descending on the Son of Man."

1. Invite the Holy Spirit into this reading, asking the Author of Scripture to speak to you through His Word
2. Read today's passage as many times as you need, take your time
3. Write down (below) what the Lord is saying to you today
4. Live with this Word in your heart through the day

---

## Sunday, August 25, 2024
### TWENTY-FIRST SUNDAY IN ORDINARY TIME

**First Reading:** Joshua 24: 1-2a, 15-17, 18b

1 Joshua gathered all the tribes of Israel to Shechem, and called for the elders of Israel, for their heads, for their judges, and for their officers; and they presented themselves before God. 2 Joshua said to all the people, "Yahweh, the God of Israel, says, 'Your fathers lived of old time beyond the River, even Terah, the father of Abraham, and the father of Nahor. They served other gods.
15 If it seems evil to you to serve Yahweh, choose today whom you will serve; whether the gods which your fathers served that were beyond the River, or the gods of the Amorites, in whose land you dwell; but as for me and my house, we will serve Yahweh."
16 The people answered, "Far be it from us that we should forsake Yahweh, to serve other gods; 17 for it is Yahweh our God who brought us and our fathers up out of the land of Egypt, from the house of bondage, and who did those great signs in our sight, and preserved us in all the way in which we went, and among all the peoples through the middle of whom we passed. 18 Yahweh drove out from before us all the peoples, even the Amorites who lived in the land. Therefore we also will serve Yahweh; for he is our God."

**Responsorial Psalm:** Psalms 34: 2-3, 16-22

2 My soul shall boast in Yahweh.
The humble shall hear of it and be glad.

3 Oh magnify Yahweh with me.
Let's exalt his name together.
16 Yahweh's face is against those who do evil,
to cut off their memory from the earth.
17 The righteous cry, and Yahweh hears,
and delivers them out of all their troubles.
18 Yahweh is near to those who have a broken heart,
and saves those who have a crushed spirit.
19 Many are the afflictions of the righteous,
but Yahweh delivers him out of them all.
20 He protects all of his bones.
Not one of them is broken.
21 Evil shall kill the wicked.
Those who hate the righteous shall be condemned.
22 Yahweh redeems the soul of his servants.
None of those who take refuge in him shall be condemned.

**Second Reading:** Ephesians 5: 21-32

21 subjecting yourselves to one another in the fear of Christ.
22 Wives, be subject to your own husbands, as to the Lord. 23 For the husband is the head of the wife, as Christ also is the head of the assembly, being himself the savior of the body. 24 But as the assembly is subject to Christ, so let the wives also be to their own husbands in everything.
25 Husbands, love your wives, even as Christ also loved the assembly and gave himself up for her, 26 that he might sanctify her, having cleansed her by the washing of water with the word, 27 that he might present the assembly to himself gloriously, not having spot or wrinkle or any such thing, but that she should be holy and without defect. 28 Even so husbands also ought to love their own wives as their own bodies. He who loves his own wife loves himself. 29 For no man ever hated his own flesh, but nourishes and cherishes it, even as the Lord also does the assembly, 30 because we are members of his body, of his flesh and bones. 31 "For this cause a man will leave his father and mother and will be joined to his wife. Then the two will become one flesh."* 32 This mystery is great, but I speak concerning Christ and the assembly.

**Gospel: John 6: 60-69**

60 Therefore many of his disciples, when they heard this, said, "This is a hard saying! Who can listen to it?"

61 But Jesus knowing in himself that his disciples murmured at this, said to them, "Does this cause you to stumble? 62 Then what if you would see the Son of Man ascending to where he was before? 63 It is the spirit who gives life. The flesh profits nothing. The words that I speak to you are spirit, and are life. 64 But there are some of you who don't believe." For Jesus knew from the beginning who they were who didn't believe, and who it was who would betray him. 65 He said, "For this cause I have said to you that no one can come to me, unless it is given to him by my Father."

66 At this, many of his disciples went back and walked no more with him. 67 Jesus said therefore to the twelve, "You don't also want to go away, do you?"

68 Simon Peter answered him, "Lord, to whom would we go? You have the words of eternal life. 69 We have come to believe and know that you are the Christ, the Son of the living God."

1. Invite the Holy Spirit into this reading, asking the Author of Scripture to speak to you through His Word
2. Read today's passage as many times as you need, take your time
3. Write down (below) what the Lord is saying to you today
4. Live with this Word in your heart through the day

_____

_____

## Monday, August 26, 2024

**First Reading:** Second Thessalonians 1: 1-5, 11-12

1 Paul, Silvanus, and Timothy, to the assembly of the Thessalonians in God our Father and the Lord Jesus Christ: 2 Grace to you and peace from God our Father and the Lord Jesus Christ.

3 We are bound to always give thanks to God for you, brothers,† even as it is appropriate, because your faith grows exceedingly, and the love of each and every one of you toward one another abounds, 4 so that we ourselves boast about you in the assemblies of God for your perseverance and faith in all your persecutions and in the afflictions which you endure. 5 This is an obvious sign of the righteous judgment of

God, to the end that you may be counted worthy of God's Kingdom, for which you also suffer.

11 To this end we also pray always for you that our God may count you worthy of your calling, and fulfill every desire of goodness and work of faith with power, 12 that the name of our Lord Jesus‡ may be glorified in you, and you in him, according to the grace of our God and the Lord Jesus Christ.

**Responsorial Psalm:** Psalms 96: 1-5

1 Sing to Yahweh a new song!
Sing to Yahweh, all the earth.
2 Sing to Yahweh!
Bless his name!
Proclaim his salvation from day to day!
3 Declare his glory among the nations,
his marvelous works among all the peoples.
4 For Yahweh is great, and greatly to be praised!
He is to be feared above all gods.
5 For all the gods of the peoples are idols,
but Yahweh made the heavens.

**Gospel: Matthew 23: 13-22**

13 "Woe to you, scribes and Pharisees, hypocrites! For you devour widows' houses, and as a pretense you make long prayers. Therefore you will receive greater condemnation.

14 "But woe to you, scribes and Pharisees, hypocrites! Because you shut up the Kingdom of Heaven against men; for you don't enter in yourselves, neither do you allow those who are entering in to enter.† 15 Woe to you, scribes and Pharisees, hypocrites! For you travel around by sea and land to make one proselyte; and when he becomes one, you make him twice as much a son of Gehenna‡ as yourselves.

16 "Woe to you, you blind guides, who say, 'Whoever swears by the temple, it is nothing; but whoever swears by the gold of the temple, he is obligated.' 17 You blind fools! For which is greater, the gold or the temple that sanctifies the gold? 18 And, 'Whoever swears by the altar, it is nothing; but whoever swears by the gift that is on it, he is obligated.' 19 You blind fools! For which is greater, the gift, or the altar that sanctifies the gift? 20 He therefore who swears by the altar, swears by it and by everything on it. 21 He who swears by the temple, swears by it and by him who has

been living§ in it. 22  He who swears by heaven, swears by the throne of God and by him who sits on it.

1. Invite the Holy Spirit into this reading, asking the Author of Scripture to speak to you through His Word
2. Read today's passage as many times as you need, take your time
3. Write down (below) what the Lord is saying to you today
4. Live with this Word in your heart through the day

---

---

## Tuesday, August 27, 2024
### Saint Monica

**First Reading:** Second Thessalonians 2: 1-3a, 14-17

1 Now, brothers, concerning the coming of our Lord Jesus Christ and our gathering together to him, we ask you 2 not to be quickly shaken in your mind or troubled, either by spirit or by word or by letter as if from us, saying that the day of Christ has already come. 3 Let no one deceive you in any way. For it will not be unless the rebellion† comes first, and the man of sin is revealed, the son of destruction.
14 to which he called you through our Good News, for the obtaining of the glory of our Lord Jesus Christ. 15 So then, brothers, stand firm and hold the traditions which you were taught by us, whether by word or by letter.
16 Now our Lord Jesus Christ himself, and God our Father, who loved us and gave us eternal comfort and good hope through grace, 17 comfort your hearts and establish you in every good work and word.

**Responsorial Psalm:** Psalms 96: 10-13

10 Say among the nations, "Yahweh reigns."
The world is also established.
It can't be moved.
He will judge the peoples with equity.
11 Let the heavens be glad, and let the earth rejoice.

Let the sea roar, and its fullness!
12 Let the field and all that is in it exult!
Then all the trees of the woods shall sing for joy
13 before Yahweh; for he comes,
for he comes to judge the earth.
He will judge the world with righteousness,
the peoples with his truth.

**Gospel: Matthew 23: 23-26**

23 "Woe to you, scribes and Pharisees, hypocrites! For you tithe mint, dill, and cumin,†
and have left undone the weightier matters of the law: justice, mercy, and faith. But
you ought to have done these, and not to have left the other undone. 24 You blind
guides, who strain out a gnat, and swallow a camel!
25 "Woe to you, scribes and Pharisees, hypocrites! For you clean the outside of the cup
and of the platter, but within they are full of extortion and unrighteousness.‡ 26 You
blind Pharisee, first clean the inside of the cup and of the platter, that its outside may
become clean also.

1. Invite the Holy Spirit into this reading, asking the Author of Scripture to speak to
you through His Word
2. Read today's passage as many times as you need, take your time
3. Write down (below) what the Lord is saying to you today
4. Live with this Word in your heart through the day

_____

_____

### Wednesday, August 28, 2024
Saint Augustine, Bishop and Doctor of the Church

**First Reading:** Second Thessalonians 3: 6-10, 16-18

6 Now we command you, brothers, in the name of our Lord Jesus Christ, that you
withdraw yourselves from every brother who walks in rebellion and not after the

tradition which they received from us. 7 For you know how you ought to imitate us. For we didn't behave ourselves rebelliously among you, 8 neither did we eat bread from anyone's hand without paying for it, but in labor and travail worked night and day, that we might not burden any of you. 9 This was not because we don't have the right, but to make ourselves an example to you, that you should imitate us. 10 For even when we were with you, we commanded you this: "If anyone is not willing to work, don't let him eat."

16 Now may the Lord of peace himself give you peace at all times in all ways. The Lord be with you all.

17 I, Paul, write this greeting with my own hand, which is the sign in every letter. This is how I write. 18 The grace of our Lord Jesus Christ be with you all. Amen.

**Responsorial Psalm:** Psalms 128: 1-2, 4-5

1 Blessed is everyone who fears Yahweh,
who walks in his ways.
2 For you will eat the labor of your hands.
You will be happy, and it will be well with you.
4 Behold, this is how the man who fears Yahweh is blessed.
5 May Yahweh bless you out of Zion,
and may you see the good of Jerusalem all the days of your life.

**Gospel: Matthew 23: 27-32**

27 "Woe to you, scribes and Pharisees, hypocrites! For you are like whitened tombs, which outwardly appear beautiful, but inwardly are full of dead men's bones and of all uncleanness. 28 Even so you also outwardly appear righteous to men, but inwardly you are full of hypocrisy and iniquity.

29 "Woe to you, scribes and Pharisees, hypocrites! For you build the tombs of the prophets and decorate the tombs of the righteous, 30 and say, 'If we had lived in the days of our fathers, we wouldn't have been partakers with them in the blood of the prophets.' 31 Therefore you testify to yourselves that you are children of those who killed the prophets. 32 Fill up, then, the measure of your fathers.

1. Invite the Holy Spirit into this reading, asking the Author of Scripture to speak to you through His Word
2. Read today's passage as many times as you need, take your time
3. Write down (below) what the Lord is saying to you today

_____

_____

## Thursday, August 29, 2024
### The Passion of Saint John the Baptist

**First Reading:** First Corinthians 1: 1-9

1 Paul, called to be an apostle of Jesus Christ† through the will of God, and our brother Sosthenes, 2 to the assembly of God which is at Corinth—those who are sanctified in Christ Jesus, called saints, with all who call on the name of our Lord Jesus Christ in every place, both theirs and ours: 3 Grace to you and peace from God our Father and the Lord Jesus Christ.

4 I always thank my God concerning you for the grace of God which was given you in Christ Jesus, 5 that in everything you were enriched in him, in all speech and all knowledge— 6 even as the testimony of Christ was confirmed in you— 7 so that you come behind in no gift, waiting for the revelation of our Lord Jesus Christ, 8 who will also confirm you until the end, blameless in the day of our Lord Jesus Christ. 9 God is faithful, through whom you were called into the fellowship of his Son, Jesus Christ our Lord.

**Responsorial Psalm:** Psalms 145: 2-7

2 Every day I will praise you.
I will extol your name forever and ever.
3 Great is Yahweh, and greatly to be praised!
His greatness is unsearchable.
4 One generation will commend your works to another,
and will declare your mighty acts.
5 I will meditate on the glorious majesty of your honor,
on your wondrous works.
6 Men will speak of the might of your awesome acts.
I will declare your greatness.

7 They will utter the memory of your great goodness,
and will sing of your righteousness.

## Gospel: Mark 6: 17-29

17 For Herod himself had sent out and arrested John and bound him in prison for the sake of Herodias, his brother Philip's wife, for he had married her. 18 For John had said to Herod, "It is not lawful for you to have your brother's wife." 19 Herodias set herself against him and desired to kill him, but she couldn't, 20 for Herod feared John, knowing that he was a righteous and holy man, and kept him safe. When he heard him, he did many things, and he heard him gladly.

21 Then a convenient day came when Herod on his birthday made a supper for his nobles, the high officers, and the chief men of Galilee. 22 When the daughter of Herodias herself came in and danced, she pleased Herod and those sitting with him. The king said to the young lady, "Ask me whatever you want, and I will give it to you."

23 He swore to her, "Whatever you ask of me, I will give you, up to half of my kingdom."

24 She went out and said to her mother, "What shall I ask?"

She said, "The head of John the Baptizer."

25 She came in immediately with haste to the king and requested, "I want you to give me right now the head of John the Baptizer on a platter."

26 The king was exceedingly sorry, but for the sake of his oaths and of his dinner guests, he didn't wish to refuse her. 27 Immediately the king sent out a soldier of his guard and commanded to bring John's head; and he went and beheaded him in the prison, 28 and brought his head on a platter, and gave it to the young lady; and the young lady gave it to her mother.

29 When his disciples heard this, they came and took up his corpse and laid it in a tomb.

1. Invite the Holy Spirit into this reading, asking the Author of Scripture to speak to you through His Word
2. Read today's passage as many times as you need, take your time
3. Write down (below) what the Lord is saying to you today
4. Live with this Word in your heart through the day

_____

_____

# Friday, August 30, 2024

**First Reading:** First Corinthians 1: 17-25

17 For Christ sent me not to baptize, but to preach the Good News—not in wisdom of words, so that the cross of Christ wouldn't be made void. 18 For the word of the cross is foolishness to those who are dying, but to us who are being saved it is the power of God. 19 For it is written,
"I will destroy the wisdom of the wise.
I will bring the discernment of the discerning to nothing."*
20 Where is the wise? Where is the scribe? Where is the debater of this age? Hasn't God made foolish the wisdom of this world? 21 For seeing that in the wisdom of God, the world through its wisdom didn't know God, it was God's good pleasure through the foolishness of the preaching to save those who believe. 22 For Jews ask for signs, Greeks seek after wisdom, 23 but we preach Christ crucified, a stumbling block to Jews and foolishness to Greeks, 24 but to those who are called, both Jews and Greeks, Christ is the power of God and the wisdom of God; 25 because the foolishness of God is wiser than men, and the weakness of God is stronger than men.

**Responsorial Psalm:** Psalms 33: 1-2, 4-5, 10-11

1 Rejoice in Yahweh, you righteous!
Praise is fitting for the upright.
2 Give thanks to Yahweh with the lyre.
Sing praises to him with the harp of ten strings.
4 For Yahweh's word is right.
All his work is done in faithfulness.
5 He loves righteousness and justice.
The earth is full of the loving kindness of Yahweh.
10 Yahweh brings the counsel of the nations to nothing.
He makes the thoughts of the peoples to be of no effect.
11 The counsel of Yahweh stands fast forever,
the thoughts of his heart to all generations.

**Gospel: Matthew 25: 1-13**

1 "Then the Kingdom of Heaven will be like ten virgins who took their lamps and went out to meet the bridegroom. 2 Five of them were foolish, and five were wise. 3 Those who were foolish, when they took their lamps, took no oil with them, 4 but the wise took oil in their vessels with their lamps. 5 Now while the bridegroom delayed, they all slumbered and slept. 6 But at midnight there was a cry, 'Behold! The bridegroom is coming! Come out to meet him!' 7 Then all those virgins arose, and trimmed their lamps.† 8 The foolish said to the wise, 'Give us some of your oil, for our lamps are going out.' 9 But the wise answered, saying, 'What if there isn't enough for us and you? You go rather to those who sell, and buy for yourselves.' 10 While they went away to buy, the bridegroom came, and those who were ready went in with him to the wedding feast, and the door was shut. 11 Afterward the other virgins also came, saying, 'Lord, Lord, open to us.' 12 But he answered, 'Most certainly I tell you, I don't know you.' 13 Watch therefore, for you don't know the day nor the hour in which the Son of Man is coming.

1. Invite the Holy Spirit into this reading, asking the Author of Scripture to speak to you through His Word
2. Read today's passage as many times as you need, take your time
3. Write down (below) what the Lord is saying to you today
4. Live with this Word in your heart through the day

---

---

## Saturday, August 31, 2024

**First Reading:** First Corinthians 1: 26-31

26 For you see your calling, brothers, that not many are wise according to the flesh, not many mighty, and not many noble; 27 but God chose the foolish things of the world that he might put to shame those who are wise. God chose the weak things of the world that he might put to shame the things that are strong. 28 God chose the lowly things of the world, and the things that are despised, and the things that don't exist, that he might bring to nothing the things that exist, 29 that no flesh should boast before God. 30 Because of him, you are in Christ Jesus, who was made to us wisdom from God, and

righteousness and sanctification, and redemption, 31 that, as it is written, "He who boasts, let him boast in the Lord."

**Responsorial Psalm:** Psalms 33: 12-13, 18-21

12 Blessed is the nation whose God is Yahweh,
the people whom he has chosen for his own inheritance.
13 Yahweh looks from heaven.
He sees all the sons of men.
18 Behold, Yahweh's eye is on those who fear him,
on those who hope in his loving kindness,
19 to deliver their soul from death,
to keep them alive in famine.
20 Our soul has waited for Yahweh.
He is our help and our shield.
21 For our heart rejoices in him,
because we have trusted in his holy name.

**Gospel: Matthew 25: 14-30**

14 "For it is like a man going into another country, who called his own servants and entrusted his goods to them. 15 To one he gave five talents,‡ to another two, to another one, to each according to his own ability. Then he went on his journey. 16 Immediately he who received the five talents went and traded with them, and made another five talents. 17 In the same way, he also who got the two gained another two. 18 But he who received the one talent went away and dug in the earth and hid his lord's money.
19 "Now after a long time the lord of those servants came, and settled accounts with them. 20 He who received the five talents came and brought another five talents, saying, 'Lord, you delivered to me five talents. Behold, I have gained another five talents in addition to them.'
21 "His lord said to him, 'Well done, good and faithful servant. You have been faithful over a few things, I will set you over many things. Enter into the joy of your lord.'
22 "He also who got the two talents came and said, 'Lord, you delivered to me two talents. Behold, I have gained another two talents in addition to them.'
23 "His lord said to him, 'Well done, good and faithful servant. You have been faithful over a few things. I will set you over many things. Enter into the joy of your lord.'
24 "He also who had received the one talent came and said, 'Lord, I knew you that you are a hard man, reaping where you didn't sow, and gathering where you didn't scatter.

25 I was afraid, and went away and hid your talent in the earth. Behold, you have what is yours.'

26 "But his lord answered him, 'You wicked and slothful servant. You knew that I reap where I didn't sow, and gather where I didn't scatter. 27 You ought therefore to have deposited my money with the bankers, and at my coming I should have received back my own with interest. 28 Take away therefore the talent from him and give it to him who has the ten talents. 29 For to everyone who has will be given, and he will have abundance, but from him who doesn't have, even that which he has will be taken away. 30 Throw out the unprofitable servant into the outer darkness, where there will be weeping and gnashing of teeth.'

1. Invite the Holy Spirit into this reading, asking the Author of Scripture to speak to you through His Word
2. Read today's passage as many times as you need, take your time
3. Write down (below) what the Lord is saying to you today
4. Live with this Word in your heart through the day

_____

_____

### Sunday, September 1, 2024
### TWENTY-SECOND SUNDAY IN ORDINARY TIME

**First Reading:** Deuteronomy 4: 1-2, 6-8

1 Now, Israel, listen to the statutes and to the ordinances which I teach you, to do them, that you may live and go in and possess the land which Yahweh, the God of your fathers, gives you. 2 You shall not add to the word which I command you, neither shall you take away from it, that you may keep the commandments of Yahweh your God which I command you.

6 Keep therefore and do them; for this is your wisdom and your understanding in the sight of the peoples who shall hear all these statutes and say, "Surely this great nation is a wise and understanding people." 7 For what great nation is there that has a god so near to them as Yahweh our God is whenever we call on him? 8 What great nation is there that has statutes and ordinances so righteous as all this law which I set before you today?

**Responsorial Psalm:** Psalms 15: 2-5

2 He who walks blamelessly and does what is right,
and speaks truth in his heart;
3 he who doesn't slander with his tongue,
nor does evil to his friend,
nor casts slurs against his fellow man;
4 in whose eyes a vile man is despised,
but who honors those who fear Yahweh;
he who keeps an oath even when it hurts, and doesn't change;
5 he who doesn't lend out his money for usury,
nor take a bribe against the innocent.

**Second Reading:** James 1: 17-18, 21b-22, 27

17 Every good gift and every perfect gift is from above, coming down from the Father of lights, with whom can be no variation nor turning shadow. 18 Of his own will he gave birth to us by the word of truth, that we should be a kind of first fruits of his creatures. 21 Therefore, putting away all filthiness and overflowing of wickedness, receive with humility the implanted word, which is able to save your souls.§
22 But be doers of the word, and not only hearers, deluding your own selves.
27 Pure religion and undefiled before our God and Father is this: to visit the fatherless and widows in their affliction, and to keep oneself unstained by the world.

**Gospel: Mark 7: 1-8, 14-15, 21-23**

1 Then the Pharisees and some of the scribes gathered together to him, having come from Jerusalem. 2 Now when they saw some of his disciples eating bread with defiled, that is unwashed, hands, they found fault. 3 (For the Pharisees and all the Jews don't eat unless they wash their hands and forearms, holding to the tradition of the elders. 4 They don't eat when they come from the marketplace unless they bathe themselves, and there are many other things which they have received to hold to: washings of cups, pitchers, bronze vessels, and couches.) 5 The Pharisees and the scribes asked him, "Why don't your disciples walk according to the tradition of the elders, but eat their bread with unwashed hands?"
6 He answered them, "Well did Isaiah prophesy of you hypocrites, as it is written,
'This people honors me with their lips,

but their heart is far from me.
7 They worship me in vain,
teaching as doctrines the commandments of men.'*
8 "For you set aside the commandment of God, and hold tightly to the tradition of men—the washing of pitchers and cups, and you do many other such things."
14 He called all the multitude to himself and said to them, "Hear me, all of you, and understand. 15 There is nothing from outside of the man that going into him can defile him; but the things which proceed out of the man are those that defile the man.
21 For from within, out of the hearts of men, proceed evil thoughts, adulteries, sexual sins, murders, thefts, 22 covetings, wickedness, deceit, lustful desires, an evil eye, blasphemy, pride, and foolishness. 23 All these evil things come from within and defile the man."

1. Invite the Holy Spirit into this reading, asking the Author of Scripture to speak to you through His Word
2. Read today's passage as many times as you need, take your time
3. Write down (below) what the Lord is saying to you today
4. Live with this Word in your heart through the day

_____

_____

## Monday, September 2, 2024

**First Reading:** First Corinthians 2: 1-5

1 When I came to you, brothers, I didn't come with excellence of speech or of wisdom, proclaiming to you the testimony of God. 2 For I determined not to know anything among you except Jesus Christ and him crucified. 3 I was with you in weakness, in fear, and in much trembling. 4 My speech and my preaching were not in persuasive words of human wisdom, but in demonstration of the Spirit and of power, 5 that your faith wouldn't stand in the wisdom of men, but in the power of God.

**Responsorial Psalm:** Psalms 119: 97-102

97 How I love your law!

It is my meditation all day.

98 Your commandments make me wiser than my enemies,

for your commandments are always with me.

99 I have more understanding than all my teachers,

for your testimonies are my meditation.

100 I understand more than the aged,

because I have kept your precepts.

101 I have kept my feet from every evil way,

that I might observe your word.

102 I have not turned away from your ordinances,

for you have taught me.

## Gospel: Luke 4: 16-30

16 He came to Nazareth, where he had been brought up. He entered, as was his custom, into the synagogue on the Sabbath day, and stood up to read. 17 The book of the prophet Isaiah was handed to him. He opened the book, and found the place where it was written,

18 "The Spirit of the Lord is on me,

because he has anointed me to preach good news to the poor.

He has sent me to heal the broken hearted,†

to proclaim release to the captives,

recovering of sight to the blind,

to deliver those who are crushed,

19 and to proclaim the acceptable year of the Lord."*

20 He closed the book, gave it back to the attendant, and sat down. The eyes of all in the synagogue were fastened on him. 21 He began to tell them, "Today, this Scripture has been fulfilled in your hearing."

22 All testified about him and wondered at the gracious words which proceeded out of his mouth; and they said, "Isn't this Joseph's son?"

23 He said to them, "Doubtless you will tell me this proverb, 'Physician, heal yourself! Whatever we have heard done at Capernaum, do also here in your hometown.' " 24 He said, "Most certainly I tell you, no prophet is acceptable in his hometown. 25 But truly I tell you, there were many widows in Israel in the days of Elijah, when the sky was shut up three years and six months, when a great famine came over all the land. 26 Elijah was sent to none of them, except to Zarephath, in the land of Sidon, to a woman who

was a widow. 27 There were many lepers in Israel in the time of Elisha the prophet, yet not one of them was cleansed, except Naaman, the Syrian."

28 They were all filled with wrath in the synagogue as they heard these things. 29 They rose up, threw him out of the city, and led him to the brow of the hill that their city was built on, that they might throw him off the cliff. 30 But he, passing through the middle of them, went his way.

1. Invite the Holy Spirit into this reading, asking the Author of Scripture to speak to you through His Word
2. Read today's passage as many times as you need, take your time
3. Write down (below) what the Lord is saying to you today
4. Live with this Word in your heart through the day

_____

_____


# Tuesday, September 3, 2024
### Saint Gregory the Great, Pope and Doctor of the Church


**First Reading:** First Corinthians 2: 10b-16

10 But to us, God revealed them through the Spirit. For the Spirit searches all things, yes, the deep things of God. 11 For who among men knows the things of a man except the spirit of the man which is in him? Even so, no one knows the things of God except God's Spirit. 12 But we received not the spirit of the world, but the Spirit which is from God, that we might know the things that were freely given to us by God. 13 We also speak these things, not in words which man's wisdom teaches but which the Holy Spirit teaches, comparing spiritual things with spiritual things. 14 Now the natural man doesn't receive the things of God's Spirit, for they are foolishness to him; and he can't know them, because they are spiritually discerned. 15 But he who is spiritual discerns all things, and he himself is to be judged by no one. 16 "For who has known the mind of the Lord that he should instruct him?" * But we have Christ's mind.

**Responsorial Psalm:** Psalms 145: 8-14

8 Yahweh is gracious, merciful,

slow to anger, and of great loving kindness.

9 Yahweh is good to all.

His tender mercies are over all his works.

10 All your works will give thanks to you, Yahweh.

Your saints will extol you.

11 They will speak of the glory of your kingdom,

and talk about your power,

12 to make known to the sons of men his mighty acts,

the glory of the majesty of his kingdom.

13 Your kingdom is an everlasting kingdom.

Your dominion endures throughout all generations.

Yahweh is faithful in all his words,

and loving in all his deeds.‡

14 Yahweh upholds all who fall,

and raises up all those who are bowed down.

**Gospel: Luke 4: 31-37**

31 He came down to Capernaum, a city of Galilee. He was teaching them on the Sabbath day, 32 and they were astonished at his teaching, for his word was with authority. 33 In the synagogue there was a man who had a spirit of an unclean demon; and he cried out with a loud voice, 34 saying, "Ah! what have we to do with you, Jesus of Nazareth? Have you come to destroy us? I know who you are: the Holy One of God!"

35 Jesus rebuked him, saying, "Be silent and come out of him!" When the demon had thrown him down in the middle of them, he came out of him, having done him no harm. 36 Amazement came on all and they spoke together, one with another, saying, "What is this word? For with authority and power he commands the unclean spirits, and they come out!" 37 News about him went out into every place of the surrounding region.

1. Invite the Holy Spirit into this reading, asking the Author of Scripture to speak to you through His Word
2. Read today's passage as many times as you need, take your time
3. Write down (below) what the Lord is saying to you today
4. Live with this Word in your heart through the day

_____

_____

# Wednesday, September 4, 2024

**First Reading:** First Corinthians 3: 1-9

1 Brothers, I couldn't speak to you as to spiritual, but as to fleshly, as to babies in Christ. 2 I fed you with milk, not with solid food, for you weren't yet ready. Indeed, you aren't ready even now, 3 for you are still fleshly. For insofar as there is jealousy, strife, and factions among you, aren't you fleshly, and don't you walk in the ways of men? 4 For when one says, "I follow Paul," and another, "I follow Apollos," aren't you fleshly? 5 Who then is Apollos, and who is Paul, but servants through whom you believed, and each as the Lord gave to him? 6 I planted. Apollos watered. But God gave the increase. 7 So then neither he who plants is anything, nor he who waters, but God who gives the increase. 8 Now he who plants and he who waters are the same, but each will receive his own reward according to his own labor. 9 For we are God's fellow workers. You are God's farming, God's building.

**Responsorial Psalm:** Psalms 33: 12-15, 20-21

12 Blessed is the nation whose God is Yahweh,
the people whom he has chosen for his own inheritance.
13 Yahweh looks from heaven.
He sees all the sons of men.
14 From the place of his habitation he looks out on all the inhabitants of the earth,
15 he who fashions all of their hearts;
and he considers all of their works.
20 Our soul has waited for Yahweh.
He is our help and our shield.
21 For our heart rejoices in him,
because we have trusted in his holy name.

**Gospel: Luke 4: 38-44**

38 He rose up from the synagogue and entered into Simon's house. Simon's mother-in-law was afflicted with a great fever, and they begged him to help her. 39 He stood over her and rebuked the fever, and it left her. Immediately she rose up and served them. 40 When the sun was setting, all those who had any sick with various diseases brought them to him; and he laid his hands on every one of them, and healed them. 41

Demons also came out of many, crying out and saying, "You are the Christ, the Son of God!" Rebuking them, he didn't allow them to speak, because they knew that he was the Christ.

42 When it was day, he departed and went into an uninhabited place and the multitudes looked for him, and came to him, and held on to him, so that he wouldn't go away from them. 43 But he said to them, "I must preach the good news of God's Kingdom to the other cities also. For this reason I have been sent." 44 He was preaching in the synagogues of Galilee.

1. Invite the Holy Spirit into this reading, asking the Author of Scripture to speak to you through His Word
2. Read today's passage as many times as you need, take your time
3. Write down (below) what the Lord is saying to you today
4. Live with this Word in your heart through the day

---

---

## Thursday, September 5, 2024

**First Reading:** First Corinthians 3: 18-23

18 Let no one deceive himself. If anyone thinks that he is wise among you in this world, let him become a fool that he may become wise. 19 For the wisdom of this world is foolishness with God. For it is written, "He has taken the wise in their craftiness."* 20 And again, "The Lord knows the reasoning of the wise, that it is worthless."* 21 Therefore let no one boast in men. For all things are yours, 22 whether Paul, or Apollos, or Cephas, or the world, or life, or death, or things present, or things to come. All are yours, 23 and you are Christ's, and Christ is God's.

**Responsorial Psalm:** Psalms 24: 1bc-6

1 The earth is Yahweh's, with its fullness;
the world, and those who dwell in it.

2 For he has founded it on the seas,
and established it on the floods.
3 Who may ascend to Yahweh's hill?
Who may stand in his holy place?
4 He who has clean hands and a pure heart;
who has not lifted up his soul to falsehood,
and has not sworn deceitfully.
5 He shall receive a blessing from Yahweh,
righteousness from the God of his salvation.
6 This is the generation of those who seek Him,
who seek your face—even Jacob.

## Gospel: Luke 5: 1-11

1 Now while the multitude pressed on him and heard the word of God, he was standing by the lake of Gennesaret. 2 He saw two boats standing by the lake, but the fishermen had gone out of them and were washing their nets. 3 He entered into one of the boats, which was Simon's, and asked him to put out a little from the land. He sat down and taught the multitudes from the boat.
4 When he had finished speaking, he said to Simon, "Put out into the deep and let down your nets for a catch."
5 Simon answered him, "Master, we worked all night and caught nothing; but at your word I will let down the net." 6 When they had done this, they caught a great multitude of fish, and their net was breaking. 7 They beckoned to their partners in the other boat, that they should come and help them. They came and filled both boats, so that they began to sink. 8 But Simon Peter, when he saw it, fell down at Jesus' knees, saying, "Depart from me, for I am a sinful man, Lord." 9 For he was amazed, and all who were with him, at the catch of fish which they had caught; 10 and so also were James and John, sons of Zebedee, who were partners with Simon.
Jesus said to Simon, "Don't be afraid. From now on you will be catching people alive."
11 When they had brought their boats to land, they left everything, and followed him.

1. Invite the Holy Spirit into this reading, asking the Author of Scripture to speak to you through His Word
2. Read today's passage as many times as you need, take your time
3. Write down (below) what the Lord is saying to you today
4. Live with this Word in your heart through the day

## Friday, September 6, 2024

**First Reading:** First Corinthians 4: 1-5

1 So let a man think of us as Christ's servants and stewards of God's mysteries. 2 Here, moreover, it is required of stewards that they be found faithful. 3 But with me it is a very small thing that I should be judged by you, or by a human court. Yes, I don't even judge my own self. 4 For I know nothing against myself. Yet I am not justified by this, but he who judges me is the Lord. 5 Therefore judge nothing before the time, until the Lord comes, who will both bring to light the hidden things of darkness and reveal the counsels of the hearts. Then each man will get his praise from God.

**Responsorial Psalm:** Psalms 37: 3-6, 27-28, 39-40

3 Trust in Yahweh, and do good.
Dwell in the land, and enjoy safe pasture.
4 Also delight yourself in Yahweh,
and he will give you the desires of your heart.
5 Commit your way to Yahweh.
Trust also in him, and he will do this:
6 he will make your righteousness shine out like light,
and your justice as the noon day sun.
27 Depart from evil, and do good.
Live securely forever.
28 For Yahweh loves justice,
and doesn't forsake his saints.
They are preserved forever,
but the children of the wicked shall be cut off.
39 But the salvation of the righteous is from Yahweh.
He is their stronghold in the time of trouble.
40 Yahweh helps them and rescues them.
He rescues them from the wicked and saves them,

because they have taken refuge in him.

## Gospel: Luke 5: 33-39

33 They said to him, "Why do John's disciples often fast and pray, likewise also the disciples of the Pharisees, but yours eat and drink?"

34 He said to them, "Can you make the friends of the bridegroom fast while the bridegroom is with them? 35 But the days will come when the bridegroom will be taken away from them. Then they will fast in those days."

36 He also told a parable to them. "No one puts a piece from a new garment on an old garment, or else he will tear the new, and also the piece from the new will not match the old. 37 No one puts new wine into old wine skins, or else the new wine will burst the skins, and it will be spilled and the skins will be destroyed. 38 But new wine must be put into fresh wine skins, and both are preserved. 39 No man having drunk old wine immediately desires new, for he says, 'The old is better.'"

1. Invite the Holy Spirit into this reading, asking the Author of Scripture to speak to you through His Word
2. Read today's passage as many times as you need, take your time
3. Write down (below) what the Lord is saying to you today
4. Live with this Word in your heart through the day

_____

_____

## Saturday, September 7, 2024

**First Reading:** First Corinthians 4: 6b-15

6 Now these things, brothers, I have in a figure transferred to myself and Apollos for your sakes, that in us you might learn not to think beyond the things which are written, that none of you be puffed up against one another. 7 For who makes you different? And what do you have that you didn't receive? But if you did receive it, why do you boast as if you had not received it?

8 You are already filled. You have already become rich. You have come to reign without us. Yes, and I wish that you did reign, that we also might reign with you! 9 For I think

that God has displayed us, the apostles, last of all, like men sentenced to death. For we are made a spectacle to the world, both to angels and men. 10 We are fools for Christ's sake, but you are wise in Christ. We are weak, but you are strong. You have honor, but we have dishonor. 11 Even to this present hour we hunger, thirst, are naked, are beaten, and have no certain dwelling place. 12 We toil, working with our own hands. When people curse us, we bless. Being persecuted, we endure. 13 Being defamed, we entreat. We are made as the filth of the world, the dirt wiped off by all, even until now.

14 I don't write these things to shame you, but to admonish you as my beloved children. 15 For though you have ten thousand tutors in Christ, you don't have many fathers. For in Christ Jesus, I became your father through the Good News.

**Responsorial Psalm:** Psalms 145: 17-21

17 Yahweh is righteous in all his ways,
and gracious in all his works.
18 Yahweh is near to all those who call on him,
to all who call on him in truth.
19 He will fulfill the desire of those who fear him.
He also will hear their cry, and will save them.
20 Yahweh preserves all those who love him,
but he will destroy all the wicked.
21 My mouth will speak the praise of Yahweh.
Let all flesh bless his holy name forever and ever.

**Gospel: Luke 6: 1-5**

1 Now on the second Sabbath after the first, he was going through the grain fields. His disciples plucked the heads of grain and ate, rubbing them in their hands. 2 But some of the Pharisees said to them, "Why do you do that which is not lawful to do on the Sabbath day?"
3 Jesus, answering them, said, "Haven't you read what David did when he was hungry, he and those who were with him, 4 how he entered into God's house, and took and ate the show bread, and gave also to those who were with him, which is not lawful to eat except for the priests alone?" 5 He said to them, "The Son of Man is lord of the Sabbath."

1. Invite the Holy Spirit into this reading, asking the Author of Scripture to speak to you through His Word

2. Read today's passage as many times as you need, take your time
3. Write down (below) what the Lord is saying to you today
4. Live with this Word in your heart through the day

---

## Sunday, September 8, 2024
### TWENTY-THIRD SUNDAY IN ORDINARY TIME

**First Reading:** Isaiah 35: 4-7a

4 Tell those who have a fearful heart, "Be strong!
Don't be afraid!
Behold, your God will come with vengeance, God's retribution.
He will come and save you.
5 Then the eyes of the blind will be opened,
and the ears of the deaf will be unstopped.
6 Then the lame man will leap like a deer,
and the tongue of the mute will sing;
for waters will break out in the wilderness,
and streams in the desert.
7 The burning sand will become a pool,
and the thirsty ground springs of water.

**Responsorial Psalm:** Psalms 146: 7-10

7 who executes justice for the oppressed;
who gives food to the hungry.
Yahweh frees the prisoners.
8 Yahweh opens the eyes of the blind.
Yahweh raises up those who are bowed down.
Yahweh loves the righteous.
9 Yahweh preserves the foreigners.
He upholds the fatherless and widow,
but he turns the way of the wicked upside down.

10 Yahweh will reign forever;
your God, O Zion, to all generations.
Praise Yah!

**Second Reading:** James 2: 1-5

1 My brothers, don't hold the faith of our glorious Lord Jesus Christ with partiality. 2 For if a man with a gold ring, in fine clothing, comes into your synagogue,† and a poor man in filthy clothing also comes in, 3 and you pay special attention to him who wears the fine clothing and say, "Sit here in a good place;" and you tell the poor man, "Stand there," or "Sit by my footstool" 4 haven't you shown partiality among yourselves, and become judges with evil thoughts? 5 Listen, my beloved brothers. Didn't God choose those who are poor in this world to be rich in faith and heirs of the Kingdom which he promised to those who love him?

**Gospel: Mark 7: 31-37**

31 Again he departed from the borders of Tyre and Sidon, and came to the sea of Galilee through the middle of the region of Decapolis. 32 They brought to him one who was deaf and had an impediment in his speech. They begged him to lay his hand on him. 33 He took him aside from the multitude privately and put his fingers into his ears; and he spat and touched his tongue. 34 Looking up to heaven, he sighed, and said to him, "Ephphatha!" that is, "Be opened!" 35 Immediately his ears were opened, and the impediment of his tongue was released, and he spoke clearly. 36 He commanded them that they should tell no one, but the more he commanded them, so much the more widely they proclaimed it. 37 They were astonished beyond measure, saying, "He has done all things well. He makes even the deaf hear and the mute speak!"

1. Invite the Holy Spirit into this reading, asking the Author of Scripture to speak to you through His Word
2. Read today's passage as many times as you need, take your time
3. Write down (below) what the Lord is saying to you today
4. Live with this Word in your heart through the day

_____

_____

<h1 style="text-align:center">Monday, September 9, 2024</h1>
Saint Peter Claver, Priest

**First Reading:** First Corinthians 5: 1-8

1 It is actually reported that there is sexual immorality among you, and such sexual immorality as is not even named among the Gentiles, that one has his father's wife. 2 You are arrogant, and didn't mourn instead, that he who had done this deed might be removed from among you. 3 For I most certainly, as being absent in body but present in spirit, have already, as though I were present, judged him who has done this thing. 4 In the name of our Lord Jesus Christ, when you are gathered together with my spirit with the power of our Lord Jesus Christ, 5 you are to deliver such a one to Satan for the destruction of the flesh, that the spirit may be saved in the day of the Lord Jesus.
6 Your boasting is not good. Don't you know that a little yeast leavens the whole lump? 7 Purge out the old yeast, that you may be a new lump, even as you are unleavened. For indeed Christ, our Passover, has been sacrificed in our place. 8 Therefore let's keep the feast, not with old yeast, neither with the yeast of malice and wickedness, but with the unleavened bread of sincerity and truth.

**Responsorial Psalm:** Psalms 5: 5-7, 12

5 The arrogant will not stand in your sight.
You hate all workers of iniquity.
6 You will destroy those who speak lies.
Yahweh abhors the bloodthirsty and deceitful man.
7 But as for me, in the abundance of your loving kindness I will come into your house.
I will bow toward your holy temple in reverence of you.
12 For you will bless the righteous.
Yahweh, you will surround him with favor as with a shield.

**Gospel: Luke 6: 6-11**

6 It also happened on another Sabbath that he entered into the synagogue and taught. There was a man there, and his right hand was withered. 7 The scribes and the Pharisees watched him, to see whether he would heal on the Sabbath, that they might find an accusation against him. 8 But he knew their thoughts; and he said to the man who had the withered hand, "Rise up and stand in the middle." He arose and stood. 9 Then Jesus said to them, "I will ask you something: Is it lawful on the Sabbath to do

good, or to do harm? To save a life, or to kill?" 10 He looked around at them all, and said to the man, "Stretch out your hand." He did, and his hand was restored as sound as the other. 11 But they were filled with rage, and talked with one another about what they might do to Jesus.

1. Invite the Holy Spirit into this reading, asking the Author of Scripture to speak to you through His Word
2. Read today's passage as many times as you need, take your time
3. Write down (below) what the Lord is saying to you today
4. Live with this Word in your heart through the day

_____

_____

## Tuesday, September 10, 2024

**First Reading:** First Corinthians 6: 1-11

1 Dare any of you, having a matter against his neighbor, go to law before the unrighteous, and not before the saints? 2 Don't you know that the saints will judge the world? And if the world is judged by you, are you unworthy to judge the smallest matters? 3 Don't you know that we will judge angels? How much more, things that pertain to this life? 4 If then you have to judge things pertaining to this life, do you set them to judge who are of no account in the assembly? 5 I say this to move you to shame. Isn't there even one wise man among you who would be able to decide between his brothers? 6 But brother goes to law with brother, and that before unbelievers! 7 Therefore it is already altogether a defect in you that you have lawsuits one with another. Why not rather be wronged? Why not rather be defrauded? 8 No, but you yourselves do wrong and defraud, and that against your brothers.
9 Or don't you know that the unrighteous will not inherit God's Kingdom? Don't be deceived. Neither the sexually immoral, nor idolaters, nor adulterers, nor male prostitutes, nor homosexuals, 10 nor thieves, nor covetous, nor drunkards, nor slanderers, nor extortionists, will inherit God's Kingdom. 11 Some of you were such, but you were washed. You were sanctified. You were justified in the name of the Lord Jesus, and in the Spirit of our God.

**Responsorial Psalm:** Psalms 149: 1b-6a and 9b

1 Praise Yahweh!
Sing to Yahweh a new song,
his praise in the assembly of the saints.
2 Let Israel rejoice in him who made them.
Let the children of Zion be joyful in their King.
3 Let them praise his name in the dance!
Let them sing praises to him with tambourine and harp!
4 For Yahweh takes pleasure in his people.
He crowns the humble with salvation.
5 Let the saints rejoice in honor.
Let them sing for joy on their beds.
6 May the high praises of God be in their mouths,
and a two-edged sword in their hand,
9b All his saints have this honor.
Praise Yah!

**Gospel: Luke 6: 12-19**

12 In these days, he went out to the mountain to pray, and he continued all night in prayer to God. 13 When it was day, he called his disciples, and from them he chose twelve, whom he also named apostles: 14 Simon, whom he also named Peter; Andrew, his brother; James; John; Philip; Bartholomew; 15 Matthew; Thomas; James the son of Alphaeus; Simon who was called the Zealot; 16 Judas the son of James; and Judas Iscariot, who also became a traitor.

17 He came down with them and stood on a level place, with a crowd of his disciples and a great number of the people from all Judea and Jerusalem and the sea coast of Tyre and Sidon, who came to hear him and to be healed of their diseases, 18 as well as those who were troubled by unclean spirits; and they were being healed. 19 All the multitude sought to touch him, for power came out of him and healed them all.

1. Invite the Holy Spirit into this reading, asking the Author of Scripture to speak to you through His Word
2. Read today's passage as many times as you need, take your time
3. Write down (below) what the Lord is saying to you today
4. Live with this Word in your heart through the day

## Wednesday, September 11, 2024

**First Reading:** First Corinthians 7: 25-31

25 Now concerning virgins, I have no commandment from the Lord, but I give my judgment as one who has obtained mercy from the Lord to be trustworthy. 26 Therefore I think that because of the distress that is on us, it's good for a man to remain as he is. 27 Are you bound to a wife? Don't seek to be freed. Are you free from a wife? Don't seek a wife. 28 But if you marry, you have not sinned. If a virgin marries, she has not sinned. Yet such will have oppression in the flesh, and I want to spare you. 29 But I say this, brothers: the time is short. From now on, both those who have wives may be as though they had none; 30 and those who weep, as though they didn't weep; and those who rejoice, as though they didn't rejoice; and those who buy, as though they didn't possess; 31 and those who use the world, as not using it to the fullest. For the mode of this world passes away.

**Responsorial Psalm:** Psalms 45: 11-12, 14-17

11 So the king will desire your beauty,
honor him, for he is your lord.
12 The daughter of Tyre comes with a gift.
The rich among the people entreat your favor.
14 She shall be led to the king in embroidered work.
The virgins, her companions who follow her, shall be brought to you.
15 With gladness and rejoicing they shall be led.
They shall enter into the king's palace.
16 Your sons will take the place of your fathers.
You shall make them princes in all the earth.
17 I will make your name to be remembered in all generations.
Therefore the peoples shall give you thanks forever and ever.

## Gospel: Luke 6: 20-26

20 He lifted up his eyes to his disciples, and said:
"Blessed are you who are poor,
for God's Kingdom is yours.
21 Blessed are you who hunger now,
for you will be filled.
Blessed are you who weep now,
for you will laugh.
22 Blessed are you when men hate you, and when they exclude and mock you, and throw out your name as evil, for the Son of Man's sake.
23 Rejoice in that day and leap for joy, for behold, your reward is great in heaven, for their fathers did the same thing to the prophets.
24 "But woe to you who are rich!
For you have received your consolation.
25 Woe to you, you who are full now,
for you will be hungry.
Woe to you who laugh now,
for you will mourn and weep.
26 Woe,† when‡ men speak well of you,
for their fathers did the same thing to the false prophets.

1. Invite the Holy Spirit into this reading, asking the Author of Scripture to speak to you through His Word
2. Read today's passage as many times as you need, take your time
3. Write down (below) what the Lord is saying to you today
4. Live with this Word in your heart through the day

---

---

### Thursday, September 12, 2024
The Most Holy Name of Mary

**First Reading:** First Corinthians 8: 1b-7, 11-13

1 Now concerning things sacrificed to idols: We know that we all have knowledge. Knowledge puffs up, but love builds up. 2 But if anyone thinks that he knows anything, he doesn't yet know as he ought to know. 3 But anyone who loves God is known by him. 4 Therefore concerning the eating of things sacrificed to idols, we know that no idol is anything in the world, and that there is no other God but one. 5 For though there are things that are called "gods", whether in the heavens or on earth—as there are many "gods" and many "lords"— 6 yet to us there is one God, the Father, of whom are all things, and we for him; and one Lord, Jesus Christ, through whom are all things, and we live through him.

7 However, that knowledge isn't in all men. But some, with consciousness of an idol until now, eat as of a thing sacrificed to an idol, and their conscience, being weak, is defiled.

11 And through your knowledge, he who is weak perishes, the brother for whose sake Christ died. 12 Thus, sinning against the brothers, and wounding their conscience when it is weak, you sin against Christ. 13 Therefore, if food causes my brother to stumble, I will eat no meat forever more, that I don't cause my brother to stumble.

**Responsorial Psalm:** Psalms 139: 1b-3, 13-14ab, 23-24

1 Yahweh, you have searched me,
and you know me.
2 You know my sitting down and my rising up.
You perceive my thoughts from afar.
3 You search out my path and my lying down,
and are acquainted with all my ways.
13 For you formed my inmost being.
You knit me together in my mother's womb.
14 I will give thanks to you,
for I am fearfully and wonderfully made.
Your works are wonderful.
My soul knows that very well.
23 Search me, God, and know my heart.
Try me, and know my thoughts.
24 See if there is any wicked way in me,
and lead me in the everlasting way.

**Gospel: Luke 6: 27-38**

27 "But I tell you who hear: love your enemies, do good to those who hate you, 28 bless those who curse you, and pray for those who mistreat you. 29 To him who strikes you on the cheek, offer also the other; and from him who takes away your cloak, don't withhold your coat also. 30 Give to everyone who asks you, and don't ask him who takes away your goods to give them back again.

31 "As you would like people to do to you, do exactly so to them.

32 "If you love those who love you, what credit is that to you? For even sinners love those who love them. 33 If you do good to those who do good to you, what credit is that to you? For even sinners do the same. 34 If you lend to those from whom you hope to receive, what credit is that to you? Even sinners lend to sinners, to receive back as much. 35 But love your enemies, and do good, and lend, expecting nothing back; and your reward will be great, and you will be children of the Most High; for he is kind toward the unthankful and evil.

36 "Therefore be merciful,
even as your Father is also merciful.
37 Don't judge,
and you won't be judged.
Don't condemn,
and you won't be condemned.
Set free,
and you will be set free.
38 "Give, and it will be given to you: good measure, pressed down, shaken together, and running over, will be given to you.§ For with the same measure you measure it will be measured back to you."

1. Invite the Holy Spirit into this reading, asking the Author of Scripture to speak to you through His Word
2. Read today's passage as many times as you need, take your time
3. Write down (below) what the Lord is saying to you today
4. Live with this Word in your heart through the day

_____

_____

**Friday, September 13, 2024**
Saint John Chrysostom, Bishop and Doctor of the Church

**First Reading:** First Corinthians 9: 16-19, 22b-27

16 For if I preach the Good News, I have nothing to boast about, for necessity is laid on me; but woe is to me if I don't preach the Good News. 17 For if I do this of my own will, I have a reward. But if not of my own will, I have a stewardship entrusted to me. 18 What then is my reward? That when I preach the Good News, I may present the Good News of Christ without charge, so as not to abuse my authority in the Good News.
19 For though I was free from all, I brought myself under bondage to all, that I might gain the more.
22 To the weak I became as weak, that I might gain the weak. I have become all things to all men, that I may by all means save some. 23 Now I do this for the sake of the Good News, that I may be a joint partaker of it. 24 Don't you know that those who run in a race all run, but one receives the prize? Run like that, so that you may win. 25 Every man who strives in the games exercises self-control in all things. Now they do it to receive a corruptible crown, but we an incorruptible. 26 I therefore run like that, not aimlessly. I fight like that, not beating the air, 27 but I beat my body and bring it into submission, lest by any means, after I have preached to others, I myself should be disqualified.

**Responsorial Psalm:** Psalms 84: 3-6, 12

3 Yes, the sparrow has found a home,
and the swallow a nest for herself, where she may have her young,
near your altars, Yahweh of Armies, my King, and my God.
4 Blessed are those who dwell in your house.
They are always praising you.
5 Blessed are those whose strength is in you,
who have set their hearts on a pilgrimage.
6 Passing through the valley of Weeping, they make it a place of springs.
Yes, the autumn rain covers it with blessings.
12 Yahweh of Armies,
blessed is the man who trusts in you.

**Gospel: Luke 6: 39-42**

39 He spoke a parable to them. "Can the blind guide the blind? Won't they both fall into a pit? 40 A disciple is not above his teacher, but everyone when he is fully trained will be like his teacher. 41 Why do you see the speck of chaff that is in your brother's eye, but don't consider the beam that is in your own eye? 42 Or how can you tell your brother, 'Brother, let me remove the speck of chaff that is in your eye,' when you yourself don't see the beam that is in your own eye? You hypocrite! First remove the beam from your own eye, and then you can see clearly to remove the speck of chaff that is in your brother's eye.

1. Invite the Holy Spirit into this reading, asking the Author of Scripture to speak to you through His Word
2. Read today's passage as many times as you need, take your time
3. Write down (below) what the Lord is saying to you today
4. Live with this Word in your heart through the day

_____

_____

### Saturday, September 14, 2024
The Exaltation of the Holy Cross

**First Reading:** Numbers 21: 4b-9

4 They traveled from Mount Hor by the way to the Red Sea, to go around the land of Edom. The soul of the people was very discouraged because of the journey. 5 The people spoke against God and against Moses: "Why have you brought us up out of Egypt to die in the wilderness? For there is no bread, there is no water, and our soul loathes this disgusting food!"
6 Yahweh sent venomous snakes among the people, and they bit the people. Many people of Israel died. 7 The people came to Moses, and said, "We have sinned, because we have spoken against Yahweh and against you. Pray to Yahweh, that he take away the serpents from us." Moses prayed for the people.
8 Yahweh said to Moses, "Make a venomous snake, and set it on a pole. It shall happen that everyone who is bitten, when he sees it, shall live." 9 Moses made a serpent of

bronze, and set it on the pole. If a serpent had bitten any man, when he looked at the serpent of bronze, he lived.

**Responsorial Psalm:** Psalms 78: 1bc-2, 34-38

1 Hear my teaching, my people.
Turn your ears to the words of my mouth.
2 I will open my mouth in a parable.
I will utter dark sayings of old,
34 When he killed them, then they inquired after him.
They returned and sought God earnestly.
35 They remembered that God was their rock,
the Most High God, their redeemer.
36 But they flattered him with their mouth,
and lied to him with their tongue.
37 For their heart was not right with him,
neither were they faithful in his covenant.
38 But he, being merciful, forgave iniquity, and didn't destroy them.
Yes, many times he turned his anger away,
and didn't stir up all his wrath.

**Second Reading:** Philippians 2: 6-11

6 who, existing in the form of God, didn't consider equality with God a thing to be grasped, 7 but emptied himself, taking the form of a servant, being made in the likeness of men. 8 And being found in human form, he humbled himself, becoming obedient to the point of death, yes, the death of the cross. 9 Therefore God also highly exalted him, and gave to him the name which is above every name, 10 that at the name of Jesus every knee should bow, of those in heaven, those on earth, and those under the earth, 11 and that every tongue should confess that Jesus Christ is Lord, to the glory of God the Father.

**Gospel: John 3: 13-17**

13 No one has ascended into heaven but he who descended out of heaven, the Son of Man, who is in heaven. 14 As Moses lifted up the serpent in the wilderness, even so must the Son of Man be lifted up, 15 that whoever believes in him should not perish, but have eternal life. 16 For God so loved the world, that he gave his only born§ Son,

that whoever believes in him should not perish, but have eternal life. 17 For God didn't send his Son into the world to judge the world, but that the world should be saved through him.

1. Invite the Holy Spirit into this reading, asking the Author of Scripture to speak to you through His Word
2. Read today's passage as many times as you need, take your time
3. Write down (below) what the Lord is saying to you today
4. Live with this Word in your heart through the day

_____

_____


## Sunday, September 15, 2024
### TWENTY-FOURTH SUNDAY IN ORDINARY TIME


**First Reading:** Isaiah 50: 5-9a

5 The Lord Yahweh has opened my ear.
I was not rebellious.
I have not turned back.
6 I gave my back to those who beat me,
and my cheeks to those who plucked off the hair.
I didn't hide my face from shame and spitting.
7 For the Lord Yahweh will help me.
Therefore I have not been confounded.
Therefore I have set my face like a flint,
and I know that I won't be disappointed.
8 He who justifies me is near.
Who will bring charges against me?
Let us stand up together.
Who is my adversary?
Let him come near to me.
9 Behold, the Lord Yahweh will help me!
Who is he who will condemn me?

Behold, they will all grow old like a garment.
The moths will eat them up.

**Responsorial Psalm:** Psalms 116: 1-6, 8-9

1 I love Yahweh, because he listens to my voice,
and my cries for mercy.
2 Because he has turned his ear to me,
therefore I will call on him as long as I live.
3 The cords of death surrounded me,
the pains of Sheol† got a hold of me.
I found trouble and sorrow.
4 Then I called on Yahweh's name:
"Yahweh, I beg you, deliver my soul."
5 Yahweh is gracious and righteous.
Yes, our God is merciful.
6 Yahweh preserves the simple.
I was brought low, and he saved me.
8 For you have delivered my soul from death,
my eyes from tears,
and my feet from falling.
9 I will walk before Yahweh in the land of the living.

**Second Reading:** James 2: 14-18

14 What good is it, my brothers, if a man says he has faith, but has no works? Can faith save him? 15 And if a brother or sister is naked and in lack of daily food, 16 and one of you tells them, "Go in peace. Be warmed and filled;" yet you didn't give them the things the body needs, what good is it? 17 Even so faith, if it has no works, is dead in itself. 18 Yes, a man will say, "You have faith, and I have works." Show me your faith without works, and I will show you my faith by my works.

**Gospel: Mark 8: 27-35**

27 Jesus went out, with his disciples, into the villages of Caesarea Philippi. On the way he asked his disciples, "Who do men say that I am?"
28 They told him, "John the Baptizer, and others say Elijah, but others, one of the prophets."
29 He said to them, "But who do you say that I am?"

Peter answered, "You are the Christ."

30 He commanded them that they should tell no one about him. 31 He began to teach them that the Son of Man must suffer many things, and be rejected by the elders, the chief priests, and the scribes, and be killed, and after three days rise again. 32 He spoke to them openly. Peter took him and began to rebuke him. 33 But he, turning around and seeing his disciples, rebuked Peter, and said, "Get behind me, Satan! For you have in mind not the things of God, but the things of men."

34 He called the multitude to himself with his disciples and said to them, "Whoever wants to come after me, let him deny himself, and take up his cross, and follow me. 35 For whoever wants to save his life will lose it; and whoever will lose his life for my sake and the sake of the Good News will save it.

1. Invite the Holy Spirit into this reading, asking the Author of Scripture to speak to you through His Word
2. Read today's passage as many times as you need, take your time
3. Write down (below) what the Lord is saying to you today
4. Live with this Word in your heart through the day

_____

_____

### Monday, September 16, 2024
Saints Cornelius, Pope, and Cyprian, Bishop, Martyrs

**First Reading:** First Corinthians 11: 17-26, 33

17 But in giving you this command I don't praise you, because you come together not for the better but for the worse. 18 For first of all, when you come together in the assembly, I hear that divisions exist among you, and I partly believe it. 19 For there also must be factions among you, that those who are approved may be revealed among you. 20 When therefore you assemble yourselves together, it is not the Lord's supper that you eat. 21 For in your eating each one takes his own supper first. One is hungry, and another is drunken. 22 What, don't you have houses to eat and to drink in? Or do you despise God's assembly and put them to shame who don't have enough? What shall I tell you? Shall I praise you? In this I don't praise you.

23 For I received from the Lord that which also I delivered to you, that the Lord Jesus on the night in which he was betrayed took bread. 24 When he had given thanks, he broke it and said, "Take, eat. This is my body, which is broken for you. Do this in memory of me." 25 In the same way he also took the cup after supper, saying, "This cup is the new covenant in my blood. Do this, as often as you drink, in memory of me." 26 For as often as you eat this bread and drink this cup, you proclaim the Lord's death until he comes.

33 Therefore, my brothers, when you come together to eat, wait for one another.

**Responsorial Psalm:** Psalms 40: 7-10, 17

7 Then I said, "Behold, I have come.
It is written about me in the book in the scroll.
8 I delight to do your will, my God.
Yes, your law is within my heart."
9 I have proclaimed glad news of righteousness in the great assembly.
Behold, I will not seal my lips, Yahweh, you know.
10 I have not hidden your righteousness within my heart.
I have declared your faithfulness and your salvation.
I have not concealed your loving kindness and your truth from the great assembly.
17 But I am poor and needy.
May the Lord think about me.
You are my help and my deliverer.
Don't delay, my God.

**Gospel: Luke 7: 1-10**

1 After he had finished speaking in the hearing of the people, he entered into Capernaum. 2 A certain centurion's servant, who was dear to him, was sick and at the point of death. 3 When he heard about Jesus, he sent to him elders of the Jews, asking him to come and save his servant. 4 When they came to Jesus, they begged him earnestly, saying, "He is worthy for you to do this for him, 5 for he loves our nation, and he built our synagogue for us." 6 Jesus went with them. When he was now not far from the house, the centurion sent friends to him, saying to him, "Lord, don't trouble yourself, for I am not worthy for you to come under my roof. 7 Therefore I didn't even think myself worthy to come to you; but say the word, and my servant will be healed. 8 For I also am a man placed under authority, having under myself soldiers. I tell this

one, 'Go!' and he goes; and to another, 'Come!' and he comes; and to my servant, 'Do this,' and he does it."

9 When Jesus heard these things, he marveled at him, and turned and said to the multitude who followed him, "I tell you, I have not found such great faith, no, not in Israel." 10 Those who were sent, returning to the house, found that the servant who had been sick was well.

1. Invite the Holy Spirit into this reading, asking the Author of Scripture to speak to you through His Word
2. Read today's passage as many times as you need, take your time
3. Write down (below) what the Lord is saying to you today
4. Live with this Word in your heart through the day

---

## Tuesday, September 17, 2024
### Saint Robert Bellarmine, Bishop and Doctor of the Church; Saint Hildegard of Bingen, Virgin and Doctor of the Church

**First Reading:** First Corinthians 12: 12-14, 27-31a

12 For as the body is one and has many members, and all the members of the body, being many, are one body; so also is Christ. 13 For in one Spirit we were all baptized into one body, whether Jews or Greeks, whether bond or free; and were all given to drink into one Spirit.
14 For the body is not one member, but many.
27 Now you are the body of Christ, and members individually. 28 God has set some in the assembly: first apostles, second prophets, third teachers, then miracle workers, then gifts of healings, helps, governments, and various kinds of languages. 29 Are all apostles? Are all prophets? Are all teachers? Are all miracle workers? 30 Do all have gifts of healings? Do all speak with various languages? Do all interpret? 31 But earnestly desire the best gifts. Moreover, I show a most excellent way to you.

**Responsorial Psalm:** Psalms 100: 1b-5

1 Shout for joy to Yahweh, all you lands!
2 Serve Yahweh with gladness.
Come before his presence with singing.
3 Know that Yahweh, he is God.
It is he who has made us, and we are his.
We are his people, and the sheep of his pasture.
4 Enter into his gates with thanksgiving,
and into his courts with praise.
Give thanks to him, and bless his name.
5 For Yahweh is good.
His loving kindness endures forever,
his faithfulness to all generations.

**Gospel: Luke 7: 11-17**

11 Soon afterwards, he went to a city called Nain. Many of his disciples, along with a great multitude, went with him. 12 Now when he came near to the gate of the city, behold, one who was dead was carried out, the only born† son of his mother, and she was a widow. Many people of the city were with her. 13 When the Lord saw her, he had compassion on her and said to her, "Don't cry." 14 He came near and touched the coffin, and the bearers stood still. He said, "Young man, I tell you, arise!" 15 He who was dead sat up and began to speak. Then he gave him to his mother.
16 Fear took hold of all, and they glorified God, saying, "A great prophet has arisen among us!" and, "God has visited his people!" 17 This report went out concerning him in the whole of Judea and in all the surrounding region.

1. Invite the Holy Spirit into this reading, asking the Author of Scripture to speak to you through His Word
2. Read today's passage as many times as you need, take your time
3. Write down (below) what the Lord is saying to you today
4. Live with this Word in your heart through the day

_____

_____

**First Reading:** First Corinthians 12: 31 – 13: 13

31 But earnestly desire the best gifts. Moreover, I show a most excellent way to you.
1 If I speak with the languages of men and of angels, but don't have love, I have become sounding brass or a clanging cymbal. 2 If I have the gift of prophecy, and know all mysteries and all knowledge, and if I have all faith, so as to remove mountains, but don't have love, I am nothing. 3 If I give away all my goods to feed the poor, and if I give my body to be burned, but don't have love, it profits me nothing.
4 Love is patient and is kind. Love doesn't envy. Love doesn't brag, is not proud, 5 doesn't behave itself inappropriately, doesn't seek its own way, is not provoked, takes no account of evil; 6 doesn't rejoice in unrighteousness, but rejoices with the truth; 7 bears all things, believes all things, hopes all things, and endures all things.
8 Love never fails. But where there are prophecies, they will be done away with. Where there are various languages, they will cease. Where there is knowledge, it will be done away with. 9 For we know in part and we prophesy in part; 10 but when that which is complete has come, then that which is partial will be done away with. 11 When I was a child, I spoke as a child, I felt as a child, I thought as a child. Now that I have become a man, I have put away childish things. 12 For now we see in a mirror, dimly, but then face to face. Now I know in part, but then I will know fully, even as I was also fully known. 13 But now faith, hope, and love remain—these three. The greatest of these is love.

**Responsorial Psalm:** Psalms 33: 2-5, 12 and 22

2 Give thanks to Yahweh with the lyre.
Sing praises to him with the harp of ten strings.
3 Sing to him a new song.
Play skillfully with a shout of joy!
4 For Yahweh's word is right.
All his work is done in faithfulness.
5 He loves righteousness and justice.
The earth is full of the loving kindness of Yahweh.
12 Blessed is the nation whose God is Yahweh,
the people whom he has chosen for his own inheritance.
22 Let your loving kindness be on us, Yahweh,

since we have hoped in you.

**Gospel: Luke 7: 31-35**

31 ‡ "To what then should I compare the people of this generation? What are they like? 32 They are like children who sit in the marketplace and call to one another, saying, 'We piped to you, and you didn't dance. We mourned, and you didn't weep.' 33 For John the Baptizer came neither eating bread nor drinking wine, and you say, 'He has a demon.' 34 The Son of Man has come eating and drinking, and you say, 'Behold, a glutton and a drunkard, a friend of tax collectors and sinners!' 35 Wisdom is justified by all her children."

1. Invite the Holy Spirit into this reading, asking the Author of Scripture to speak to you through His Word
2. Read today's passage as many times as you need, take your time
3. Write down (below) what the Lord is saying to you today
4. Live with this Word in your heart through the day

_____

_____

## Thursday, September 19, 2024
Saint Januarius, Bishop and Martyr

**First Reading:** First Corinthians 15: 1-11

1 Now I declare to you, brothers, the Good News which I preached to you, which also you received, in which you also stand, 2 by which also you are saved, if you hold firmly the word which I preached to you—unless you believed in vain.
3 For I delivered to you first of all that which I also received: that Christ died for our sins according to the Scriptures, 4 that he was buried, that he was raised on the third day according to the Scriptures, 5 and that he appeared to Cephas, then to the twelve. 6 Then he appeared to over five hundred brothers at once, most of whom remain until now, but some have also fallen asleep. 7 Then he appeared to James, then to all the apostles, 8 and last of all, as to the child born at the wrong time, he appeared to me

also. 9 For I am the least of the apostles, who is not worthy to be called an apostle, because I persecuted the assembly of God. 10 But by the grace of God I am what I am. His grace which was given to me was not futile, but I worked more than all of them; yet not I, but the grace of God which was with me. 11 Whether then it is I or they, so we preach, and so you believed.

**Responsorial Psalm:** Psalms 118: 1b-2, 16ab-17, 28

1 Give thanks to Yahweh, for he is good,
for his loving kindness endures forever.
2 Let Israel now say
that his loving kindness endures forever.
16 The right hand of Yahweh is exalted!
The right hand of Yahweh does valiantly!"
17 I will not die, but live,
and declare Yah's works.
28 You are my God, and I will give thanks to you.
You are my God, I will exalt you.

**Gospel: Luke 7: 36-50**

36 One of the Pharisees invited him to eat with him. He entered into the Pharisee's house and sat at the table. 37 Behold, a woman in the city who was a sinner, when she knew that he was reclining in the Pharisee's house, brought an alabaster jar of ointment. 38 Standing behind at his feet weeping, she began to wet his feet with her tears, and she wiped them with the hair of her head, kissed his feet, and anointed them with the ointment. 39 Now when the Pharisee who had invited him saw it, he said to himself, "This man, if he were a prophet, would have perceived who and what kind of woman this is who touches him, that she is a sinner."
40 Jesus answered him, "Simon, I have something to tell you."
He said, "Teacher, say on."
41 "A certain lender had two debtors. The one owed five hundred denarii, and the other fifty. 42 When they couldn't pay, he forgave them both. Which of them therefore will love him most?"
43 Simon answered, "He, I suppose, to whom he forgave the most."
He said to him, "You have judged correctly." 44 Turning to the woman, he said to Simon, "Do you see this woman? I entered into your house, and you gave me no water for my feet, but she has wet my feet with her tears, and wiped them with the hair of her

head. 45 You gave me no kiss, but she, since the time I came in, has not ceased to kiss my feet. 46 You didn't anoint my head with oil, but she has anointed my feet with ointment. 47 Therefore I tell you, her sins, which are many, are forgiven, for she loved much. But one to whom little is forgiven, loves little." 48 He said to her, "Your sins are forgiven."

49 Those who sat at the table with him began to say to themselves, "Who is this who even forgives sins?"

50 He said to the woman, "Your faith has saved you. Go in peace."

1. Invite the Holy Spirit into this reading, asking the Author of Scripture to speak to you through His Word
2. Read today's passage as many times as you need, take your time
3. Write down (below) what the Lord is saying to you today
4. Live with this Word in your heart through the day

———————————————————————

———————————————————————

### Friday, September 20, 2024
Saints Andrew Kim Tae-gŏn, Priest, and Paul Chŏng Ha-sang, red
and Companions, Martyrs

**First Reading:** First Corinthians 15: 12-20

12 Now if Christ is preached, that he has been raised from the dead, how do some among you say that there is no resurrection of the dead? 13 But if there is no resurrection of the dead, neither has Christ been raised. 14 If Christ has not been raised, then our preaching is in vain and your faith also is in vain. 15 Yes, we are also found false witnesses of God, because we testified about God that he raised up Christ, whom he didn't raise up if it is true that the dead are not raised. 16 For if the dead aren't raised, neither has Christ been raised. 17 If Christ has not been raised, your faith is vain; you are still in your sins. 18 Then they also who are fallen asleep in Christ have perished. 19 If we have only hoped in Christ in this life, we are of all men most pitiable. 20 But now Christ has been raised from the dead. He became the first fruit of those who are asleep.

**Responsorial Psalm:** Psalms 17: 1bcd, 6-7, 8b and 15

1 Hear, Yahweh, my righteous plea.
Give ear to my prayer that doesn't go out of deceitful lips.
6 I have called on you, for you will answer me, God.
Turn your ear to me.
Hear my speech.
7 Show your marvelous loving kindness,
you who save those who take refuge by your right hand from their enemies.
8 Keep me as the apple of your eye.
Hide me under the shadow of your wings,
15 As for me, I shall see your face in righteousness.
I shall be satisfied, when I awake, with seeing your form.

**Gospel: Luke 8: 1-3**

1 Soon afterwards, he went about through cities and villages, preaching and bringing the good news of God's Kingdom. With him were the twelve, 2 and certain women who had been healed of evil spirits and infirmities: Mary who was called Magdalene, from whom seven demons had gone out; 3 and Joanna, the wife of Chuzas, Herod's steward; Susanna; and many others who served them† from their possessions.

1. Invite the Holy Spirit into this reading, asking the Author of Scripture to speak to you through His Word
2. Read today's passage as many times as you need, take your time
3. Write down (below) what the Lord is saying to you today
4. Live with this Word in your heart through the day

---

---

## Saturday, September 21, 2024
### Saint Matthew, Apostle and Evangelist

**First Reading:** Ephesians 4: 1-7, 11-13

1 I therefore, the prisoner in the Lord, beg you to walk worthily of the calling with which you were called, 2 with all lowliness and humility, with patience, bearing with one another in love, 3 being eager to keep the unity of the Spirit in the bond of peace. 4 There is one body and one Spirit, even as you also were called in one hope of your calling, 5 one Lord, one faith, one baptism, 6 one God and Father of all, who is over all and through all and in us all. 7 But to each one of us, the grace was given according to the measure of the gift of Christ.

11 He gave some to be apostles; and some, prophets; and some, evangelists; and some, shepherds† and teachers; 12 for the perfecting of the saints, to the work of serving, to the building up of the body of Christ, 13 until we all attain to the unity of the faith and of the knowledge of the Son of God, to a full grown man, to the measure of the stature of the fullness of Christ,

## Responsorial Psalm: Psalms 19: 2-5

2 Day after day they pour out speech,
and night after night they display knowledge.
3 There is no speech nor language
where their voice is not heard.
4 Their voice has gone out through all the earth,
their words to the end of the world.
In them he has set a tent for the sun,
5 which is as a bridegroom coming out of his room,
like a strong man rejoicing to run his course.

## Gospel: Matthew 9: 9-13

9 As Jesus passed by from there, he saw a man called Matthew sitting at the tax collection office. He said to him, "Follow me." He got up and followed him. 10 As he sat in the house, behold, many tax collectors and sinners came and sat down with Jesus and his disciples. 11 When the Pharisees saw it, they said to his disciples, "Why does your teacher eat with tax collectors and sinners?"
12 When Jesus heard it, he said to them, "Those who are healthy have no need for a physician, but those who are sick do. 13 But you go and learn what this means: 'I desire mercy, and not sacrifice,'* for I came not to call the righteous, but sinners to repentance."

1. Invite the Holy Spirit into this reading, asking the Author of Scripture to speak to you through His Word
2. Read today's passage as many times as you need, take your time
3. Write down (below) what the Lord is saying to you today
4. Live with this Word in your heart through the day

_____

_____

## Sunday, September 22, 2024
### TWENTY-FIFTH SUNDAY IN ORDINARY TIME

**First Reading:** Wisdom 2: 12, 17-20

12 But let's lie in wait for the righteous man,
because he annoys us,
is contrary to our works,
reproaches us with sins against the law,
and charges us with sins against our training.
17 Let's see if his words are true.
Let's test what will happen at the end of his life.
18 For if the righteous man is God's son, he will uphold him,
and he will deliver him out of the hand of his adversaries.
19 Let's test him with insult and torture,
that we may find out how gentle he is,
and test his patience.
20 Let's condemn him to a shameful death,
for he will be protected, according to his words."

**Responsorial Psalm:** Psalms 54: 3-7

3 For strangers have risen up against me.
Violent men have sought after my soul.
They haven't set God before them.

4 Behold, God is my helper.
The Lord is the one who sustains my soul.
5 He will repay the evil to my enemies.
Destroy them in your truth.
6 With a free will offering, I will sacrifice to you.
I will give thanks to your name, Yahweh, for it is good.
7 For he has delivered me out of all trouble.
My eye has seen triumph over my enemies.

**Second Reading:** James 3: 16 – 4: 3

16 For where jealousy and selfish ambition are, there is confusion and every evil deed. 17 But the wisdom that is from above is first pure, then peaceful, gentle, reasonable, full of mercy and good fruits, without partiality, and without hypocrisy. 18 Now the fruit of righteousness is sown in peace by those who make peace.
1 Where do wars and fightings among you come from? Don't they come from your pleasures that war in your members? 2 You lust, and don't have. You murder and covet, and can't obtain. You fight and make war. You don't have, because you don't ask. 3 You ask, and don't receive, because you ask with wrong motives, so that you may spend it on your pleasures.

**Gospel: Mark 9: 30-37**

30 Then their eyes were opened. Jesus strictly commanded them, saying, "See that no one knows about this." 31 But they went out and spread abroad his fame in all that land.
32 As they went out, behold, a mute man who was demon possessed was brought to him. 33 When the demon was cast out, the mute man spoke. The multitudes marveled, saying, "Nothing like this has ever been seen in Israel!"
34 But the Pharisees said, "By the prince of the demons, he casts out demons."
35 Jesus went about all the cities and the villages, teaching in their synagogues and preaching the Good News of the Kingdom, and healing every disease and every sickness among the people. 36 But when he saw the multitudes, he was moved with compassion for them because they were harassed§ and scattered, like sheep without a shepherd. 37 Then he said to his disciples, "The harvest indeed is plentiful, but the laborers are few.

1. Invite the Holy Spirit into this reading, asking the Author of Scripture to speak to you through His Word

2. Read today's passage as many times as you need, take your time
3. Write down (below) what the Lord is saying to you today
4. Live with this Word in your heart through the day

---

---

## Monday, September 23, 2024
### Saint Pio of Pietrelcina, Priest

**First Reading:** Proverbs 3: 27-34

27 Don't withhold good from those to whom it is due,
when it is in the power of your hand to do it.
28 Don't say to your neighbor, "Go, and come again;
tomorrow I will give it to you,"
when you have it by you.
29 Don't devise evil against your neighbor,
since he dwells securely by you.
30 Don't strive with a man without cause,
if he has done you no harm.
31 Don't envy the man of violence.
Choose none of his ways.
32 For the perverse is an abomination to Yahweh,
but his friendship is with the upright.
33 Yahweh's curse is in the house of the wicked,
but he blesses the habitation of the righteous.
34 Surely he mocks the mockers,
but he gives grace to the humble.

**Responsorial Psalm:** Psalms 15: 2-5

2 He who walks blamelessly and does what is right,
and speaks truth in his heart;

3 he who doesn't slander with his tongue,
nor does evil to his friend,
nor casts slurs against his fellow man;
4 in whose eyes a vile man is despised,
but who honors those who fear Yahweh;
he who keeps an oath even when it hurts, and doesn't change;
5 he who doesn't lend out his money for usury,
nor take a bribe against the innocent.

## Gospel: Luke 8: 16-18

16 "No one, when he has lit a lamp, covers it with a container or puts it under a bed; but puts it on a stand, that those who enter in may see the light. 17 For nothing is hidden that will not be revealed, nor anything secret that will not be known and come to light. 18 Be careful therefore how you hear. For whoever has, to him will be given; and whoever doesn't have, from him will be taken away even that which he thinks he has."

1. Invite the Holy Spirit into this reading, asking the Author of Scripture to speak to you through His Word
2. Read today's passage as many times as you need, take your time
3. Write down (below) what the Lord is saying to you today
4. Live with this Word in your heart through the day

_____

_____

## Tuesday, September 24, 2024

**First Reading:** Proverbs 21: 1-6, 10-13

1 The king's heart is in Yahweh's hand like the watercourses.
He turns it wherever he desires.
2 Every way of a man is right in his own eyes,
but Yahweh weighs the hearts.

3 To do righteousness and justice
is more acceptable to Yahweh than sacrifice.
4 A high look and a proud heart,
the lamp of the wicked, is sin.
5 The plans of the diligent surely lead to profit;
and everyone who is hasty surely rushes to poverty.
6 Getting treasures by a lying tongue
is a fleeting vapor for those who seek death.
10 The soul of the wicked desires evil;
his neighbor finds no mercy in his eyes.
11 When the mocker is punished, the simple gains wisdom.
When the wise is instructed, he receives knowledge.
12 The Righteous One considers the house of the wicked,
and brings the wicked to ruin.
13 Whoever stops his ears at the cry of the poor,
he will also cry out, but shall not be heard.

**Responsorial Psalm:** Psalms 119: 1, 27, 30, 34, 35, 44

1 Blessed are those whose ways are blameless,
who walk according to Yahweh's law.
27 Let me understand the teaching of your precepts!
Then I will meditate on your wondrous works.
30 I have chosen the way of truth.
I have set your ordinances before me.
34 Give me understanding, and I will keep your law.
Yes, I will obey it with my whole heart.
35 Direct me in the path of your commandments,
for I delight in them.
44 So I will obey your law continually,
forever and ever.

**Gospel: Luke 8: 19-21**

19 His mother and brothers came to him, and they could not come near him for the crowd. 20 Some people told him, "Your mother and your brothers stand outside, desiring to see you."

21 But he answered them, "My mother and my brothers are these who hear the word of God and do it."

_____

_____

## Wednesday, September 25, 2024

**First Reading:** Proverbs 30: 5-9

5 "Every word of God is flawless.
He is a shield to those who take refuge in him.
6 Don't you add to his words,
lest he reprove you, and you be found a liar.
7 "Two things I have asked of you.
Don't deny me before I die.
8 Remove far from me falsehood and lies.
Give me neither poverty nor riches.
Feed me with the food that is needful for me,
9 lest I be full, deny you, and say, 'Who is Yahweh?'
or lest I be poor, and steal,
and so dishonor the name of my God.

**Responsorial Psalm:** Psalms 119: 29, 72, 89, 101, 104, 163

29 Keep me from the way of deceit.
Grant me your law graciously!
72 The law of your mouth is better to me than thousands of pieces of gold and silver.
89 Yahweh, your word is settled in heaven forever.

101 I have kept my feet from every evil way,
that I might observe your word.
104 Through your precepts, I get understanding;
therefore I hate every false way.
163 I hate and abhor falsehood.
I love your law.

**Gospel: Luke 9: 1-6**

1 He called the twelve† together and gave them power and authority over all demons, and to cure diseases. 2 He sent them out to preach God's Kingdom and to heal the sick. 3 He said to them, "Take nothing for your journey—no staffs, nor wallet, nor bread, nor money. Don't have two tunics each. 4 Into whatever house you enter, stay there, and depart from there. 5 As many as don't receive you, when you depart from that city, shake off even the dust from your feet for a testimony against them."
6 They departed and went throughout the villages, preaching the Good News and healing everywhere.

1. Invite the Holy Spirit into this reading, asking the Author of Scripture to speak to you through His Word
2. Read today's passage as many times as you need, take your time
3. Write down (below) what the Lord is saying to you today
4. Live with this Word in your heart through the day

_____

_____

### Thursday, September 26, 2024
Saints Cosmas and Damian, Martyrs

**First Reading:** Ecclesiastes 1: 2-11

2 "Vanity of vanities," says the Preacher; "Vanity of vanities, all is vanity." 3 What does man gain from all his labor in which he labors under the sun? 4 One generation goes, and another generation comes; but the earth remains forever. 5 The sun also rises, and

the sun goes down, and hurries to its place where it rises. 6 The wind goes toward the south, and turns around to the north. It turns around continually as it goes, and the wind returns again to its courses. 7 All the rivers run into the sea, yet the sea is not full. To the place where the rivers flow, there they flow again. 8 All things are full of weariness beyond uttering. The eye is not satisfied with seeing, nor the ear filled with hearing. 9 That which has been is that which shall be, and that which has been done is that which shall be done; and there is no new thing under the sun. 10 Is there a thing of which it may be said, "Behold,† this is new"? It has been long ago, in the ages which were before us. 11 There is no memory of the former; neither shall there be any memory of the latter that are to come, among those that shall come after.

**Responsorial Psalm:** Psalms 90: 3-6, 12-14 and 17bc

3 You turn man to destruction, saying,
"Return, you children of men."
4 For a thousand years in your sight are just like yesterday when it is past,
like a watch in the night.
5 You sweep them away as they sleep.
In the morning they sprout like new grass.
6 In the morning it sprouts and springs up.
By evening, it is withered and dry.
12 So teach us to count our days,
that we may gain a heart of wisdom.
13 Relent, Yahweh!§
How long?
Have compassion on your servants!
14 Satisfy us in the morning with your loving kindness,
that we may rejoice and be glad all our days.
17b Establish the work of our hands for us.
Yes, establish the work of our hands.

**Gospel: Luke 9: 7-9**

7 Now Herod the tetrarch heard of all that was done by him; and he was very perplexed, because it was said by some that John had risen from the dead, 8 and by some that Elijah had appeared, and by others that one of the old prophets had risen again. 9 Herod said, "I beheaded John, but who is this about whom I hear such things?" He sought to see him.

1. Invite the Holy Spirit into this reading, asking the Author of Scripture to speak to you through His Word
2. Read today's passage as many times as you need, take your time
3. Write down (below) what the Lord is saying to you today
4. Live with this Word in your heart through the day

_____

_____

## Friday, September 27, 2024
### Saint Vincent de Paul, Priest

**First Reading:** Ecclesiastes 3: 1-11

1 For everything there is a season, and a time for every purpose under heaven:
2 a time to be born, and a time to die; a time to plant, and a time to pluck up that which is planted;
3 a time to kill, and a time to heal; a time to break down, and a time to build up;
4 a time to weep, and a time to laugh; a time to mourn, and a time to dance;
5 a time to cast away stones, and a time to gather stones together; a time to embrace, and a time to refrain from embracing;
6 a time to seek, and a time to lose; a time to keep, and a time to cast away;
7 a time to tear, and a time to sew; a time to keep silence, and a time to speak;
8 a time to love, and a time to hate; a time for war, and a time for peace.
9 What profit has he who works in that in which he labors? 10 I have seen the burden which God has given to the sons of men to be afflicted with. 11 He has made everything beautiful in its time. He has also set eternity in their hearts, yet so that man can't find out the work that God has done from the beginning even to the end.

**Responsorial Psalm:** Psalms 144: 1b-4

1 Blessed be Yahweh, my rock,
who trains my hands to war,
and my fingers to battle—

2 my loving kindness, my fortress,
my high tower, my deliverer,
my shield, and he in whom I take refuge,
who subdues my people under me.
3 Yahweh, what is man, that you care for him?
Or the son of man, that you think of him?
4 Man is like a breath.
His days are like a shadow that passes away.

**Gospel: Luke 9: 18-22**

18 As he was praying alone, the disciples were near him, and he asked them, "Who do the multitudes say that I am?"
19 They answered, " 'John the Baptizer,' but others say, 'Elijah,' and others, that one of the old prophets has risen again."
20 He said to them, "But who do you say that I am?"
Peter answered, "The Christ of God."
21 But he warned them and commanded them to tell this to no one, 22 saying, "The Son of Man must suffer many things, and be rejected by the elders, chief priests, and scribes, and be killed, and the third day be raised up."

1. Invite the Holy Spirit into this reading, asking the Author of Scripture to speak to you through His Word
2. Read today's passage as many times as you need, take your time
3. Write down (below) what the Lord is saying to you today
4. Live with this Word in your heart through the day

_____

_____

### Saturday, September 28, 2024
Saint Wenceslaus, Martyr; Saint Lawrence Ruiz
and Companions, Martyrs; BVM

**First Reading:** Ecclesiastes 11: 9 – 12: 8

9 Rejoice, young man, in your youth,

and let your heart cheer you in the days of your youth,

and walk in the ways of your heart,

and in the sight of your eyes;

but know that for all these things God will bring you into judgment.

10 Therefore remove sorrow from your heart,

and put away evil from your flesh;

for youth and the dawn of life are vanity.

1 Remember also your Creator in the days of your youth,

before the evil days come, and the years draw near,

when you will say, "I have no pleasure in them;"

2 Before the sun, the light, the moon, and the stars are darkened,

and the clouds return after the rain;

3 in the day when the keepers of the house shall tremble,

and the strong men shall bow themselves,

and the grinders cease because they are few,

and those who look out of the windows are darkened,

4 and the doors shall be shut in the street;

when the sound of the grinding is low,

and one shall rise up at the voice of a bird,

and all the daughters of music shall be brought low;

5 yes, they shall be afraid of heights,

and terrors will be on the way;

and the almond tree shall blossom,

and the grasshopper shall be a burden,

and desire shall fail;

because man goes to his everlasting home,

and the mourners go about the streets;

6 before the silver cord is severed,

or the golden bowl is broken,

or the pitcher is broken at the spring,

or the wheel broken at the cistern,

7 and the dust returns to the earth as it was,

and the spirit returns to God who gave it.

8 "Vanity of vanities," says the Preacher.

"All is vanity!"

**Responsorial Psalm:** Psalms 90: 3-6, 12-14 and 17

3 You turn man to destruction, saying,
"Return, you children of men."
4 For a thousand years in your sight are just like yesterday when it is past,
like a watch in the night.
5 You sweep them away as they sleep.
In the morning they sprout like new grass.
6 In the morning it sprouts and springs up.
By evening, it is withered and dry.
12 So teach us to count our days,
that we may gain a heart of wisdom.
13 Relent, Yahweh!§
How long?
Have compassion on your servants!
14 Satisfy us in the morning with your loving kindness,
that we may rejoice and be glad all our days.
17 Let the favor of the Lord our God be on us.
Establish the work of our hands for us.
Yes, establish the work of our hands.

## Gospel: Luke 9: 43b-45

43 They were all astonished at the majesty of God.
But while all were marveling at all the things which Jesus did, he said to his disciples,
44 "Let these words sink into your ears, for the Son of Man will be delivered up into the hands of men." 45 But they didn't understand this saying. It was concealed from them, that they should not perceive it, and they were afraid to ask him about this saying.

1. Invite the Holy Spirit into this reading, asking the Author of Scripture to speak to you through His Word
2. Read today's passage as many times as you need, take your time
3. Write down (below) what the Lord is saying to you today
4. Live with this Word in your heart through the day

_____

_____

## Sunday, September 29, 2024
### TWENTY-SIXTH SUNDAY IN ORDINARY TIME

**First Reading:** Numbers 11: 25-29

25 Yahweh came down in the cloud, and spoke to him, and took of the Spirit that was on him, and put it on the seventy elders. When the Spirit rested on them, they prophesied, but they did so no more. 26 But two men remained in the camp. The name of one was Eldad, and the name of the other Medad; and the Spirit rested on them. They were of those who were written, but had not gone out to the Tent; and they prophesied in the camp. 27 A young man ran, and told Moses, and said, "Eldad and Medad are prophesying in the camp!"

28 Joshua the son of Nun, the servant of Moses, one of his chosen men, answered, "My lord Moses, forbid them!"

29 Moses said to him, "Are you jealous for my sake? I wish that all Yahweh's people were prophets, that Yahweh would put his Spirit on them!"

**Responsorial Psalm:** Psalms 19: 8, 10, 12-13, 14

8 Yahweh's precepts are right, rejoicing the heart.
Yahweh's commandment is pure, enlightening the eyes.
10 They are more to be desired than gold, yes, than much fine gold,
sweeter also than honey and the extract of the honeycomb.
12 Who can discern his errors?
Forgive me from hidden errors.
13 Keep back your servant also from presumptuous sins.
Let them not have dominion over me.
Then I will be upright.
I will be blameless and innocent of great transgression.
14 Let the words of my mouth and the meditation of my heart
be acceptable in your sight,
Yahweh, my rock, and my redeemer.

**Second Reading:** James 5: 1-6

1 Come now, you rich, weep and howl for your miseries that are coming on you. 2 Your riches are corrupted and your garments are moth-eaten. 3 Your gold and your silver

are corroded, and their corrosion will be for a testimony against you and will eat your flesh like fire. You have laid up your treasure in the last days. 4 Behold, the wages of the laborers who mowed your fields, which you have kept back by fraud, cry out; and the cries of those who reaped have entered into the ears of the Lord of Armies.† 5 You have lived in luxury on the earth, and taken your pleasure. You have nourished your hearts as in a day of slaughter. 6 You have condemned and you have murdered the righteous one. He doesn't resist you.

## Gospel: Mark 9: 38-43, 45, 47-48

38 John said to him, "Teacher, we saw someone who doesn't follow us casting out demons in your name; and we forbade him, because he doesn't follow us."
39 But Jesus said, "Don't forbid him, for there is no one who will do a mighty work in my name and be able quickly to speak evil of me. 40  For whoever is not against us is on our side. 41  For whoever will give you a cup of water to drink in my name because you are Christ's, most certainly I tell you, he will in no way lose his reward.
42 "Whoever will cause one of these little ones who believe in me to stumble, it would be better for him if he were thrown into the sea with a millstone hung around his neck. 43  If your hand causes you to stumble, cut it off. It is better for you to enter into life maimed, rather than having your two hands to go into Gehenna, † into the unquenchable fire, 45  If your foot causes you to stumble, cut it off. It is better for you to enter into life lame, rather than having your two feet to be cast into Gehenna, § into the fire that will never be quenched—47  If your eye causes you to stumble, throw it out. It is better for you to enter into God's Kingdom with one eye, rather than having two eyes to be cast into the Gehenna‡ of fire, 48  'where their worm doesn't die, and the fire is not quenched.'

1. Invite the Holy Spirit into this reading, asking the Author of Scripture to speak to you through His Word
2. Read today's passage as many times as you need, take your time
3. Write down (below) what the Lord is saying to you today
4. Live with this Word in your heart through the day

_____

_____

**First Reading:** Job 1: 6-22

6 Now on the day when God's sons came to present themselves before Yahweh,‡ Satan also came among them. 7 Yahweh said to Satan, "Where have you come from?"
Then Satan answered Yahweh, and said, "From going back and forth in the earth, and from walking up and down in it."
8 Yahweh said to Satan, "Have you considered my servant, Job? For there is no one like him in the earth, a blameless and an upright man, one who fears God, and turns away from evil."
9 Then Satan answered Yahweh, and said, "Does Job fear God for nothing? 10 Haven't you made a hedge around him, and around his house, and around all that he has, on every side? You have blessed the work of his hands, and his substance is increased in the land. 11 But stretch out your hand now, and touch all that he has, and he will renounce you to your face."
12 Yahweh said to Satan, "Behold,§ all that he has is in your power. Only on himself don't stretch out your hand."
So Satan went out from the presence of Yahweh. 13 It fell on a day when his sons and his daughters were eating and drinking wine in their oldest brother's house, 14 that a messenger came to Job, and said, "The oxen were plowing, and the donkeys feeding beside them, 15 and the Sabeans attacked, and took them away. Yes, they have killed the servants with the edge of the sword, and I alone have escaped to tell you."
16 While he was still speaking, another also came and said, "The fire of God has fallen from the sky, and has burned up the sheep and the servants, and consumed them, and I alone have escaped to tell you."
17 While he was still speaking, another also came and said, "The Chaldeans made three bands, and swept down on the camels, and have taken them away, yes, and killed the servants with the edge of the sword; and I alone have escaped to tell you."
18 While he was still speaking, there came also another, and said, "Your sons and your daughters were eating and drinking wine in their oldest brother's house, 19 and behold, there came a great wind from the wilderness, and struck the four corners of the house, and it fell on the young men, and they are dead. I alone have escaped to tell you."
20 Then Job arose, and tore his robe, and shaved his head, and fell down on the ground, and worshiped. 21 He said, "Naked I came out of my mother's womb, and naked will I

return there. Yahweh gave, and Yahweh has taken away. Blessed be Yahweh's name." 22 In all this, Job didn't sin, nor charge God with wrongdoing.

**Responsorial Psalm:** Psalms 17: 1bcd, 2-3, 6-7

1b Give ear to my prayer that doesn't go out of deceitful lips.
2 Let my sentence come out of your presence.
Let your eyes look on equity.
3 You have proved my heart.
You have visited me in the night.
You have tried me, and found nothing.
I have resolved that my mouth shall not disobey.
6 I have called on you, for you will answer me, God.
Turn your ear to me.
Hear my speech.
7 Show your marvelous loving kindness,
you who save those who take refuge by your right hand from their enemies.

**Gospel: Luke 9: 46-50**

46 An argument arose among them about which of them was the greatest. 47 Jesus, perceiving the reasoning of their hearts, took a little child, and set him by his side, 48 and said to them, "Whoever receives this little child in my name receives me. Whoever receives me receives him who sent me. For whoever is least among you all, this one will be great."
49 John answered, "Master, we saw someone casting out demons in your name, and we forbade him, because he doesn't follow with us."
50 Jesus said to him, "Don't forbid him, for he who is not against us is for us."

1. Invite the Holy Spirit into this reading, asking the Author of Scripture to speak to you through His Word
2. Read today's passage as many times as you need, take your time
3. Write down (below) what the Lord is saying to you today
4. Live with this Word in your heart through the day

_____

_____

Saint Thérèse of the Child Jesus, Virgin and Doctor of the Church

**First Reading:** Job 3: 1-3, 11-17, 20-23

1 After this Job opened his mouth, and cursed the day of his birth. 2 Job answered:
3 "Let the day perish in which I was born,
the night which said, 'There is a boy conceived.'
11 "Why didn't I die from the womb?
Why didn't I give up the spirit when my mother bore me?
12 Why did the knees receive me?
Or why the breast, that I should nurse?
13 For now I should have lain down and been quiet.
I should have slept, then I would have been at rest,
14 with kings and counselors of the earth,
who built up waste places for themselves;
15 or with princes who had gold,
who filled their houses with silver;
16 or as a hidden untimely birth I had not been,
as infants who never saw light.
17 There the wicked cease from troubling.
There the weary are at rest.
20 "Why is light given to him who is in misery,
life to the bitter in soul,
21 who long for death, but it doesn't come;
and dig for it more than for hidden treasures,
22 who rejoice exceedingly,
and are glad, when they can find the grave?
23 Why is light given to a man whose way is hidden,
whom God has hedged in?

**Responsorial Psalm:** Psalms 88: 2-8

2 Let my prayer enter into your presence.
Turn your ear to my cry.
3 For my soul is full of troubles.
My life draws near to Sheol.†

4 I am counted among those who go down into the pit.
I am like a man who has no help,
5 set apart among the dead,
like the slain who lie in the grave,
whom you remember no more.
They are cut off from your hand.
6 You have laid me in the lowest pit,
in the darkest depths.
7 Your wrath lies heavily on me.
You have afflicted me with all your waves.
8 You have taken my friends from me.
You have made me an abomination to them.
I am confined, and I can't escape.

## Gospel: Luke 9: 51-56

51 It came to pass, when the days were near that he should be taken up, he intently set his face to go to Jerusalem 52 and sent messengers before his face. They went and entered into a village of the Samaritans, so as to prepare for him. 53 They didn't receive him, because he was traveling with his face set toward Jerusalem. 54 When his disciples, James and John, saw this, they said, "Lord, do you want us to command fire to come down from the sky and destroy them, just as Elijah did?"
55 But he turned and rebuked them, "You don't know of what kind of spirit you are. 56 For the Son of Man didn't come to destroy men's lives, but to save them."
They went to another village.

1. Invite the Holy Spirit into this reading, asking the Author of Scripture to speak to you through His Word
2. Read today's passage as many times as you need, take your time
3. Write down (below) what the Lord is saying to you today
4. Live with this Word in your heart through the day

_____

_____

# Wednesday, October 2, 2024
## The Holy Guardian Angels

**First Reading:** Job 9: 1-12, 14-16

1 Then Job answered,
2 "Truly I know that it is so,
but how can man be just with God?
3 If he is pleased to contend with him,
he can't answer him one time in a thousand.
4 God is wise in heart, and mighty in strength.
Who has hardened himself against him and prospered?
5 He removes the mountains, and they don't know it,
when he overturns them in his anger.
6 He shakes the earth out of its place.
Its pillars tremble.
7 He commands the sun and it doesn't rise,
and seals up the stars.
8 He alone stretches out the heavens,
and treads on the waves of the sea.
9 He makes the Bear, Orion, and the Pleiades,
and the rooms of the south.
10 He does great things past finding out;
yes, marvelous things without number.
11 Behold, he goes by me, and I don't see him.
He passes on also, but I don't perceive him.
12 Behold, he snatches away.
Who can hinder him?
Who will ask him, 'What are you doing?'
14 How much less will I answer him,
and choose my words to argue with him?
15 Though I were righteous, yet I wouldn't answer him.
I would make supplication to my judge.
16 If I had called, and he had answered me,
yet I wouldn't believe that he listened to my voice.

**Responsorial Psalm:** Psalms 88: 10bc-15

10 Do you show wonders to the dead?
Do the departed spirits rise up and praise you?
11 Is your loving kindness declared in the grave?
Or your faithfulness in Destruction?
12 Are your wonders made known in the dark?
Or your righteousness in the land of forgetfulness?
13 But to you, Yahweh, I have cried.
In the morning, my prayer comes before you.
14 Yahweh, why do you reject my soul?
Why do you hide your face from me?
15 I am afflicted and ready to die from my youth up.
While I suffer your terrors, I am distracted.

## Gospel: Matthew 18: 1-5, 10

1 In that hour the disciples came to Jesus, saying, "Who then is greatest in the Kingdom of Heaven?"
2 Jesus called a little child to himself, and set him in the middle of them 3 and said, "Most certainly I tell you, unless you turn and become as little children, you will in no way enter into the Kingdom of Heaven. 4 Whoever therefore humbles himself as this little child is the greatest in the Kingdom of Heaven. 5 Whoever receives one such little child in my name receives me,
10 See that you don't despise one of these little ones, for I tell you that in heaven their angels always see the face of my Father who is in heaven. 11 For the Son of Man came to save that which was lost.

1. Invite the Holy Spirit into this reading, asking the Author of Scripture to speak to you through His Word
2. Read today's passage as many times as you need, take your time
3. Write down (below) what the Lord is saying to you today
4. Live with this Word in your heart through the day

_____

_____

**First Reading:** Job 19: 21-27

21 "Have pity on me. Have pity on me, you my friends,
for the hand of God has touched me.
22 Why do you persecute me as God,
and are not satisfied with my flesh?
23 "Oh that my words were now written!
Oh that they were inscribed in a book!
24 That with an iron pen and lead
they were engraved in the rock forever!
25 But as for me, I know that my Redeemer lives.
In the end, he will stand upon the earth.
26 After my skin is destroyed,
then I will see God in my flesh,
27 whom I, even I, will see on my side.
My eyes will see, and not as a stranger.
"My heart is consumed within me.

**Responsorial Psalm:** Psalms 27: 7-9, 13-14

7 Hear, Yahweh, when I cry with my voice.
Have mercy also on me, and answer me.
8 When you said, "Seek my face,"
my heart said to you, "I will seek your face, Yahweh."
9 Don't hide your face from me.
Don't put your servant away in anger.
You have been my help.
Don't abandon me,
neither forsake me, God of my salvation.
13 I am still confident of this:
I will see the goodness of Yahweh in the land of the living.
14 Wait for Yahweh.
Be strong, and let your heart take courage.
Yes, wait for Yahweh.

**Gospel: Luke 10: 1-12**

1 Now after these things, the Lord also appointed seventy others, and sent them two by two ahead of him† into every city and place where he was about to come. 2 Then he said to them, "The harvest is indeed plentiful, but the laborers are few. Pray therefore to the Lord of the harvest, that he may send out laborers into his harvest. 3 Go your ways. Behold, I send you out as lambs among wolves. 4 Carry no purse, nor wallet, nor sandals. Greet no one on the way. 5 Into whatever house you enter, first say, 'Peace be to this house.' 6 If a son of peace is there, your peace will rest on him; but if not, it will return to you. 7 Remain in that same house, eating and drinking the things they give, for the laborer is worthy of his wages. Don't go from house to house. 8 Into whatever city you enter and they receive you, eat the things that are set before you. 9 Heal the sick who are there and tell them, 'God's Kingdom has come near to you.' 10 But into whatever city you enter and they don't receive you, go out into its streets and say, 11 'Even the dust from your city that clings to us, we wipe off against you. Nevertheless know this, that God's Kingdom has come near to you.' 12 I tell you, it will be more tolerable in that day for Sodom than for that city.

1. Invite the Holy Spirit into this reading, asking the Author of Scripture to speak to you through His Word
2. Read today's passage as many times as you need, take your time
3. Write down (below) what the Lord is saying to you today
4. Live with this Word in your heart through the day

_____

_____

**Friday, October 4, 2024**
Saint Francis of Assisi

**First Reading:** Job 38: 1, 12-21; 40: 3-5

1 Then Yahweh answered Job out of the whirlwind,
12 "Have you commanded the morning in your days,
and caused the dawn to know its place,

13 that it might take hold of the ends of the earth,
and shake the wicked out of it?
14 It is changed as clay under the seal,
and presented as a garment.
15 From the wicked, their light is withheld.
The high arm is broken.
 16 "Have you entered into the springs of the sea?
Or have you walked in the recesses of the deep?
17 Have the gates of death been revealed to you?
Or have you seen the gates of the shadow of death?
18 Have you comprehended the earth in its width?
Declare, if you know it all.
 19 "What is the way to the dwelling of light?
As for darkness, where is its place,
20 that you should take it to its bound,
that you should discern the paths to its house?
21 Surely you know, for you were born then,
and the number of your days is great!
3 Then Job answered Yahweh,
4 "Behold, I am of small account. What will I answer you?
I lay my hand on my mouth.
5 I have spoken once, and I will not answer;
Yes, twice, but I will proceed no further."

**Responsorial Psalm:** Psalms 139: 1-3, 7-10, 13-14ab

1 Yahweh, you have searched me,
and you know me.
2 You know my sitting down and my rising up.
You perceive my thoughts from afar.
3 You search out my path and my lying down,
and are acquainted with all my ways.
7 Where could I go from your Spirit?
Or where could I flee from your presence?
8 If I ascend up into heaven, you are there.
If I make my bed in Sheol,† behold, you are there!
9 If I take the wings of the dawn,
and settle in the uttermost parts of the sea,

10 even there your hand will lead me,
and your right hand will hold me.
13 For you formed my inmost being.
You knit me together in my mother's womb.
14 I will give thanks to you,
for I am fearfully and wonderfully made.
Your works are wonderful.
My soul knows that very well.

**Gospel: Luke 10: 13-16**

13 "Woe to you, Chorazin! Woe to you, Bethsaida! For if the mighty works had been done in Tyre and Sidon which were done in you, they would have repented long ago, sitting in sackcloth and ashes. 14 But it will be more tolerable for Tyre and Sidon in the judgment than for you. 15 You, Capernaum, who are exalted to heaven, will be brought down to Hades. ‡ 16 Whoever listens to you listens to me, and whoever rejects you rejects me. Whoever rejects me rejects him who sent me."

1. Invite the Holy Spirit into this reading, asking the Author of Scripture to speak to you through His Word
2. Read today's passage as many times as you need, take your time
3. Write down (below) what the Lord is saying to you today
4. Live with this Word in your heart through the day

---

---

### Saturday, October 5, 2024
Saint Faustina Kowalska, Virgin;
USA: Blessed Francis Xavier Seelos, Priest

**First Reading:** Job 42: 1-3, 5-6, 12-17

1 Then Job answered Yahweh:
2 "I know that you can do all things,
and that no purpose of yours can be restrained.

3 You asked, 'Who is this who hides counsel without knowledge?'
therefore I have uttered that which I didn't understand,
things too wonderful for me, which I didn't know.
5 I had heard of you by the hearing of the ear,
but now my eye sees you.
6 Therefore I abhor myself,
and repent in dust and ashes."
12 So Yahweh blessed the latter end of Job more than his beginning. He had fourteen thousand sheep, six thousand camels, one thousand yoke of oxen, and a thousand female donkeys. 13 He had also seven sons and three daughters. 14 He called the name of the first, Jemimah; and the name of the second, Keziah; and the name of the third, Keren Happuch. 15 In all the land were no women found so beautiful as the daughters of Job. Their father gave them an inheritance among their brothers. 16 After this Job lived one hundred forty years, and saw his sons, and his sons' sons, to four generations. 17 So Job died, being old and full of days.

**Responsorial Psalm:** Psalms 119: 66, 71, 75, 91, 125, 130

65 You have treated your servant well,
according to your word, Yahweh.
71 It is good for me that I have been afflicted,
that I may learn your statutes.
75 Yahweh, I know that your judgments are righteous,
that in faithfulness you have afflicted me.
91 Your laws remain to this day,
for all things serve you.
125 I am your servant. Give me understanding,
that I may know your testimonies.
130 The entrance of your words gives light.
It gives understanding to the simple.

**Gospel: Luke 10: 17-24**

17 The seventy returned with joy, saying, "Lord, even the demons are subject to us in your name!"
18 He said to them, "I saw Satan having fallen like lightning from heaven. 19 Behold, I give you authority to tread on serpents and scorpions, and over all the power of the

enemy. Nothing will in any way hurt you. 20 Nevertheless, don't rejoice in this, that the spirits are subject to you, but rejoice that your names are written in heaven."

21 In that same hour, Jesus rejoiced in the Holy Spirit, and said, "I thank you, O Father, Lord of heaven and earth, that you have hidden these things from the wise and understanding, and revealed them to little children. Yes, Father, for so it was well-pleasing in your sight."

22 Turning to the disciples, he said, "All things have been delivered to me by my Father. No one knows who the Son is, except the Father, and who the Father is, except the Son, and he to whomever the Son desires to reveal him."

23 Turning to the disciples, he said privately, "Blessed are the eyes which see the things that you see, 24 for I tell you that many prophets and kings desired to see the things which you see, and didn't see them, and to hear the things which you hear, and didn't hear them."

1. Invite the Holy Spirit into this reading, asking the Author of Scripture to speak to you through His Word
2. Read today's passage as many times as you need, take your time
3. Write down (below) what the Lord is saying to you today
4. Live with this Word in your heart through the day

_____

_____

### Sunday, October 6, 2024
### TWENTY-SEVENTH SUNDAY IN ORDINARY TIME

**First Reading:** Genesis 2: 18-24

18 Yahweh God said, "It is not good for the man to be alone. I will make him a helper comparable to§ him." 19 Out of the ground Yahweh God formed every animal of the field, and every bird of the sky, and brought them to the man to see what he would call them. Whatever the man called every living creature became its name. 20 The man gave names to all livestock, and to the birds of the sky, and to every animal of the field; but for man there was not found a helper comparable to him. 21 Yahweh God caused the man to fall into a deep sleep. As the man slept, he took one of his ribs, and closed up the flesh in its place. 22 Yahweh God made a woman from the rib which he had

taken from the man, and brought her to the man. 23 The man said, "This is now bone of my bones, and flesh of my flesh. She will be called 'woman,' because she was taken out of Man." 24 Therefore a man will leave his father and his mother, and will join with his wife, and they will be one flesh.

**Responsorial Psalm:** Psalms 128: 1-6

1 Blessed is everyone who fears Yahweh,
who walks in his ways.
2 For you will eat the labor of your hands.
You will be happy, and it will be well with you.
3 Your wife will be as a fruitful vine in the innermost parts of your house,
your children like olive shoots around your table.
4 Behold, this is how the man who fears Yahweh is blessed.
5 May Yahweh bless you out of Zion,
and may you see the good of Jerusalem all the days of your life.
6 Yes, may you see your children's children.
Peace be upon Israel.

**Second Reading:** Hebrews 2: 9-11

9 But we see him who has been made a little lower than the angels, Jesus, because of the suffering of death crowned with glory and honor, that by the grace of God he should taste of death for everyone.
10 For it became him, for whom are all things and through whom are all things, in bringing many children to glory, to make the author of their salvation perfect through sufferings. 11 For both he who sanctifies and those who are sanctified are all from one, for which cause he is not ashamed to call them brothers,

**Gospel: Mark 10: 2-16**

2 Pharisees came to him testing him, and asked him, "Is it lawful for a man to divorce his wife?"
3 He answered, "What did Moses command you?"
4 They said, "Moses allowed a certificate of divorce to be written, and to divorce her."
5 But Jesus said to them, "For your hardness of heart, he wrote you this commandment. 6 But from the beginning of the creation, God made them male and female.* 7 For this cause a man will leave his father and mother, and will join to his

wife, 8 and the two will become one flesh,* so that they are no longer two, but one flesh. 9 What therefore God has joined together, let no man separate."

10 In the house, his disciples asked him again about the same matter. 11 He said to them, "Whoever divorces his wife and marries another commits adultery against her. 12 If a woman herself divorces her husband and marries another, she commits adultery."

13 They were bringing to him little children, that he should touch them, but the disciples rebuked those who were bringing them. 14 But when Jesus saw it, he was moved with indignation and said to them, "Allow the little children to come to me! Don't forbid them, for God's Kingdom belongs to such as these. 15 Most certainly I tell you, whoever will not receive God's Kingdom like a little child, he will in no way enter into it." 16 He took them in his arms and blessed them, laying his hands on them.

1. Invite the Holy Spirit into this reading, asking the Author of Scripture to speak to you through His Word
2. Read today's passage as many times as you need, take your time
3. Write down (below) what the Lord is saying to you today
4. Live with this Word in your heart through the day

_____

_____

## Monday, October 7, 2024
### Our Lady of the Rosary

**First Reading:** Galatians 1: 6-12

6 I marvel that you are so quickly deserting him who called you in the grace of Christ to a different "good news", 7 but there isn't another "good news." Only there are some who trouble you and want to pervert the Good News of Christ. 8 But even though we, or an angel from heaven, should preach to you any "good news" other than that which we preached to you, let him be cursed. 9 As we have said before, so I now say again: if any man preaches to you any "good news" other than that which you received, let him be cursed.

10 For am I now seeking the favor of men, or of God? Or am I striving to please men? For if I were still pleasing men, I wouldn't be a servant of Christ.

11 But I make known to you, brothers, concerning the Good News which was preached by me, that it is not according to man. 12 For I didn't receive it from man, nor was I taught it, but it came to me through revelation of Jesus Christ.

**Responsorial Psalm:** Psalms 111: 1b-2, 7-9 and 10c

1b I will give thanks to Yahweh with my whole heart,
in the council of the upright, and in the congregation.
2 Yahweh's works are great,
pondered by all those who delight in them.
7 The works of his hands are truth and justice.
All his precepts are sure.
8 They are established forever and ever.
They are done in truth and uprightness.
9 He has sent redemption to his people.
He has ordained his covenant forever.
His name is holy and awesome!
10c His praise endures forever!

**Gospel: Luke 10: 25-37**

25 Behold, a certain lawyer stood up and tested him, saying, "Teacher, what shall I do to inherit eternal life?"
26 He said to him, "What is written in the law? How do you read it?"
27 He answered, "You shall love the Lord your God with all your heart, with all your soul, with all your strength, and with all your mind;* and your neighbor as yourself."*
28 He said to him, "You have answered correctly. Do this, and you will live."
29 But he, desiring to justify himself, asked Jesus, "Who is my neighbor?"
30 Jesus answered, "A certain man was going down from Jerusalem to Jericho, and he fell among robbers, who both stripped him and beat him, and departed, leaving him half dead. 31 By chance a certain priest was going down that way. When he saw him, he passed by on the other side. 32 In the same way a Levite also, when he came to the place and saw him, passed by on the other side. 33 But a certain Samaritan, as he traveled, came where he was. When he saw him, he was moved with compassion, 34 came to him, and bound up his wounds, pouring on oil and wine. He set him on his own animal, brought him to an inn, and took care of him. 35 On the next day, when he

departed, he took out two denarii, gave them to the host, and said to him, 'Take care of him. Whatever you spend beyond that, I will repay you when I return.' 36 Now which of these three do you think seemed to be a neighbor to him who fell among the robbers?"

37 He said, "He who showed mercy on him."

Then Jesus said to him, "Go and do likewise."

1. Invite the Holy Spirit into this reading, asking the Author of Scripture to speak to you through His Word
2. Read today's passage as many times as you need, take your time
3. Write down (below) what the Lord is saying to you today
4. Live with this Word in your heart through the day

_____

_____

## Tuesday, October 8, 2024

**First Reading:** Galatians 1: 13-24

13 For you have heard of my way of living in time past in the Jews' religion, how that beyond measure I persecuted the assembly of God and ravaged it. 14 I advanced in the Jews' religion beyond many of my own age among my countrymen, being more exceedingly zealous for the traditions of my fathers. 15 But when it was the good pleasure of God, who separated me from my mother's womb and called me through his grace, 16 to reveal his Son in me, that I might preach him among the Gentiles, I didn't immediately confer with flesh and blood, 17 nor did I go up to Jerusalem to those who were apostles before me, but I went away into Arabia. Then I returned to Damascus.

18 Then after three years I went up to Jerusalem to visit Peter, and stayed with him fifteen days. 19 But of the other apostles I saw no one except James, the Lord's brother. 20 Now about the things which I write to you, behold,§ before God, I'm not lying. 21 Then I came to the regions of Syria and Cilicia. 22 I was still unknown by face to the assemblies of Judea which were in Christ, 23 but they only heard, "He who once persecuted us now preaches the faith that he once tried to destroy." 24 So they glorified God in me.

**Responsorial Psalm:** Psalms 139: 1b-3, 13-15

1 Yahweh, you have searched me,
and you know me.
2 You know my sitting down and my rising up.
You perceive my thoughts from afar.
3 You search out my path and my lying down,
and are acquainted with all my ways.
13 For you formed my inmost being.
You knit me together in my mother's womb.
14 I will give thanks to you,
for I am fearfully and wonderfully made.
Your works are wonderful.
My soul knows that very well.
15 My frame wasn't hidden from you,
when I was made in secret,
woven together in the depths of the earth.

**Gospel: Luke 10: 38-42**

38 As they went on their way, he entered into a certain village, and a certain woman named Martha received him into her house. 39 She had a sister called Mary, who also sat at Jesus' feet and heard his word. 40 But Martha was distracted with much serving, and she came up to him, and said, "Lord, don't you care that my sister left me to serve alone? Ask her therefore to help me."
41 Jesus answered her, "Martha, Martha, you are anxious and troubled about many things, 42  but one thing is needed. Mary has chosen the good part, which will not be taken away from her."

1. Invite the Holy Spirit into this reading, asking the Author of Scripture to speak to you through His Word
2. Read today's passage as many times as you need, take your time
3. Write down (below) what the Lord is saying to you today
4. Live with this Word in your heart through the day

_____

_____

**First Reading:** Galatians 2: 1-2, 7-14

1 Then after a period of fourteen years I went up again to Jerusalem with Barnabas, taking Titus also with me. 2 I went up by revelation, and I laid before them the Good News which I preach among the Gentiles, but privately before those who were respected, for fear that I might be running, or had run, in vain.

7 but to the contrary, when they saw that I had been entrusted with the Good News for the uncircumcised, even as Peter with the Good News for the circumcised— 8 for he who worked through Peter in the apostleship with the circumcised also worked through me with the Gentiles— 9 and when they perceived the grace that was given to me, James and Cephas and John, those who were reputed to be pillars, gave to Barnabas and me the right hand of fellowship, that we should go to the Gentiles, and they to the circumcision. 10 They only asked us to remember the poor—which very thing I was also zealous to do.

11 But when Peter came to Antioch, I resisted him to his face, because he stood condemned. 12 For before some people came from James, he ate with the Gentiles. But when they came, he drew back and separated himself, fearing those who were of the circumcision. 13 And the rest of the Jews joined him in his hypocrisy, so that even Barnabas was carried away with their hypocrisy. 14 But when I saw that they didn't walk uprightly according to the truth of the Good News, I said to Peter before them all, "If you, being a Jew, live as the Gentiles do, and not as the Jews do, why do you compel the Gentiles to live as the Jews do?

**Responsorial Psalm:** Psalms 117: 1bc, 2

1 Praise Yahweh, all you nations!
Extol him, all you peoples!
2 For his loving kindness is great toward us.
Yahweh's faithfulness endures forever.
Praise Yah!

**Gospel: Luke 11: 1-4**

1 When he finished praying in a certain place, one of his disciples said to him, "Lord, teach us to pray, just as John also taught his disciples."
2 He said to them, "When you pray, say,
'Our Father in heaven,
may your name be kept holy.
May your Kingdom come.
May your will be done on earth, as it is in heaven.
3 Give us day by day our daily bread.
4 Forgive us our sins,
for we ourselves also forgive everyone who is indebted to us.
Bring us not into temptation,
but deliver us from the evil one.' "

1. Invite the Holy Spirit into this reading, asking the Author of Scripture to speak to you through His Word
2. Read today's passage as many times as you need, take your time
3. Write down (below) what the Lord is saying to you today
4. Live with this Word in your heart through the day

_____

_____

## Thursday, October 10, 2024

**First Reading:** Galatians 3: 1-5

1 Foolish Galatians, who has bewitched you not to obey the truth, before whose eyes Jesus Christ was openly portrayed among you as crucified? 2 I just want to learn this from you: Did you receive the Spirit by the works of the law, or by hearing of faith? 3 Are you so foolish? Having begun in the Spirit, are you now completed in the flesh? 4 Did you suffer so many things in vain, if it is indeed in vain? 5 He therefore who supplies the Spirit to you and does miracles among you, does he do it by the works of the law, or by hearing of faith?

**Responsorial Psalm:** Luke 1: 69-75

69 and has raised up a horn of salvation for us in the house of his servant David
70 (as he spoke by the mouth of his holy prophets who have been from of old),
71 salvation from our enemies and from the hand of all who hate us;
72 to show mercy toward our fathers,
to remember his holy covenant,
73 the oath which he swore to Abraham our father,
74 to grant to us that we, being delivered out of the hand of our enemies,
should serve him without fear,
75 in holiness and righteousness before him all the days of our life.

## Gospel: Luke 11: 5-13

5 He said to them, "Which of you, if you go to a friend at midnight and tell him, 'Friend, lend me three loaves of bread, 6 for a friend of mine has come to me from a journey, and I have nothing to set before him,' 7 and he from within will answer and say, 'Don't bother me. The door is now shut, and my children are with me in bed. I can't get up and give it to you'? 8 I tell you, although he will not rise and give it to him because he is his friend, yet because of his persistence, he will get up and give him as many as he needs.
9 "I tell you, keep asking, and it will be given you. Keep seeking, and you will find. Keep knocking, and it will be opened to you. 10 For everyone who asks receives. He who seeks finds. To him who knocks it will be opened.
11 "Which of you fathers, if your son asks for bread, will give him a stone? Or if he asks for a fish, he won't give him a snake instead of a fish, will he? 12 Or if he asks for an egg, he won't give him a scorpion, will he? 13 If you then, being evil, know how to give good gifts to your children, how much more will your heavenly Father give the Holy Spirit to those who ask him?"

1. Invite the Holy Spirit into this reading, asking the Author of Scripture to speak to you through His Word
2. Read today's passage as many times as you need, take your time
3. Write down (below) what the Lord is saying to you today
4. Live with this Word in your heart through the day

_____

_____

# Friday, October 11, 2024
## Saint John XXIII, Pope

**First Reading:** Galatians 3: 7-14

7 Know therefore that those who are of faith are children of Abraham. 8 The Scripture, foreseeing that God would justify the Gentiles by faith, preached the Good News beforehand to Abraham, saying, "In you all the nations will be blessed."* 9 So then, those who are of faith are blessed with the faithful Abraham.
10 For as many as are of the works of the law are under a curse. For it is written, "Cursed is everyone who doesn't continue in all things that are written in the book of the law, to do them."* 11 Now that no man is justified by the law before God is evident, for, "The righteous will live by faith."* 12 The law is not of faith, but, "The man who does them will live by them."*
13 Christ redeemed us from the curse of the law, having become a curse for us. For it is written, "Cursed is everyone who hangs on a tree,"* 14 that the blessing of Abraham might come on the Gentiles through Christ Jesus, that we might receive the promise of the Spirit through faith.

**Responsorial Psalm:** Psalms 111: 1b-6

1b I will give thanks to Yahweh with my whole heart,
in the council of the upright, and in the congregation.
2 Yahweh's works are great,
pondered by all those who delight in them.
3 His work is honor and majesty.
His righteousness endures forever.
4 He has caused his wonderful works to be remembered.
Yahweh is gracious and merciful.
5 He has given food to those who fear him.
He always remembers his covenant.
6 He has shown his people the power of his works,
in giving them the heritage of the nations.

**Gospel: Luke 11: 15-26**

15 But some of them said, "He casts out demons by Beelzebul, the prince of the demons." 16 Others, testing him, sought from him a sign from heaven. 17 But he, knowing their thoughts, said to them, "Every kingdom divided against itself is brought to desolation. A house divided against itself falls. 18 If Satan also is divided against himself, how will his kingdom stand? For you say that I cast out demons by Beelzebul. 19 But if I cast out demons by Beelzebul, by whom do your children cast them out? Therefore they will be your judges. 20 But if I by God's finger cast out demons, then God's Kingdom has come to you.

21 "When the strong man, fully armed, guards his own dwelling, his goods are safe. 22 But when someone stronger attacks him and overcomes him, he takes from him his whole armor in which he trusted, and divides his plunder.

23 "He who is not with me is against me. He who doesn't gather with me scatters.

24 The unclean spirit, when he has gone out of the man, passes through dry places, seeking rest; and finding none, he says, 'I will turn back to my house from which I came out.' 25 When he returns, he finds it swept and put in order. 26 Then he goes and takes seven other spirits more evil than himself, and they enter in and dwell there. The last state of that man becomes worse than the first."

1. Invite the Holy Spirit into this reading, asking the Author of Scripture to speak to you through His Word
2. Read today's passage as many times as you need, take your time
3. Write down (below) what the Lord is saying to you today
4. Live with this Word in your heart through the day

_____

_____

## Saturday, October 12, 2024

**First Reading:** Galatians 3: 22-29

2 But the Scripture imprisoned all things under sin, that the promise by faith in Jesus Christ might be given to those who believe.

23 But before faith came, we were kept in custody under the law, confined for the faith which should afterwards be revealed. 24 So that the law has become our tutor to bring

us to Christ, that we might be justified by faith. 25 But now that faith has come, we are no longer under a tutor. 26 For you are all children of God, through faith in Christ Jesus. 27 For as many of you as were baptized into Christ have put on Christ. 28 There is neither Jew nor Greek, there is neither slave nor free man, there is neither male nor female; for you are all one in Christ Jesus. 29 If you are Christ's, then you are Abraham's offspring and heirs according to promise.

**Responsorial Psalm:** Psalms 105: 2-7

2 Sing to him, sing praises to him!
Tell of all his marvelous works.
3 Glory in his holy name.
Let the heart of those who seek Yahweh rejoice.
4 Seek Yahweh and his strength.
Seek his face forever more.
5 Remember his marvelous works that he has done:
his wonders, and the judgments of his mouth,
6 you offspring of Abraham, his servant,
you children of Jacob, his chosen ones.
7 He is Yahweh, our God.
His judgments are in all the earth.

**Gospel: Luke 11: 27-28**

27 It came to pass, as he said these things, a certain woman out of the multitude lifted up her voice and said to him, "Blessed is the womb that bore you, and the breasts which nursed you!"
28 But he said, "On the contrary, blessed are those who hear the word of God, and keep it."

1. Invite the Holy Spirit into this reading, asking the Author of Scripture to speak to you through His Word
2. Read today's passage as many times as you need, take your time
3. Write down (below) what the Lord is saying to you today
4. Live with this Word in your heart through the day

_____

_____

Sunday, October 13, 2024<br>TWENTY-EIGHTH SUNDAY IN ORDINARY TIME

**First Reading:** Wisdom 7: 7-11

7 For this cause I prayed, and understanding was given to me.
I asked, and a spirit of wisdom came to me.
8 I preferred her before sceptres and thrones.
I considered riches nothing in comparison to her.
9 Neither did I liken to her any priceless gem,
because all gold in her presence is a little sand,
and silver will be considered as clay before her.
10 I loved her more than health and beauty,
and I chose to have her rather than light,
because her bright shining is never laid to sleep.
11 All good things came to me with her,
and innumerable riches are in her hands.

**Responsorial Psalm:** Psalms 90: 12-17

12 So teach us to count our days,
that we may gain a heart of wisdom.
13 Relent, Yahweh!§
How long?
Have compassion on your servants!
14 Satisfy us in the morning with your loving kindness,
that we may rejoice and be glad all our days.
15 Make us glad for as many days as you have afflicted us,
for as many years as we have seen evil.
16 Let your work appear to your servants,
your glory to their children.
17 Let the favor of the Lord our God be on us.
Establish the work of our hands for us.
Yes, establish the work of our hands.

**Second Reading:** Hebrews 4: 12-13

12 For the word of God is living and active, and sharper than any two-edged sword, piercing even to the dividing of soul and spirit, of both joints and marrow, and is able to discern the thoughts and intentions of the heart. 13 There is no creature that is hidden from his sight, but all things are naked and laid open before the eyes of him to whom we must give an account.

## Gospel: Mark 10: 17-30

17 As he was going out into the way, one ran to him, knelt before him, and asked him, "Good Teacher, what shall I do that I may inherit eternal life?"

18 Jesus said to him, "Why do you call me good? No one is good except one—God. 19 You know the commandments: 'Do not murder,' 'Do not commit adultery,' 'Do not steal,' 'Do not give false testimony,' 'Do not defraud,' 'Honor your father and mother.' "*

20 He said to him, "Teacher, I have observed all these things from my youth."

21 Jesus looking at him loved him, and said to him, "One thing you lack. Go, sell whatever you have and give to the poor, and you will have treasure in heaven; and come, follow me, taking up the cross."

22 But his face fell at that saying, and he went away sorrowful, for he was one who had great possessions.

23 Jesus looked around and said to his disciples, "How difficult it is for those who have riches to enter into God's Kingdom!"

24 The disciples were amazed at his words. But Jesus answered again, "Children, how hard it is for those who trust in riches to enter into God's Kingdom! 25 It is easier for a camel to go through a needle's eye than for a rich man to enter into God's Kingdom."

26 They were exceedingly astonished, saying to him, "Then who can be saved?"

27 Jesus, looking at them, said, "With men it is impossible, but not with God, for all things are possible with God."

28 Peter began to tell him, "Behold, we have left all and have followed you."

29 Jesus said, "Most certainly I tell you, there is no one who has left house, or brothers, or sisters, or father, or mother, or wife, or children, or land, for my sake, and for the sake of the Good News, 30 but he will receive one hundred times more now in this time: houses, brothers, sisters, mothers, children, and land, with persecutions; and in the age to come eternal life.

1. Invite the Holy Spirit into this reading, asking the Author of Scripture to speak to you through His Word

2. Read today's passage as many times as you need, take your time
3. Write down (below) what the Lord is saying to you today
4. Live with this Word in your heart through the day

_____

_____

## Monday, October 14, 2024
### Saint Callistus I, Pope and Martyr

**First Reading:** Galatians 4: 22-24, 26-27, 31 – 5: 1

22 For it is written that Abraham had two sons, one by the servant, and one by the free woman. 23 However, the son by the servant was born according to the flesh, but the son by the free woman was born through promise. 24 These things contain an allegory, for these are two covenants. One is from Mount Sinai, bearing children to bondage, which is Hagar.
26 But the Jerusalem that is above is free, which is the mother of us all. 27 For it is written,
"Rejoice, you barren who don't bear.
Break out and shout, you who don't travail.
For the desolate women have more children than her who has a husband."
31 So then, brothers, we are not children of a servant, but of the free woman.
1 Stand firm therefore in the liberty by which Christ has made us free, and don't be entangled again with a yoke of bondage.

**Responsorial Psalm:** Psalms 113: 1b-7

1b Praise, you servants of Yahweh,
praise Yahweh's name.
2 Blessed be Yahweh's name,
from this time forward and forever more.
3 From the rising of the sun to its going down,
Yahweh's name is to be praised.
4 Yahweh is high above all nations,

his glory above the heavens.
5 Who is like Yahweh, our God,
who has his seat on high,
6 who stoops down to see in heaven and in the earth?
7 He raises up the poor out of the dust,
and lifts up the needy from the ash heap,

**Gospel: Luke 11: 29-32**

29 When the multitudes were gathering together to him, he began to say, "This is an evil generation. It seeks after a sign. No sign will be given to it but the sign of Jonah the prophet. 30 For even as Jonah became a sign to the Ninevites, so the Son of Man will also be to this generation. 31 The Queen of the South will rise up in the judgment with the men of this generation and will condemn them, for she came from the ends of the earth to hear the wisdom of Solomon; and behold, one greater than Solomon is here. 32 The men of Nineveh will stand up in the judgment with this generation, and will condemn it, for they repented at the preaching of Jonah; and behold, one greater than Jonah is here.

1. Invite the Holy Spirit into this reading, asking the Author of Scripture to speak to you through His Word
2. Read today's passage as many times as you need, take your time
3. Write down (below) what the Lord is saying to you today
4. Live with this Word in your heart through the day

_____

_____


**Tuesday, October 15, 2024**
Saint Teresa of Jesus, Virgin and Doctor of the Church


**First Reading:** Galatians 5: 1-6

1 Stand firm therefore in the liberty by which Christ has made us free, and don't be entangled again with a yoke of bondage.

2 Behold, I, Paul, tell you that if you receive circumcision, Christ will profit you nothing. 3 Yes, I testify again to every man who receives circumcision that he is a debtor to do the whole law. 4 You are alienated from Christ, you who desire to be justified by the law. You have fallen away from grace. 5 For we through the Spirit, by faith wait for the hope of righteousness. 6 For in Christ Jesus neither circumcision nor uncircumcision amounts to anything, but faith working through love.

**Responsorial Psalm:** Psalms 119: 41, 43, 44, 45, 47, 48

41 Let your loving kindness also come to me, Yahweh,
your salvation, according to your word.
43 Don't snatch the word of truth out of my mouth,
for I put my hope in your ordinances.
44 So I will obey your law continually,
forever and ever.
45 I will walk in liberty,
for I have sought your precepts.
47 I will delight myself in your commandments,
because I love them.
48 I reach out my hands for your commandments, which I love.
I will meditate on your statutes.

**Gospel: Luke 11: 37-41**

37 Now as he spoke, a certain Pharisee asked him to dine with him. He went in and sat at the table. 38 When the Pharisee saw it, he marveled that he had not first washed himself before dinner. 39 The Lord said to him, "Now you Pharisees cleanse the outside of the cup and of the platter, but your inward part is full of extortion and wickedness. 40 You foolish ones, didn't he who made the outside make the inside also? 41 But give for gifts to the needy those things which are within, and behold, all things will be clean to you.

1. Invite the Holy Spirit into this reading, asking the Author of Scripture to speak to you through His Word
2. Read today's passage as many times as you need, take your time
3. Write down (below) what the Lord is saying to you today
4. Live with this Word in your heart through the day

## Wednesday, October 16, 2024
### Saint Hedwig, Religious; Saint Margaret Mary Alacoque, Virgin

**First Reading:** Galatians 5: 18-25

18 But if you are led by the Spirit, you are not under the law. 19 Now the deeds of the flesh are obvious, which are: adultery, sexual immorality, uncleanness, lustfulness, 20 idolatry, sorcery, hatred, strife, jealousies, outbursts of anger, rivalries, divisions, heresies, 21 envy, murders, drunkenness, orgies, and things like these; of which I forewarn you, even as I also forewarned you, that those who practice such things will not inherit God's Kingdom.
22 But the fruit of the Spirit is love, joy, peace, patience, kindness, goodness, faith,† 23 gentleness, and self-control. Against such things there is no law. 24 Those who belong to Christ have crucified the flesh with its passions and lusts.
25 If we live by the Spirit, let's also walk by the Spirit.

**Responsorial Psalm:** Psalms 1: 1-2, 3, 4 and 6

1 Blessed is the man who doesn't walk in the counsel of the wicked,
nor stand on the path of sinners,
nor sit in the seat of scoffers;
2 but his delight is in Yahweh's† law.
On his law he meditates day and night.
3 He will be like a tree planted by the streams of water,
that produces its fruit in its season,
whose leaf also does not wither.
Whatever he does shall prosper.
4 The wicked are not so,
but are like the chaff which the wind drives away.
6 For Yahweh knows the way of the righteous,

but the way of the wicked shall perish.

## Gospel: Luke 11: 42-46

42 But woe to you Pharisees! For you tithe mint and rue and every herb, but you bypass justice and God's love. You ought to have done these, and not to have left the other undone. 43 Woe to you Pharisees! For you love the best seats in the synagogues and the greetings in the marketplaces. 44 Woe to you, scribes and Pharisees, hypocrites! For you are like hidden graves, and the men who walk over them don't know it."
45 One of the lawyers answered him, "Teacher, in saying this you insult us also."
46 He said, "Woe to you lawyers also! For you load men with burdens that are difficult to carry, and you yourselves won't even lift one finger to help carry those burdens.

1. Invite the Holy Spirit into this reading, asking the Author of Scripture to speak to you through His Word
2. Read today's passage as many times as you need, take your time
3. Write down (below) what the Lord is saying to you today
4. Live with this Word in your heart through the day

---

## Thursday, October 17, 2024
Saint Ignatius of Antioch, Bishop and Martyr

**First Reading:** Ephesians 1: 1-10

1 Paul, an apostle of Christ† Jesus through the will of God, to the saints who are at Ephesus, and the faithful in Christ Jesus: 2 Grace to you and peace from God our Father and the Lord Jesus Christ.
3 Blessed be the God and Father of our Lord Jesus Christ, who has blessed us with every spiritual blessing in the heavenly places in Christ, 4 even as he chose us in him before the foundation of the world, that we would be holy and without defect before him in love, 5 having predestined us for adoption as children through Jesus Christ to himself, according to the good pleasure of his desire, 6 to the praise of the glory of his

grace, by which he freely gave us favor in the Beloved. 7 In him we have our redemption through his blood, the forgiveness of our trespasses, according to the riches of his grace 8 which he made to abound toward us in all wisdom and prudence, 9 making known to us the mystery of his will, according to his good pleasure which he purposed in him 10 to an administration of the fullness of the times, to sum up all things in Christ, the things in the heavens and the things on the earth, in him.

**Responsorial Psalm:** Psalms 98: 1-6

1 Sing to Yahweh a new song,
for he has done marvelous things!
His right hand and his holy arm have worked salvation for him.
2 Yahweh has made known his salvation.
He has openly shown his righteousness in the sight of the nations.
3 He has remembered his loving kindness and his faithfulness toward the house of Israel.
All the ends of the earth have seen the salvation of our God.
4 Make a joyful noise to Yahweh, all the earth!
Burst out and sing for joy, yes, sing praises!
5 Sing praises to Yahweh with the harp,
with the harp and the voice of melody.
6 With trumpets and sound of the ram's horn,
make a joyful noise before the King, Yahweh.

**Gospel: Luke 11: 47-54**

47 Woe to you! For you build the tombs of the prophets, and your fathers killed them. 48 So you testify and consent to the works of your fathers. For they killed them, and you build their tombs. 49 Therefore also the wisdom of God said, 'I will send to them prophets and apostles; and some of them they will kill and persecute, 50 that the blood of all the prophets, which was shed from the foundation of the world, may be required of this generation, 51 from the blood of Abel to the blood of Zachariah, who perished between the altar and the sanctuary.' Yes, I tell you, it will be required of this generation. 52 Woe to you lawyers! For you took away the key of knowledge. You didn't enter in yourselves, and those who were entering in, you hindered."
53 As he said these things to them, the scribes and the Pharisees began to be terribly angry, and to draw many things out of him, 54 lying in wait for him, and seeking to catch him in something he might say, that they might accuse him.

1. Invite the Holy Spirit into this reading, asking the Author of Scripture to speak to you through His Word
2. Read today's passage as many times as you need, take your time
3. Write down (below) what the Lord is saying to you today
4. Live with this Word in your heart through the day

_____

_____

## Friday, October 18, 2024
### Saint Luke, Evangelist

**First Reading:** Second Timothy 4: 10-17b

10 for Demas left me, having loved this present world, and went to Thessalonica; Crescens to Galatia; and Titus to Dalmatia. 11 Only Luke is with me. Take Mark and bring him with you, for he is useful to me for service. 12 But I sent Tychicus to Ephesus. 13 Bring the cloak that I left at Troas with Carpus when you come—and the books, especially the parchments. 14 Alexander the coppersmith did much evil to me. The Lord will repay him according to his deeds. 15 Beware of him, for he greatly opposed our words.

16 At my first defense, no one came to help me, but all left me. May it not be held against them. 17 But the Lord stood by me and strengthened me, that through me the message might be fully proclaimed, and that all the Gentiles might hear.

**Responsorial Psalm:** Psalms 145: 10-13, 17-18

10 All your works will give thanks to you, Yahweh.
Your saints will extol you.
11 They will speak of the glory of your kingdom,
and talk about your power,
12 to make known to the sons of men his mighty acts,
the glory of the majesty of his kingdom.
13 Your kingdom is an everlasting kingdom.

Your dominion endures throughout all generations.
Yahweh is faithful in all his words,
and loving in all his deeds.‡
17 Yahweh is righteous in all his ways,
and gracious in all his works.
18 Yahweh is near to all those who call on him,
to all who call on him in truth.

## Gospel: Luke 10: 1-9

1 Now after these things, the Lord also appointed seventy others, and sent them two by two ahead of him† into every city and place where he was about to come. 2 Then he said to them, "The harvest is indeed plentiful, but the laborers are few. Pray therefore to the Lord of the harvest, that he may send out laborers into his harvest. 3 Go your ways. Behold, I send you out as lambs among wolves. 4 Carry no purse, nor wallet, nor sandals. Greet no one on the way. 5 Into whatever house you enter, first say, 'Peace be to this house.' 6 If a son of peace is there, your peace will rest on him; but if not, it will return to you. 7 Remain in that same house, eating and drinking the things they give, for the laborer is worthy of his wages. Don't go from house to house. 8 Into whatever city you enter and they receive you, eat the things that are set before you. 9 Heal the sick who are there and tell them, 'God's Kingdom has come near to you.'

1. Invite the Holy Spirit into this reading, asking the Author of Scripture to speak to you through His Word
2. Read today's passage as many times as you need, take your time
3. Write down (below) what the Lord is saying to you today
4. Live with this Word in your heart through the day

---

---

**Saturday, October 19, 2024**
Saints John de Brébeuf and Isaac Jogues, Priests, red
and Companions, Martyrs

**First Reading:** Ephesians 1: 15-23

15 For this cause I also, having heard of the faith in the Lord Jesus which is among you and the love which you have toward all the saints, 16 don't cease to give thanks for you, making mention of you in my prayers, 17 that the God of our Lord Jesus Christ, the Father of glory, may give to you a spirit of wisdom and revelation in the knowledge of him, 18 having the eyes of your hearts‡ enlightened, that you may know what is the hope of his calling, and what are the riches of the glory of his inheritance in the saints, 19 and what is the exceeding greatness of his power toward us who believe, according to that working of the strength of his might 20 which he worked in Christ when he raised him from the dead and made him to sit at his right hand in the heavenly places, 21 far above all rule, authority, power, dominion, and every name that is named, not only in this age, but also in that which is to come. 22 He put all things in subjection under his feet, and gave him to be head over all things for the assembly, 23 which is his body, the fullness of him who fills all in all.

**Responsorial Psalm:** Psalms 8: 2-7

2 From the lips of babes and infants you have established strength,
because of your adversaries, that you might silence the enemy and the avenger.
3 When I consider your heavens, the work of your fingers,
the moon and the stars, which you have ordained,
4 what is man, that you think of him?
What is the son of man, that you care for him?
5 For you have made him a little lower than the angels,†
and crowned him with glory and honor.
6 You make him ruler over the works of your hands.
You have put all things under his feet:
7 All sheep and cattle,
yes, and the animals of the field,

**Gospel: Luke 12: 8-12**

8 "I tell you, everyone who confesses me before men, the Son of Man will also confess before the angels of God; 9 but he who denies me in the presence of men will be denied in the presence of God's angels. 10 Everyone who speaks a word against the Son of Man will be forgiven, but those who blaspheme against the Holy Spirit will not be forgiven. 11 When they bring you before the synagogues, the rulers, and the

authorities, don't be anxious how or what you will answer or what you will say; 12 for the Holy Spirit will teach you in that same hour what you must say."

1. Invite the Holy Spirit into this reading, asking the Author of Scripture to speak to you through His Word
2. Read today's passage as many times as you need, take your time
3. Write down (below) what the Lord is saying to you today
4. Live with this Word in your heart through the day

_____

_____

## Sunday, October 20, 2024
### TWENTY-NINTH SUNDAY IN ORDINARY TIME

**First Reading:** Isaiah 53: 10-11

10 Yet it pleased Yahweh to bruise him.
He has caused him to suffer.
When you make his soul an offering for sin,
he will see his offspring.
He will prolong his days
and Yahweh's pleasure will prosper in his hand.
11 After the suffering of his soul,
he will see the light† and be satisfied.
My righteous servant will justify many by the knowledge of himself;
and he will bear their iniquities.

**Responsorial Psalm:** Psalms 33: 4-5, 18-20, 22

4 For Yahweh's word is right.
All his work is done in faithfulness.
5 He loves righteousness and justice.
The earth is full of the loving kindness of Yahweh.
18 Behold, Yahweh's eye is on those who fear him,

on those who hope in his loving kindness,
19 to deliver their soul from death,
to keep them alive in famine.
20 Our soul has waited for Yahweh.
He is our help and our shield.
22 Let your loving kindness be on us, Yahweh,
since we have hoped in you.

**Second Reading:** Hebrews 4: 14-16

14 Having then a great high priest who has passed through the heavens, Jesus, the Son of God, let's hold tightly to our confession. 15 For we don't have a high priest who can't be touched with the feeling of our infirmities, but one who has been in all points tempted like we are, yet without sin. 16 Let's therefore draw near with boldness to the throne of grace, that we may receive mercy and may find grace for help in time of need.

**Gospel: Mark 10: 42-45**

42 Jesus summoned them and said to them, "You know that they who are recognized as rulers over the nations lord it over them, and their great ones exercise authority over them. 43 But it shall not be so among you, but whoever wants to become great among you shall be your servant. 44 Whoever of you wants to become first among you shall be bondservant of all. 45 For the Son of Man also came not to be served but to serve, and to give his life as a ransom for many."

1. Invite the Holy Spirit into this reading, asking the Author of Scripture to speak to you through His Word
2. Read today's passage as many times as you need, take your time
3. Write down (below) what the Lord is saying to you today
4. Live with this Word in your heart through the day

_____

_____

# Monday, October 21, 2024

**First Reading:** Ephesians 2: 1-10

1 You were made alive when you were dead in transgressions and sins, 2 in which you once walked according to the course of this world, according to the prince of the power of the air, the spirit who now works in the children of disobedience. 3 We also all once lived among them in the lusts of our flesh, doing the desires of the flesh and of the mind, and were by nature children of wrath, even as the rest. 4 But God, being rich in mercy, for his great love with which he loved us, 5 even when we were dead through our trespasses, made us alive together with Christ—by grace you have been saved— 6 and raised us up with him, and made us to sit with him in the heavenly places in Christ Jesus, 7 that in the ages to come he might show the exceeding riches of his grace in kindness toward us in Christ Jesus; 8 for by grace you have been saved through faith, and that not of yourselves; it is the gift of God, 9 not of works, that no one would boast. 10 For we are his workmanship, created in Christ Jesus for good works, which God prepared before that we would walk in them.

**Responsorial Psalm:** Psalms 100: 2-5

2 Serve Yahweh with gladness.
Come before his presence with singing.
3 Know that Yahweh, he is God.
It is he who has made us, and we are his.
We are his people, and the sheep of his pasture.
4 Enter into his gates with thanksgiving,
and into his courts with praise.
Give thanks to him, and bless his name.
5 For Yahweh is good.
His loving kindness endures forever,
his faithfulness to all generations.

**Gospel: Luke 12: 13-21**

13 One of the multitude said to him, "Teacher, tell my brother to divide the inheritance with me."

14 But he said to him, "Man, who made me a judge or an arbitrator over you?" 15 He said to them, "Beware! Keep yourselves from covetousness, for a man's life doesn't consist of the abundance of the things which he possesses."

16 He spoke a parable to them, saying, "The ground of a certain rich man produced abundantly. 17 He reasoned within himself, saying, 'What will I do, because I don't have room to store my crops?' 18 He said, 'This is what I will do. I will pull down my barns, build bigger ones, and there I will store all my grain and my goods. 19 I will tell my soul, "Soul, you have many goods laid up for many years. Take your ease, eat, drink, and be merry."'

20 "But God said to him, 'You foolish one, tonight your soul is required of you. The things which you have prepared—whose will they be?' 21 So is he who lays up treasure for himself, and is not rich toward God."

1. Invite the Holy Spirit into this reading, asking the Author of Scripture to speak to you through His Word
2. Read today's passage as many times as you need, take your time
3. Write down (below) what the Lord is saying to you today
4. Live with this Word in your heart through the day

_____

_____

### Tuesday, October 22, 2024
Saint John Paul II, Pope

**First Reading:** Ephesians 2: 12-22

12 that you were at that time separate from Christ, alienated from the commonwealth of Israel, and strangers from the covenants of the promise, having no hope and without God in the world. 13 But now in Christ Jesus you who once were far off are made near in the blood of Christ. 14 For he is our peace, who made both one, and broke down the middle wall of separation, 15 having abolished in his flesh the hostility, the law of commandments contained in ordinances, that he might create in himself one new man of the two, making peace, 16 and might reconcile them both in one body to God through the cross, having killed the hostility through it. 17 He came and preached peace to you

who were far off and to those who were near. 18 For through him we both have our access in one Spirit to the Father. 19 So then you are no longer strangers and foreigners, but you are fellow citizens with the saints and of the household of God, 20 being built on the foundation of the apostles and prophets, Christ Jesus himself being the chief cornerstone; 21 in whom the whole building, fitted together, grows into a holy temple in the Lord; 22 in whom you also are built together for a habitation of God in the Spirit.

**Responsorial Psalm:** Psalms 85: 9ab-13

9 Surely his salvation is near those who fear him,
that glory may dwell in our land.
10 Mercy and truth meet together.
Righteousness and peace have kissed each other.
11 Truth springs out of the earth.
Righteousness has looked down from heaven.
12 Yes, Yahweh will give that which is good.
Our land will yield its increase.
13 Righteousness goes before him,
and prepares the way for his steps.

**Gospel: Luke 12: 35-38**

35 "Let your waist be dressed and your lamps burning. 36 Be like men watching for their lord when he returns from the wedding feast, that when he comes and knocks, they may immediately open to him. 37 Blessed are those servants whom the lord will find watching when he comes. Most certainly I tell you that he will dress himself, make them recline, and will come and serve them. 38 They will be blessed if he comes in the second or third watch and finds them so.

1. Invite the Holy Spirit into this reading, asking the Author of Scripture to speak to you through His Word
2. Read today's passage as many times as you need, take your time
3. Write down (below) what the Lord is saying to you today
4. Live with this Word in your heart through the day

_____

_____

**First Reading:** Ephesians 3: 2-12

2 if it is so that you have heard of the administration of that grace of God which was given me toward you, 3 how that by revelation the mystery was made known to me, as I wrote before in few words, 4 by which, when you read, you can perceive my understanding in the mystery of Christ, 5 which in other generations was not made known to the children of men, as it has now been revealed to his holy apostles and prophets in the Spirit, 6 that the Gentiles are fellow heirs and fellow members of the body, and fellow partakers of his promise in Christ Jesus through the Good News, 7 of which I was made a servant according to the gift of that grace of God which was given me according to the working of his power. 8 To me, the very least of all saints, was this grace given, to preach to the Gentiles the unsearchable riches of Christ, 9 and to make all men see what is the administration† of the mystery which for ages has been hidden in God, who created all things through Jesus Christ, 10 to the intent that now through the assembly the manifold wisdom of God might be made known to the principalities and the powers in the heavenly places, 11 according to the eternal purpose which he accomplished in Christ Jesus our Lord. 12 In him we have boldness and access in confidence through our faith in him.

**Responsorial Psalm:** Isaiah 12: 2-3, 4bcd, 5-6

2 Behold, God is my salvation. I will trust, and will not be afraid; for Yah, Yahweh, is my strength and song; and he has become my salvation." 3 Therefore with joy you will draw water out of the wells of salvation. 4b "Give thanks to Yahweh! Call on his name! Declare his doings among the peoples! Proclaim that his name is exalted! 5 Sing to Yahweh, for he has done excellent things! Let this be known in all the earth! 6 Cry aloud and shout, you inhabitant of Zion, for the Holy One of Israel is great among you!"

**Gospel: Luke 12: 39-48**

39 But know this, that if the master of the house had known in what hour the thief was coming, he would have watched and not allowed his house to be broken into. 40 Therefore be ready also, for the Son of Man is coming in an hour that you don't expect him."

41 Peter said to him, "Lord, are you telling this parable to us, or to everybody?"

42 The Lord said, "Who then is the faithful and wise steward, whom his lord will set over his household, to give them their portion of food at the right times? 43 Blessed is that servant whom his lord will find doing so when he comes. 44 Truly I tell you that he will set him over all that he has. 45 But if that servant says in his heart, 'My lord delays his coming,' and begins to beat the menservants and the maidservants, and to eat and drink and to be drunken, 46 then the lord of that servant will come in a day when he isn't expecting him and in an hour that he doesn't know, and will cut him in two, and place his portion with the unfaithful. 47 That servant who knew his lord's will, and didn't prepare nor do what he wanted, will be beaten with many stripes, 48 but he who didn't know, and did things worthy of stripes, will be beaten with few stripes. To whomever much is given, of him will much be required; and to whom much was entrusted, of him more will be asked.

1. Invite the Holy Spirit into this reading, asking the Author of Scripture to speak to you through His Word
2. Read today's passage as many times as you need, take your time
3. Write down (below) what the Lord is saying to you today
4. Live with this Word in your heart through the day

_____

_____

### Thursday, October 24, 2024
Saint Anthony Mary Claret, Bishop

**First Reading:** Ephesians 3: 14-21

14 For this cause, I bow my knees to the Father of our Lord Jesus Christ, 15 from whom every family in heaven and on earth is named, 16 that he would grant you, according to the riches of his glory, that you may be strengthened with power through his Spirit in the inner person, 17 that Christ may dwell in your hearts through faith, to the end that you, being rooted and grounded in love, 18 may be strengthened to comprehend with all the saints what is the width and length and height and depth, 19 and to know

Christ's love which surpasses knowledge, that you may be filled with all the fullness of God.

20 Now to him who is able to do exceedingly abundantly above all that we ask or think, according to the power that works in us, 21 to him be the glory in the assembly and in Christ Jesus to all generations, forever and ever. Amen.

**Responsorial Psalm:** Psalms 33: 1-2, 4-5, 11-12, 18-19

1 Rejoice in Yahweh, you righteous!
Praise is fitting for the upright.
2 Give thanks to Yahweh with the lyre.
Sing praises to him with the harp of ten strings.
4 For Yahweh's word is right.
All his work is done in faithfulness.
5 He loves righteousness and justice.
The earth is full of the loving kindness of Yahweh.
11 The counsel of Yahweh stands fast forever,
the thoughts of his heart to all generations.
12 Blessed is the nation whose God is Yahweh,
the people whom he has chosen for his own inheritance.
18 Behold, Yahweh's eye is on those who fear him,
on those who hope in his loving kindness,
19 to deliver their soul from death,
to keep them alive in famine.

**Gospel: Luke 12: 49-53**

49 "I came to throw fire on the earth. I wish it were already kindled. 50 But I have a baptism to be baptized with, and how distressed I am until it is accomplished! 51 Do you think that I have come to give peace in the earth? I tell you, no, but rather division. 52 For from now on, there will be five in one house divided, three against two, and two against three. 53 They will be divided, father against son, and son against father; mother against daughter, and daughter against her mother; mother-in-law against her daughter-in-law, and daughter-in-law against her mother-in-law."

1. Invite the Holy Spirit into this reading, asking the Author of Scripture to speak to you through His Word
2. Read today's passage as many times as you need, take your time

3. Write down (below) what the Lord is saying to you today
4. Live with this Word in your heart through the day

---

---

**Friday, October 25, 2024**

**First Reading:** Ephesians 4: 1-6

1 I therefore, the prisoner in the Lord, beg you to walk worthily of the calling with which you were called, 2 with all lowliness and humility, with patience, bearing with one another in love, 3 being eager to keep the unity of the Spirit in the bond of peace. 4 There is one body and one Spirit, even as you also were called in one hope of your calling, 5 one Lord, one faith, one baptism, 6 one God and Father of all, who is over all and through all and in us all.

**Responsorial Psalm:** Psalms 24: 1-6

1 The earth is Yahweh's, with its fullness;
the world, and those who dwell in it.
2 For he has founded it on the seas,
and established it on the floods.
3 Who may ascend to Yahweh's hill?
Who may stand in his holy place?
4 He who has clean hands and a pure heart;
who has not lifted up his soul to falsehood,
and has not sworn deceitfully.
5 He shall receive a blessing from Yahweh,
righteousness from the God of his salvation.
6 This is the generation of those who seek Him,
who seek your face—even Jacob.

**Gospel: Luke 12: 54-59**

54 He said to the multitudes also, "When you see a cloud rising from the west, immediately you say, 'A shower is coming,' and so it happens. 55 When a south wind blows, you say, 'There will be a scorching heat,' and it happens. 56 You hypocrites! You know how to interpret the appearance of the earth and the sky, but how is it that you don't interpret this time?

57 "Why don't you judge for yourselves what is right? 58 For when you are going with your adversary before the magistrate, try diligently on the way to be released from him, lest perhaps he drag you to the judge, and the judge deliver you to the officer, and the officer throw you into prison. 59 I tell you, you will by no means get out of there until you have paid the very last penny.†"

1. Invite the Holy Spirit into this reading, asking the Author of Scripture to speak to you through His Word
2. Read today's passage as many times as you need, take your time
3. Write down (below) what the Lord is saying to you today
4. Live with this Word in your heart through the day

_____

_____

## Saturday, October 26, 2024

**First Reading:** Ephesians 4: 7-16

7 But to each one of us, the grace was given according to the measure of the gift of Christ. 8 Therefore he says,
"When he ascended on high,
he led captivity captive,
and gave gifts to people."*
9 Now this, "He ascended", what is it but that he also first descended into the lower parts of the earth? 10 He who descended is the one who also ascended far above all the heavens, that he might fill all things.
11 He gave some to be apostles; and some, prophets; and some, evangelists; and some, shepherds† and teachers; 12 for the perfecting of the saints, to the work of serving, to the building up of the body of Christ, 13 until we all attain to the unity of the faith and

of the knowledge of the Son of God, to a full grown man, to the measure of the stature of the fullness of Christ, 14 that we may no longer be children, tossed back and forth and carried about with every wind of doctrine, by the trickery of men, in craftiness, after the wiles of error; 15 but speaking truth in love, we may grow up in all things into him who is the head, Christ, 16 from whom all the body, being fitted and knit together through that which every joint supplies, according to the working in measure of each individual part, makes the body increase to the building up of itself in love.

**Responsorial Psalm:** Psalms 122: 1-5

1 I was glad when they said to me,
"Let's go to Yahweh's house!"
2 Our feet are standing within your gates, Jerusalem!
3 Jerusalem is built as a city that is compact together,
4 where the tribes go up, even Yah's tribes,
according to an ordinance for Israel,
to give thanks to Yahweh's name.
5 For there are set thrones for judgment,
the thrones of David's house.

**Gospel: Luke 13: 1-9**

1 Now there were some present at the same time who told him about the Galileans whose blood Pilate had mixed with their sacrifices. 2 Jesus answered them, "Do you think that these Galileans were worse sinners than all the other Galileans, because they suffered such things? 3 I tell you, no, but unless you repent, you will all perish in the same way. 4 Or those eighteen on whom the tower in Siloam fell and killed them—do you think that they were worse offenders than all the men who dwell in Jerusalem? 5 I tell you, no, but, unless you repent, you will all perish in the same way."
6 He spoke this parable. "A certain man had a fig tree planted in his vineyard, and he came seeking fruit on it and found none. 7 He said to the vine dresser, 'Behold, these three years I have come looking for fruit on this fig tree, and found none. Cut it down! Why does it waste the soil?' 8 He answered, 'Lord, leave it alone this year also, until I dig around it and fertilize it. 9 If it bears fruit, fine; but if not, after that, you can cut it down.'"

1. Invite the Holy Spirit into this reading, asking the Author of Scripture to speak to you through His Word

2. Read today's passage as many times as you need, take your time
3. Write down (below) what the Lord is saying to you today
4. Live with this Word in your heart through the day

---

---

## Sunday, October 27, 2024
### THIRTIETH SUNDAY IN ORDINARY TIME

**First Reading:** Jeremiah 31: 7-9

7 For Yahweh says,
"Sing with gladness for Jacob,
and shout for the chief of the nations.
Publish, praise, and say,
'Yahweh, save your people,
the remnant of Israel!'
8 Behold, I will bring them from the north country,
and gather them from the uttermost parts of the earth,
along with the blind and the lame,
the woman with child and her who travails with child together.
They will return as a great company.
9 They will come with weeping.
I will lead them with petitions.
I will cause them to walk by rivers of waters,
in a straight way in which they won't stumble;
for I am a father to Israel.
Ephraim is my firstborn.

**Responsorial Psalm:** Psalms 126: 1-6

1 When Yahweh brought back those who returned to Zion,
we were like those who dream.
2 Then our mouth was filled with laughter,

and our tongue with singing.
Then they said among the nations,
"Yahweh has done great things for them."
3 Yahweh has done great things for us,
and we are glad.
4 Restore our fortunes again, Yahweh,
like the streams in the Negev.
5 Those who sow in tears will reap in joy.
6 He who goes out weeping, carrying seed for sowing,
will certainly come again with joy, carrying his sheaves.

## Second Reading: Hebrews 5: 1-6

1 For every high priest, being taken from among men, is appointed for men in things pertaining to God, that he may offer both gifts and sacrifices for sins. 2 The high priest can deal gently with those who are ignorant and going astray, because he himself is also surrounded with weakness. 3 Because of this, he must offer sacrifices for sins for the people, as well as for himself. 4 Nobody takes this honor on himself, but he is called by God, just like Aaron was. 5 So also Christ didn't glorify himself to be made a high priest, but it was he who said to him,
"You are my Son.
Today I have become your father."*
6 As he says also in another place,
"You are a priest forever,
after the order of Melchizedek."

## Gospel: Mark 10: 46-52

46 They came to Jericho. As he went out from Jericho with his disciples and a great multitude, the son of Timaeus, Bartimaeus, a blind beggar, was sitting by the road. 47 When he heard that it was Jesus the Nazarene, he began to cry out and say, "Jesus, you son of David, have mercy on me!" 48 Many rebuked him, that he should be quiet, but he cried out much more, "You son of David, have mercy on me!"
49 Jesus stood still and said, "Call him."
They called the blind man, saying to him, "Cheer up! Get up. He is calling you!"
50 He, casting away his cloak, sprang up, and came to Jesus.
51 Jesus asked him, "What do you want me to do for you?"
The blind man said to him, "Rabboni,† that I may see again."

52 Jesus said to him, "Go your way. Your faith has made you well." Immediately he received his sight and followed Jesus on the way.

1. Invite the Holy Spirit into this reading, asking the Author of Scripture to speak to you through His Word
2. Read today's passage as many times as you need, take your time
3. Write down (below) what the Lord is saying to you today
4. Live with this Word in your heart through the day

_____

_____

## Monday, October 28, 2024
### Saints Simon and Jude, Apostles

**First Reading:** Ephesians 2: 19-22

19 So then you are no longer strangers and foreigners, but you are fellow citizens with the saints and of the household of God, 20 being built on the foundation of the apostles and prophets, Christ Jesus himself being the chief cornerstone; 21 in whom the whole building, fitted together, grows into a holy temple in the Lord; 22 in whom you also are built together for a habitation of God in the Spirit.

**Responsorial Psalm:** Psalms 19: 2-5

2 Day after day they pour out speech,
and night after night they display knowledge.
3 There is no speech nor language
where their voice is not heard.
4 Their voice has gone out through all the earth,
their words to the end of the world.
In them he has set a tent for the sun,
5 which is as a bridegroom coming out of his room,
like a strong man rejoicing to run his course.

**Gospel: Luke 6: 12-16**

12 In these days, he went out to the mountain to pray, and he continued all night in prayer to God. 13 When it was day, he called his disciples, and from them he chose twelve, whom he also named apostles: 14 Simon, whom he also named Peter; Andrew, his brother; James; John; Philip; Bartholomew; 15 Matthew; Thomas; James the son of Alphaeus; Simon who was called the Zealot; 16 Judas the son of James; and Judas Iscariot, who also became a traitor.

1. Invite the Holy Spirit into this reading, asking the Author of Scripture to speak to you through His Word
2. Read today's passage as many times as you need, take your time
3. Write down (below) what the Lord is saying to you today
4. Live with this Word in your heart through the day

_____

_____

## Tuesday, October 29, 2024
### Saints Simon and Jude, Apostles

**First Reading:** Ephesians 5: 21-33

21 subjecting yourselves to one another in the fear of Christ.
22 Wives, be subject to your own husbands, as to the Lord. 23 For the husband is the head of the wife, as Christ also is the head of the assembly, being himself the savior of the body. 24 But as the assembly is subject to Christ, so let the wives also be to their own husbands in everything.
25 Husbands, love your wives, even as Christ also loved the assembly and gave himself up for her, 26 that he might sanctify her, having cleansed her by the washing of water with the word, 27 that he might present the assembly to himself gloriously, not having spot or wrinkle or any such thing, but that she should be holy and without defect. 28 Even so husbands also ought to love their own wives as their own bodies. He who loves his own wife loves himself. 29 For no man ever hated his own flesh, but nourishes and cherishes it, even as the Lord also does the assembly, 30 because we are members of

his body, of his flesh and bones. 31 "For this cause a man will leave his father and mother and will be joined to his wife. Then the two will become one flesh."* 32 This mystery is great, but I speak concerning Christ and the assembly. 33 Nevertheless each of you must also love his own wife even as himself; and let the wife see that she respects her husband.

**Responsorial Psalm:** Psalms 128: 1-5

1 Blessed is everyone who fears Yahweh,
who walks in his ways.
2 For you will eat the labor of your hands.
You will be happy, and it will be well with you.
3 Your wife will be as a fruitful vine in the innermost parts of your house,
your children like olive shoots around your table.
4 Behold, this is how the man who fears Yahweh is blessed.
5 May Yahweh bless you out of Zion,
and may you see the good of Jerusalem all the days of your life.

**Gospel: Luke 13: 18-21**

18 He said, "What is God's Kingdom like? To what shall I compare it? 19 It is like a grain of mustard seed which a man took and put in his own garden. It grew and became a large tree, and the birds of the sky live in its branches."
20 Again he said, "To what shall I compare God's Kingdom? 21 It is like yeast, which a woman took and hid in three measures † of flour, until it was all leavened."

1. Invite the Holy Spirit into this reading, asking the Author of Scripture to speak to you through His Word
2. Read today's passage as many times as you need, take your time
3. Write down (below) what the Lord is saying to you today
4. Live with this Word in your heart through the day

_____

_____

**First Reading:** Ephesians 6: 1-9

1 Children, obey your parents in the Lord, for this is right. 2 "Honor your father and mother," which is the first commandment with a promise: 3 "that it may be well with you, and you may live long on the earth." *
4 You fathers, don't provoke your children to wrath, but nurture them in the discipline and instruction of the Lord.
5 Servants, be obedient to those who according to the flesh are your masters, with fear and trembling, in singleness of your heart, as to Christ, 6 not in the way of service only when eyes are on you, as men pleasers, but as servants of Christ, doing the will of God from the heart, 7 with good will doing service as to the Lord and not to men, 8 knowing that whatever good thing each one does, he will receive the same good again from the Lord, whether he is bound or free.
9 You masters, do the same things to them, and give up threatening, knowing that he who is both their Master and yours is in heaven, and there is no partiality with him.

**Responsorial Psalm:** Psalms 145: 10-14

10 All your works will give thanks to you, Yahweh.
Your saints will extol you.
11 They will speak of the glory of your kingdom,
and talk about your power,
12 to make known to the sons of men his mighty acts,
the glory of the majesty of his kingdom.
13 Your kingdom is an everlasting kingdom.
Your dominion endures throughout all generations.
Yahweh is faithful in all his words,
and loving in all his deeds.‡
14 Yahweh upholds all who fall,
and raises up all those who are bowed down.

**Gospel: Luke 13: 22-30**

22 He went on his way through cities and villages, teaching, and traveling on to Jerusalem. 23 One said to him, "Lord, are they few who are saved?"

He said to them, 24 "Strive to enter in by the narrow door, for many, I tell you, will seek to enter in and will not be able. 25 When once the master of the house has risen up and has shut the door, and you begin to stand outside and to knock at the door, saying, 'Lord, Lord, open to us!' then he will answer and tell you, 'I don't know you or where you come from.' 26 Then you will begin to say, 'We ate and drank in your presence, and you taught in our streets.' 27 He will say, 'I tell you, I don't know where you come from. Depart from me, all you workers of iniquity.' 28 There will be weeping and gnashing of teeth when you see Abraham, Isaac, Jacob, and all the prophets in God's Kingdom, and yourselves being thrown outside. 29 They will come from the east, west, north, and south, and will sit down in God's Kingdom. 30 Behold, there are some who are last who will be first, and there are some who are first who will be last."

1. Invite the Holy Spirit into this reading, asking the Author of Scripture to speak to you through His Word
2. Read today's passage as many times as you need, take your time
3. Write down (below) what the Lord is saying to you today
4. Live with this Word in your heart through the day

_____

_____

## Thursday, October 31, 2024

**First Reading:** Ephesians 6: 10-20

10 Finally, be strong in the Lord and in the strength of his might. 11 Put on the whole armor of God, that you may be able to stand against the wiles of the devil. 12 For our wrestling is not against flesh and blood, but against the principalities, against the powers, against the world's rulers of the darkness of this age, and against the spiritual forces of wickedness in the heavenly places. 13 Therefore put on the whole armor of God, that you may be able to withstand in the evil day, and having done all, to stand. 14 Stand therefore, having the utility belt of truth buckled around your waist, and having put on the breastplate of righteousness, 15 and having fitted your feet with the preparation of the Good News of peace, 16 above all, taking up the shield of faith, with which you will be able to quench all the fiery darts of the evil one. 17 And take the

helmet of salvation, and the sword of the Spirit, which is the word† of God; 18 with all prayer and requests, praying at all times in the Spirit, and being watchful to this end in all perseverance and requests for all the saints. 19 Pray for me, that utterance may be given to me in opening my mouth, to make known with boldness the mystery of the Good News, 20 for which I am an ambassador in chains; that in it I may speak boldly, as I ought to speak.

**Responsorial Psalm:** Psalms 144: 1-2, 9-10

1 Blessed be Yahweh, my rock,
who trains my hands to war,
and my fingers to battle—
2 my loving kindness, my fortress,
my high tower, my deliverer,
my shield, and he in whom I take refuge,
who subdues my people under me.
9 I will sing a new song to you, God.
On a ten-stringed lyre, I will sing praises to you.
10 You are he who gives salvation to kings,
who rescues David, his servant, from the deadly sword.

**Gospel: Luke 13: 31-35**

31 On that same day, some Pharisees came, saying to him, "Get out of here and go away, for Herod wants to kill you."
32 He said to them, "Go and tell that fox, 'Behold, I cast out demons and perform cures today and tomorrow, and the third day I complete my mission. 33 Nevertheless I must go on my way today and tomorrow and the next day, for it can't be that a prophet would perish outside of Jerusalem.'
34 "Jerusalem, Jerusalem, you who kills the prophets and stones those who are sent to her! How often I wanted to gather your children together, like a hen gathers her own brood under her wings, and you refused! 35 Behold, your house is left to you desolate. I tell you, you will not see me until you say, 'Blessed is he who comes in the name of the Lord!' "

1. Invite the Holy Spirit into this reading, asking the Author of Scripture to speak to you through His Word
2. Read today's passage as many times as you need, take your time

3. Write down (below) what the Lord is saying to you today
4. Live with this Word in your heart through the day

_____

_____

## Friday, November 1, 2024
### ALL SAINTS

**First Reading:** Revelation 7: 2-4, 9-14

2 I saw another angel ascend from the sunrise, having the seal of the living God. He cried with a loud voice to the four angels to whom it was given to harm the earth and the sea, 3 saying, "Don't harm the earth, the sea, or the trees, until we have sealed the bondservants of our God on their foreheads!" 4 I heard the number of those who were sealed, one hundred forty-four thousand, sealed out of every tribe of the children of Israel

  9 After these things I looked, and behold, a great multitude which no man could count, out of every nation and of all tribes, peoples, and languages, standing before the throne and before the Lamb, dressed in white robes, with palm branches in their hands. 10 They cried with a loud voice, saying, "Salvation be to our God, who sits on the throne, and to the Lamb!"

11 All the angels were standing around the throne, the elders, and the four living creatures; and they fell on their faces before his throne, and worshiped God, 12 saying, "Amen! Blessing, glory, wisdom, thanksgiving, honor, power, and might, be to our God forever and ever! Amen."

13 One of the elders answered, saying to me, "These who are arrayed in the white robes, who are they, and where did they come from?"

14 I told him, "My lord, you know."

He said to me, "These are those who came out of the great suffering.† They washed their robes and made them white in the Lamb's blood.

**Responsorial Psalm:** Psalms 24: 1b-6

1 The earth is Yahweh's, with its fullness;
the world, and those who dwell in it.
2 For he has founded it on the seas,

and established it on the floods.
 3 Who may ascend to Yahweh's hill?
Who may stand in his holy place?
4 He who has clean hands and a pure heart;
who has not lifted up his soul to falsehood,
and has not sworn deceitfully.
5 He shall receive a blessing from Yahweh,
righteousness from the God of his salvation.
6 This is the generation of those who seek Him,
who seek your face—even Jacob.

**Second Reading:** First John 3: 1-3

1 See how great a love the Father has given to us, that we should be called children of God! For this cause the world doesn't know us, because it didn't know him. 2 Beloved, now we are children of God. It is not yet revealed what we will be; but we know that when he is revealed, we will be like him, for we will see him just as he is. 3 Everyone who has this hope set on him purifies himself, even as he is pure.

**Gospel: Matthew 5: 1-12a**

1 Seeing the multitudes, he went up onto the mountain. When he had sat down, his disciples came to him. 2 He opened his mouth and taught them, saying,
3 "Blessed are the poor in spirit,
for theirs is the Kingdom of Heaven.*
4 Blessed are those who mourn,
for they shall be comforted.*
5 Blessed are the gentle,
for they shall inherit the earth.†*
6 Blessed are those who hunger and thirst for righteousness,
for they shall be filled.
7 Blessed are the merciful,
for they shall obtain mercy.
8 Blessed are the pure in heart,
for they shall see God.
9 Blessed are the peacemakers,
for they shall be called children of God.
10 Blessed are those who have been persecuted for righteousness' sake,

for theirs is the Kingdom of Heaven.

11 "Blessed are you when people reproach you, persecute you, and say all kinds of evil against you falsely, for my sake. 12 Rejoice, and be exceedingly glad, for great is your reward in heaven. For that is how they persecuted the prophets who were before you.

1. Invite the Holy Spirit into this reading, asking the Author of Scripture to speak to you through His Word
2. Read today's passage as many times as you need, take your time
3. Write down (below) what the Lord is saying to you today
4. Live with this Word in your heart through the day

_____

_____

## Saturday, November 2, 2024
The Commemoration of All the Faithful Departed
(All Souls' Day)

**First Reading:** Wisdom 3: 1-9

1 But the souls of the righteous are in the hand of God,
and no torment will touch them.
2 In the eyes of the foolish they seemed to have died.
Their departure was considered a disaster,
3 and their travel away from us ruin,
but they are in peace.
4 For even if in the sight of men they are punished,
their hope is full of immortality.
5 Having borne a little chastening, they will receive great good;
because God tested them, and found them worthy of himself.
6 He tested them like gold in the furnace,
and he accepted them as a whole burnt offering.
7 In the time of their visitation they will shine.
They will run back and forth like sparks among stubble.
8 They will judge nations and have dominion over peoples.

The Lord will reign over them forever.
9 Those who trust him will understand truth.
The faithful will live with him in love,
because grace and mercy are with his chosen ones.

**Responsorial Psalm:** Psalms 23: 1-6

1 Yahweh is my shepherd;
I shall lack nothing.
2 He makes me lie down in green pastures.
He leads me beside still waters.
3 He restores my soul.
He guides me in the paths of righteousness for his name's sake.
4 Even though I walk through the valley of the shadow of death,
I will fear no evil, for you are with me.
Your rod and your staff,
they comfort me.
5 You prepare a table before me
in the presence of my enemies.
You anoint my head with oil.
My cup runs over.
6 Surely goodness and loving kindness shall follow me all the days of my life,
and I will dwell in Yahweh's house forever.

**Second Reading:** Romans 5: 5-11

5 and hope doesn't disappoint us, because God's love has been poured into our hearts through the Holy Spirit who was given to us.
6 For while we were yet weak, at the right time Christ died for the ungodly. 7 For one will hardly die for a righteous man. Yet perhaps for a good person someone would even dare to die. 8 But God commends his own love toward us, in that while we were yet sinners, Christ died for us.
9 Much more then, being now justified by his blood, we will be saved from God's wrath through him. 10 For if while we were enemies, we were reconciled to God through the death of his Son, much more, being reconciled, we will be saved by his life.
11 Not only so, but we also rejoice in God through our Lord Jesus Christ, through whom we have now received the reconciliation.

## Gospel: John 6: 37-40

37 All those whom the Father gives me will come to me. He who comes to me I will in no way throw out. 38 For I have come down from heaven, not to do my own will, but the will of him who sent me. 39 This is the will of my Father who sent me, that of all he has given to me I should lose nothing, but should raise him up at the last day. 40 This is the will of the one who sent me, that everyone who sees the Son and believes in him should have eternal life; and I will raise him up at the last day."

1. Invite the Holy Spirit into this reading, asking the Author of Scripture to speak to you through His Word
2. Read today's passage as many times as you need, take your time
3. Write down (below) what the Lord is saying to you today
4. Live with this Word in your heart through the day

_____

_____

## Sunday, November 3, 2024
### THIRTY-FIRST SUNDAY IN ORDINARY TIME

**First Reading:** Deuteronomy 6: 2-6

2 that you might fear Yahweh your God, to keep all his statutes and his commandments, which I command you—you, your son, and your son's son, all the days of your life; and that your days may be prolonged. 3 Hear therefore, Israel, and observe to do it, that it may be well with you, and that you may increase mightily, as Yahweh, the God of your fathers, has promised to you, in a land flowing with milk and honey.
4 Hear, Israel: Yahweh is our God. Yahweh is one. 5 You shall love Yahweh your God with all your heart, with all your soul, and with all your might. 6 These words, which I command you today, shall be on your heart;

**Responsorial Psalm:** Psalms 18: 2-4, 47, 50

2 Yahweh is my rock, my fortress, and my deliverer;

my God, my rock, in whom I take refuge;
my shield, and the horn of my salvation, my high tower.
3 I call on Yahweh, who is worthy to be praised;
and I am saved from my enemies.
4 The cords of death surrounded me.
The floods of ungodliness made me afraid.
47 even the God who executes vengeance for me,
and subdues peoples under me.
50 He gives great deliverance to his king,
and shows loving kindness to his anointed,
to David and to his offspring,‡ forever more.

**Second Reading:** Hebrews 7: 23-28

23 Many, indeed, have been made priests, because they are hindered from continuing by death. 24 But he, because he lives forever, has his priesthood unchangeable. 25 Therefore he is also able to save to the uttermost those who draw near to God through him, seeing that he lives forever to make intercession for them.

26 For such a high priest was fitting for us: holy, guiltless, undefiled, separated from sinners, and made higher than the heavens; 27 who doesn't need, like those high priests, to offer up sacrifices daily, first for his own sins, and then for the sins of the people. For he did this once for all, when he offered up himself. 28 For the law appoints men as high priests who have weakness, but the word of the oath, which came after the law, appoints a Son forever who has been perfected.

**Gospel: Mark 12: 28b-34**

28 One of the scribes came and heard them questioning together, and knowing that he had answered them well, asked him, "Which commandment is the greatest of all?"

29 Jesus answered, "The greatest is: 'Hear, Israel, the Lord our God, the Lord is one. 30  You shall love the Lord your God with all your heart, with all your soul, with all your mind, and with all your strength.'* This is the first commandment. 31 The second is like this: 'You shall love your neighbor as yourself.'* There is no other commandment greater than these."

32 The scribe said to him, "Truly, teacher, you have said well that he is one, and there is none other but he; 33 and to love him with all the heart, with all the understanding, all the soul, and with all the strength, and to love his neighbor as himself, is more important than all whole burnt offerings and sacrifices."

34 When Jesus saw that he answered wisely, he said to him, "You are not far from God's Kingdom."

No one dared ask him any question after that.

_____

_____

## Monday, November 4, 2024
### Saint Charles Borromeo, Bishop

**First Reading:** Philippians 2: 1-4

1 If therefore there is any exhortation in Christ, if any consolation of love, if any fellowship of the Spirit, if any tender mercies and compassion, 2 make my joy full by being like-minded, having the same love, being of one accord, of one mind; 3 doing nothing through rivalry or through conceit, but in humility, each counting others better than himself; 4 each of you not just looking to his own things, but each of you also to the things of others.

**Responsorial Psalm:** Psalms 131: 1-3

1 Yahweh, my heart isn't arrogant, nor my eyes lofty;
nor do I concern myself with great matters,
or things too wonderful for me.
2 Surely I have stilled and quieted my soul,
like a weaned child with his mother,
like a weaned child is my soul within me.
3 Israel, hope in Yahweh,
from this time forward and forever more.

**Gospel: Luke 14: 12-14**

12 He also said to the one who had invited him, "When you make a dinner or a supper, don't call your friends, nor your brothers, nor your kinsmen, nor rich neighbors, or perhaps they might also return the favor, and pay you back. 13 But when you make a feast, ask the poor, the maimed, the lame, or the blind; 14 and you will be blessed, because they don't have the resources to repay you. For you will be repaid in the resurrection of the righteous."

1. Invite the Holy Spirit into this reading, asking the Author of Scripture to speak to you through His Word
2. Read today's passage as many times as you need, take your time
3. Write down (below) what the Lord is saying to you today
4. Live with this Word in your heart through the day

_____

_____

## Tuesday, November 5, 2024

**First Reading:** Philippians 2: 5-11

5 Have this in your mind, which was also in Christ Jesus, 6 who, existing in the form of God, didn't consider equality with God a thing to be grasped, 7 but emptied himself, taking the form of a servant, being made in the likeness of men. 8 And being found in human form, he humbled himself, becoming obedient to the point of death, yes, the death of the cross. 9 Therefore God also highly exalted him, and gave to him the name which is above every name, 10 that at the name of Jesus every knee should bow, of those in heaven, those on earth, and those under the earth, 11 and that every tongue should confess that Jesus Christ is Lord, to the glory of God the Father.

**Responsorial Psalm:** Psalms 22: 26b-31

26 The humble shall eat and be satisfied.
They shall praise Yahweh who seek after him.

Let your hearts live forever.

27 All the ends of the earth shall remember and turn to Yahweh.

All the relatives of the nations shall worship before you.

28 For the kingdom is Yahweh's.

He is the ruler over the nations.

29 All the rich ones of the earth shall eat and worship.

All those who go down to the dust shall bow before him,

even he who can't keep his soul alive.

30 Posterity shall serve him.

Future generations shall be told about the Lord.

31 They shall come and shall declare his righteousness to a people that shall be born, for he has done it.

## Gospel: Luke 14: 15-24

15 When one of those who sat at the table with him heard these things, he said to him, "Blessed is he who will feast in God's Kingdom!"

16 But he said to him, "A certain man made a great supper, and he invited many people.

17 He sent out his servant at supper time to tell those who were invited, 'Come, for everything is ready now.' 18 They all as one began to make excuses.

"The first said to him, 'I have bought a field, and I must go and see it. Please have me excused.'

19 "Another said, 'I have bought five yoke of oxen, and I must go try them out. Please have me excused.'

20 "Another said, 'I have married a wife, and therefore I can't come.'

21 "That servant came, and told his lord these things. Then the master of the house, being angry, said to his servant, 'Go out quickly into the streets and lanes of the city, and bring in the poor, maimed, blind, and lame.'

1. Invite the Holy Spirit into this reading, asking the Author of Scripture to speak to you through His Word

2. Read today's passage as many times as you need, take your time

3. Write down (below) what the Lord is saying to you today

4. Live with this Word in your heart through the day

_____

_____

**First Reading:** Philippians 2: 12-18

12 So then, my beloved, even as you have always obeyed, not only in my presence, but now much more in my absence, work out your own salvation with fear and trembling. 13 For it is God who works in you both to will and to work for his good pleasure. 14 Do all things without complaining and arguing, 15 that you may become blameless and harmless, children of God without defect in the middle of a crooked and perverse generation, among whom you are seen as lights in the world, 16 holding up the word of life, that I may have something to boast in the day of Christ that I didn't run in vain nor labor in vain. 17 Yes, and if I am poured out on the sacrifice and service of your faith, I am glad and rejoice with you all. 18 In the same way, you also should be glad and rejoice with me.

**Responsorial Psalm:** Psalms 27: 1, 4, 13-14

1 Yahweh is my light and my salvation.
Whom shall I fear?
Yahweh is the strength of my life.
Of whom shall I be afraid?
4 One thing I have asked of Yahweh, that I will seek after:
that I may dwell in Yahweh's house all the days of my life,
to see Yahweh's beauty,
and to inquire in his temple.
13 I am still confident of this:
I will see the goodness of Yahweh in the land of the living.
14 Wait for Yahweh.
Be strong, and let your heart take courage.
Yes, wait for Yahweh.

**Gospel: Luke 14: 25-33**

25 Now great multitudes were going with him. He turned and said to them, 26 "If anyone comes to me, and doesn't disregard‡ his own father, mother, wife, children, brothers, and sisters, yes, and his own life also, he can't be my disciple. 27 Whoever doesn't bear his own cross and come after me, can't be my disciple. 28 For which of

you, desiring to build a tower, doesn't first sit down and count the cost, to see if he has enough to complete it? 29 Or perhaps, when he has laid a foundation and isn't able to finish, everyone who sees begins to mock him, 30 saying, 'This man began to build and wasn't able to finish.' 31 Or what king, as he goes to encounter another king in war, will not sit down first and consider whether he is able with ten thousand to meet him who comes against him with twenty thousand? 32 Or else, while the other is yet a great way off, he sends an envoy and asks for conditions of peace. 33 So therefore, whoever of you who doesn't renounce all that he has, he can't be my disciple.

1. Invite the Holy Spirit into this reading, asking the Author of Scripture to speak to you through His Word
2. Read today's passage as many times as you need, take your time
3. Write down (below) what the Lord is saying to you today
4. Live with this Word in your heart through the day

_____

_____

## Thursday, November 7, 2024

**First Reading:** Philippians 3: 3-8a

3 For we are the circumcision, who worship God in the Spirit, and rejoice in Christ Jesus, and have no confidence in the flesh; 4 though I myself might have confidence even in the flesh. If any other man thinks that he has confidence in the flesh, I yet more: 5 circumcised the eighth day, of the stock of Israel, of the tribe of Benjamin, a Hebrew of Hebrews; concerning the law, a Pharisee; 6 concerning zeal, persecuting the assembly; concerning the righteousness which is in the law, found blameless.
7 However, I consider those things that were gain to me as a loss for Christ. 8 Yes most certainly, and I count all things to be a loss for the excellency of the knowledge of Christ Jesus, my Lord, for whom I suffered the loss of all things, and count them nothing but refuse, that I may gain Christ

**Responsorial Psalm:** Psalms 105: 2-7

2 Sing to him, sing praises to him!
Tell of all his marvelous works.
3 Glory in his holy name.
Let the heart of those who seek Yahweh rejoice.
4 Seek Yahweh and his strength.
Seek his face forever more.
5 Remember his marvelous works that he has done:
his wonders, and the judgments of his mouth,
6 you offspring of Abraham, his servant,
you children of Jacob, his chosen ones.
7 He is Yahweh, our God.
His judgments are in all the earth.

## Gospel: Luke 15: 1-10

1 Now all the tax collectors and sinners were coming close to him to hear him. 2 The Pharisees and the scribes murmured, saying, "This man welcomes sinners, and eats with them."
3 He told them this parable: 4 "Which of you men, if you had one hundred sheep and lost one of them, wouldn't leave the ninety-nine in the wilderness and go after the one that was lost, until he found it? 5 When he has found it, he carries it on his shoulders, rejoicing. 6 When he comes home, he calls together his friends and his neighbors, saying to them, 'Rejoice with me, for I have found my sheep which was lost!' 7 I tell you that even so there will be more joy in heaven over one sinner who repents, than over ninety-nine righteous people who need no repentance.
8 "Or what woman, if she had ten drachma† coins, if she lost one drachma coin, wouldn't light a lamp, sweep the house, and seek diligently until she found it? 9 When she has found it, she calls together her friends and neighbors, saying, 'Rejoice with me, for I have found the drachma which I had lost!' 10 Even so, I tell you, there is joy in the presence of the angels of God over one sinner repenting."

1. Invite the Holy Spirit into this reading, asking the Author of Scripture to speak to you through His Word
2. Read today's passage as many times as you need, take your time
3. Write down (below) what the Lord is saying to you today
4. Live with this Word in your heart through the day

_____

_____

**First Reading:** Philippians 3: 17 – 4: 1

17 Brothers, be imitators together of me, and note those who walk this way, even as you have us for an example. 18 For many walk, of whom I told you often, and now tell you even weeping, as the enemies of the cross of Christ, 19 whose end is destruction, whose god is the belly, and whose glory is in their shame, who think about earthly things. 20 For our citizenship is in heaven, from where we also wait for a Savior, the Lord Jesus Christ, 21 who will change the body of our humiliation to be conformed to the body of his glory, according to the working by which he is able even to subject all things to himself.

1 Therefore, my brothers, beloved and longed for, my joy and crown, stand firm in the Lord in this way, my beloved.

**Responsorial Psalm:** Psalms 122: 1-5

1 I was glad when they said to me,
"Let's go to Yahweh's house!"
2 Our feet are standing within your gates, Jerusalem!
3 Jerusalem is built as a city that is compact together,
4 where the tribes go up, even Yah's tribes,
according to an ordinance for Israel,
to give thanks to Yahweh's name.
5 For there are set thrones for judgment,
the thrones of David's house.

**Gospel: Luke 16: 1-8**

1 He also said to his disciples, "There was a certain rich man who had a manager. An accusation was made to him that this man was wasting his possessions. 2 He called him, and said to him, 'What is this that I hear about you? Give an accounting of your management, for you can no longer be manager.'
3 "The manager said within himself, 'What will I do, seeing that my lord is taking away the management position from me? I don't have strength to dig. I am ashamed to beg. 4 I know what I will do, so that when I am removed from management, they may receive me into their houses.' 5 Calling each one of his lord's debtors to him, he said

to the first, 'How much do you owe to my lord?' 6 He said, 'A hundred batos† of oil.' He said to him, 'Take your bill, and sit down quickly and write fifty.' 7 Then he said to another, 'How much do you owe?' He said, 'A hundred cors‡ of wheat.' He said to him, 'Take your bill, and write eighty.'

8 "His lord commended the dishonest manager because he had done wisely, for the children of this world are, in their own generation, wiser than the children of the light.

1. Invite the Holy Spirit into this reading, asking the Author of Scripture to speak to you through His Word
2. Read today's passage as many times as you need, take your time
3. Write down (below) what the Lord is saying to you today
4. Live with this Word in your heart through the day

---

---

### Saturday, November 9, 2024
The Dedication of the Lateran Basilica

**First Reading:** Ezekiel 47: 1-2, 8-9, 12

1 He brought me back to the door of the temple; and behold, waters flowed out from under the threshold of the temple eastward, for the front of the temple faced toward the east. The waters came down from underneath, from the right side of the temple, on the south of the altar. 2 Then he brought me out by the way of the gate northward, and led me around by the way outside to the outer gate, by the way of the gate that looks toward the east. Behold, waters ran out on the right side.

8 Then he said to me, "These waters flow out toward the eastern region and will go down into the Arabah. Then they will go toward the sea and flow into the sea which will be made to flow out; and the waters will be healed. 9 It will happen that every living creature which swarms, in every place where the rivers come, will live. Then there will be a very great multitude of fish; for these waters have come there, and the waters of the sea will be healed, and everything will live wherever the river comes.

12 By the river banks, on both sides, will grow every tree for food, whose leaf won't wither, neither will its fruit fail. It will produce new fruit every month, because its waters issue out of the sanctuary. Its fruit will be for food, and its leaf for healing."

**Responsorial Psalm:** Psalms 46: 2-3, 5-6, 8-9

2 Therefore we won't be afraid, though the earth changes,
though the mountains are shaken into the heart of the seas;
3 though its waters roar and are troubled,
though the mountains tremble with their swelling.
5 God is within her. She shall not be moved.
God will help her at dawn.
6 The nations raged. The kingdoms were moved.
He lifted his voice and the earth melted.
8 Come, see Yahweh's works,
what desolations he has made in the earth.
9 He makes wars cease to the end of the earth.
He breaks the bow, and shatters the spear.
He burns the chariots in the fire.

**Second Reading:** First Corinthians 3: 9c-11, 16-17

9c You are God's farming, God's building. 10 According to the grace of God which was given to me, as a wise master builder I laid a foundation, and another builds on it. But let each man be careful how he builds on it. 11 For no one can lay any other foundation than that which has been laid, which is Jesus Christ.
16 Don't you know that you are God's temple and that God's Spirit lives in you? 17 If anyone destroys God's temple, God will destroy him; for God's temple is holy, which you are.

**Gospel: John 2: 13-22**

13 The Passover of the Jews was at hand, and Jesus went up to Jerusalem. 14 He found in the temple those who sold oxen, sheep, and doves, and the changers of money sitting. 15 He made a whip of cords and drove all out of the temple, both the sheep and the oxen; and he poured out the changers' money and overthrew their tables. 16 To those who sold the doves, he said, "Take these things out of here! Don't make my

er's house a marketplace!" 17 His disciples remembered that it was written, "Zeal your house will eat me up."*

.8 The Jews therefore answered him, "What sign do you show us, seeing that you do these things?"

19 Jesus answered them, "Destroy this temple, and in three days I will raise it up."

20 The Jews therefore said, "It took forty-six years to build this temple! Will you raise it up in three days?" 21 But he spoke of the temple of his body. 22 When therefore he was raised from the dead, his disciples remembered that he said this, and they believed the Scripture and the word which Jesus had said.

1. Invite the Holy Spirit into this reading, asking the Author of Scripture to speak to you through His Word
2. Read today's passage as many times as you need, take your time
3. Write down (below) what the Lord is saying to you today
4. Live with this Word in your heart through the day

---

---

## Sunday, November 10, 2024
### THIRTY-SECOND SUNDAY IN ORDINARY TIME

**First Reading:** First Kings 17: 10-16

10 So he arose and went to Zarephath; and when he came to the gate of the city, behold, a widow was there gathering sticks. He called to her and said, "Please get me a little water in a jar, that I may drink."

11 As she was going to get it, he called to her and said, "Please bring me a morsel of bread in your hand."

12 She said, "As Yahweh your God lives, I don't have anything baked, but only a handful of meal in a jar and a little oil in a jar. Behold, I am gathering two sticks, that I may go in and bake it for me and my son, that we may eat it, and die."

13 Elijah said to her, "Don't be afraid. Go and do as you have said; but make me a little cake from it first, and bring it out to me, and afterward make some for you and for your

son. 14 For Yahweh, the God of Israel, says, 'The jar of meal will not run out, and the jar of oil will not fail, until the day that Yahweh sends rain on the earth.' "

15 She went and did according to the saying of Elijah; and she, he, and her household ate many days. 16 The jar of meal didn't run out and the jar of oil didn't fail, according to Yahweh's word, which he spoke by Elijah.

**Responsorial Psalm:** Psalms 146: 7-10

7 who executes justice for the oppressed;
who gives food to the hungry.
Yahweh frees the prisoners.
8 Yahweh opens the eyes of the blind.
Yahweh raises up those who are bowed down.
Yahweh loves the righteous.
9 Yahweh preserves the foreigners.
He upholds the fatherless and widow,
but he turns the way of the wicked upside down.
10 Yahweh will reign forever;
your God, O Zion, to all generations.
Praise Yah!

**Second Reading:** Hebrews 9: 24-28

24 For Christ hasn't entered into holy places made with hands, which are representations of the true, but into heaven itself, now to appear in the presence of God for us; 25 nor yet that he should offer himself often, as the high priest enters into the holy place year by year with blood not his own, 26 or else he must have suffered often since the foundation of the world. But now once at the end of the ages, he has been revealed to put away sin by the sacrifice of himself. 27 Inasmuch as it is appointed for men to die once, and after this, judgment, 28 so Christ also, having been offered once to bear the sins of many, will appear a second time, not to deal with sin, but to save those who are eagerly waiting for him.

**Gospel: Mark 12: 41-44**

41 Jesus sat down opposite the treasury and saw how the multitude cast money into the treasury. Many who were rich cast in much. 42 A poor widow came and she cast in two small brass coins,† which equal a quadrans coin.‡ 43 He called his disciples to

himself and said to them, "Most certainly I tell you, this poor widow gave more than all those who are giving into the treasury, 44 for they all gave out of their abundance, but she, out of her poverty, gave all that she had to live on."

1. Invite the Holy Spirit into this reading, asking the Author of Scripture to speak to you through His Word
2. Read today's passage as many times as you need, take your time
3. Write down (below) what the Lord is saying to you today
4. Live with this Word in your heart through the day

_____

_____

## Monday, November 11, 2024
### Saint Martin of Tours, Bishop

**First Reading:** Titus 1: 1-9

1 Paul, a servant of God and an apostle of Jesus Christ,† according to the faith of God's chosen ones and the knowledge of the truth which is according to godliness, 2 in hope of eternal life, which God, who can't lie, promised before time began; 3 but in his own time revealed his word in the message with which I was entrusted according to the commandment of God our Savior, 4 to Titus, my true child according to a common faith: Grace, mercy, and peace from God the Father and the Lord Jesus Christ our Savior.
5 I left you in Crete for this reason, that you would set in order the things that were lacking and appoint elders in every city, as I directed you— 6 if anyone is blameless, the husband of one wife, having children who believe, who are not accused of loose or unruly behavior. 7 For the overseer must be blameless, as God's steward, not self-pleasing, not easily angered, not given to wine, not violent, not greedy for dishonest gain; 8 but given to hospitality, a lover of good, sober minded, fair, holy, self-controlled, 9 holding to the faithful word which is according to the teaching, that he may be able to exhort in the sound doctrine, and to convict those who contradict him.

**Responsorial Psalm:** Psalms 24: 1b-6

1 The earth is Yahweh's, with its fullness;
the world, and those who dwell in it.
2 For he has founded it on the seas,
and established it on the floods.
3 Who may ascend to Yahweh's hill?
Who may stand in his holy place?
4 He who has clean hands and a pure heart;
who has not lifted up his soul to falsehood,
and has not sworn deceitfully.
5 He shall receive a blessing from Yahweh,
righteousness from the God of his salvation.
6 This is the generation of those who seek Him,
who seek your face—even Jacob.

**Gospel: Luke 17: 1-6**

1 He said to the disciples, "It is impossible that no occasions of stumbling should come, but woe to him through whom they come! 2 It would be better for him if a millstone were hung around his neck, and he were thrown into the sea, rather than that he should cause one of these little ones to stumble. 3 Be careful. If your brother sins against you, rebuke him. If he repents, forgive him. 4 If he sins against you seven times in the day, and seven times returns, saying, 'I repent,' you shall forgive him."
5 The apostles said to the Lord, "Increase our faith."
6 The Lord said, "If you had faith like a grain of mustard seed, you would tell this sycamore tree, 'Be uprooted and be planted in the sea,' and it would obey you.

1. Invite the Holy Spirit into this reading, asking the Author of Scripture to speak to you through His Word
2. Read today's passage as many times as you need, take your time
3. Write down (below) what the Lord is saying to you today
4. Live with this Word in your heart through the day

_____

_____

# Tuesday, November 12, 2024
### Saint Josaphat, Bishop and Martyr

**First Reading:** Titus 2: 1-8, 11-14

1 But say the things which fit sound doctrine, 2 that older men should be temperate, sensible, sober minded, sound in faith, in love, and in perseverance, 3 and that older women likewise be reverent in behavior, not slanderers nor enslaved to much wine, teachers of that which is good, 4 that they may train the young wives to love their husbands, to love their children, 5 to be sober minded, chaste, workers at home, kind, being in subjection to their own husbands, that God's word may not be blasphemed.

6 Likewise, exhort the younger men to be sober minded. 7 In all things show yourself an example of good works. In your teaching, show integrity, seriousness, incorruptibility, 8 and soundness of speech that can't be condemned, that he who opposes you may be ashamed, having no evil thing to say about us.

11 For the grace of God has appeared, bringing salvation to all men, 12 instructing us to the intent that, denying ungodliness and worldly lusts, we would live soberly, righteously, and godly in this present age; 13 looking for the blessed hope and appearing of the glory of our great God and Savior, Jesus Christ, 14 who gave himself for us, that he might redeem us from all iniquity and purify for himself a people for his own possession, zealous for good works.

**Responsorial Psalm:** Psalms 37: 3-4, 18 and 23, 27 and 29

3 Trust in Yahweh, and do good.
Dwell in the land, and enjoy safe pasture.
4 Also delight yourself in Yahweh,
and he will give you the desires of your heart.
18 Yahweh knows the days of the perfect.
Their inheritance shall be forever.
23 A man's steps are established by Yahweh.
He delights in his way.
27 Depart from evil, and do good.
Live securely forever.
29 The righteous shall inherit the land,
and live in it forever.

## Gospel: Luke 17: 7-10

7 But who is there among you, having a servant plowing or keeping sheep, that will say when he comes in from the field, 'Come immediately and sit down at the table'? 8 Wouldn't he rather tell him, 'Prepare my supper, clothe yourself properly, and serve me while I eat and drink. Afterward you shall eat and drink'? 9 Does he thank that servant because he did the things that were commanded? I think not. 10 Even so you also, when you have done all the things that are commanded you, say, 'We are unworthy servants. We have done our duty.' "

1. Invite the Holy Spirit into this reading, asking the Author of Scripture to speak to you through His Word
2. Read today's passage as many times as you need, take your time
3. Write down (below) what the Lord is saying to you today
4. Live with this Word in your heart through the day

---

## Wednesday, November 13, 2024
### Saint Frances Xavier Cabrini, Virgin

**First Reading:** Titus 3: 1-7

1 Remind them to be in subjection to rulers and to authorities, to be obedient, to be ready for every good work, 2 to speak evil of no one, not to be contentious, to be gentle, showing all humility toward all men. 3 For we were also once foolish, disobedient, deceived, serving various lusts and pleasures, living in malice and envy, hateful, and hating one another. 4 But when the kindness of God our Savior and his love toward mankind appeared, 5 not by works of righteousness which we did ourselves, but according to his mercy, he saved us through the washing of regeneration and renewing by the Holy Spirit, 6 whom he poured out on us richly through Jesus Christ our Savior; 7 that being justified by his grace, we might be made heirs according to the hope of eternal life.

**Responsorial Psalm:** Psalms 23: 1b-6

1 Yahweh is my shepherd;
I shall lack nothing.
2 He makes me lie down in green pastures.
He leads me beside still waters.
3 He restores my soul.
He guides me in the paths of righteousness for his name's sake.
4 Even though I walk through the valley of the shadow of death,
I will fear no evil, for you are with me.
Your rod and your staff,
they comfort me.
5 You prepare a table before me
in the presence of my enemies.
You anoint my head with oil.
My cup runs over.
6 Surely goodness and loving kindness shall follow me all the days of my life,
and I will dwell in Yahweh's house forever.

**Gospel: Luke 17: 11-19**

11 As he was on his way to Jerusalem, he was passing along the borders of Samaria and Galilee. 12 As he entered into a certain village, ten men who were lepers met him, who stood at a distance. 13 They lifted up their voices, saying, "Jesus, Master, have mercy on us!"
14 When he saw them, he said to them, "Go and show yourselves to the priests." As they went, they were cleansed. 15 One of them, when he saw that he was healed, turned back, glorifying God with a loud voice. 16 He fell on his face at Jesus' feet, giving him thanks; and he was a Samaritan.
17 Jesus answered, "Weren't the ten cleansed? But where are the nine? 18 Were there none found who returned to give glory to God, except this foreigner?" 19 Then he said to him, "Get up, and go your way. Your faith has healed you."

1. Invite the Holy Spirit into this reading, asking the Author of Scripture to speak to you through His Word
2. Read today's passage as many times as you need, take your time
3. Write down (below) what the Lord is saying to you today
4. Live with this Word in your heart through the day

## Thursday, November 14, 2024

**First Reading:** Philemon 1: 7-20

7 For we have much joy and comfort in your love, because the hearts of the saints have been refreshed through you, brother.

8 Therefore though I have all boldness in Christ to command you that which is appropriate, 9 yet for love's sake I rather appeal to you, being such a one as Paul, the aged, but also a prisoner of Jesus Christ. 10 I appeal to you for my child Onesimus, whom I have become the father of in my chains,‡ 11 who once was useless to you, but now is useful to you and to me. 12 I am sending him back. Therefore receive him, that is, my own heart, 13 whom I desired to keep with me, that on your behalf he might serve me in my chains for the Good News. 14 But I was willing to do nothing without your consent, that your goodness would not be as of necessity, but of free will. 15 For perhaps he was therefore separated from you for a while that you would have him forever, 16 no longer as a slave, but more than a slave, a beloved brother—especially to me, but how much rather to you, both in the flesh and in the Lord.

17 If then you count me a partner, receive him as you would receive me. 18 But if he has wronged you at all or owes you anything, put that to my account. 19 I, Paul, write this with my own hand: I will repay it (not to mention to you that you owe to me even your own self besides). 20 Yes, brother, let me have joy from you in the Lord. Refresh my heart in the Lord.

**Responsorial Psalm:** Psalms 146: 7-10

7 who executes justice for the oppressed;
who gives food to the hungry.
Yahweh frees the prisoners.
8 Yahweh opens the eyes of the blind.
Yahweh raises up those who are bowed down.
Yahweh loves the righteous.

9 Yahweh preserves the foreigners.
He upholds the fatherless and widow,
but he turns the way of the wicked upside down.
10 Yahweh will reign forever;
your God, O Zion, to all generations.
Praise Yah!

**Gospel: Luke 17: 20-25**

20 Being asked by the Pharisees when God's Kingdom would come, he answered them, "God's Kingdom doesn't come with observation; 21 neither will they say, 'Look, here!' or, 'Look, there!' for behold, God's Kingdom is within you."
22 He said to the disciples, "The days will come when you will desire to see one of the days of the Son of Man, and you will not see it. 23 They will tell you, 'Look, here!' or 'Look, there!' Don't go away or follow after them, 24 for as the lightning, when it flashes out of one part under the sky, shines to another part under the sky, so will the Son of Man be in his day. 25 But first, he must suffer many things and be rejected by this generation.

1. Invite the Holy Spirit into this reading, asking the Author of Scripture to speak to you through His Word
2. Read today's passage as many times as you need, take your time
3. Write down (below) what the Lord is saying to you today
4. Live with this Word in your heart through the day

_____

_____

### Friday, November 15, 2024
Saint Albert the Great, Bishop and Doctor of the Church

**First Reading:** Second John 1: 4-9

4 I rejoice greatly that I have found some of your children walking in truth, even as we have been commanded by the Father. 5 Now I beg you, dear lady, not as though I wrote to you a new commandment, but that which we had from the beginning, that we love

one another. 6 This is love, that we should walk according to his commandments. This is the commandment, even as you heard from the beginning, that you should walk in it.

7 For many deceivers have gone out into the world, those who don't confess that Jesus Christ came in the flesh. This is the deceiver and the Antichrist. 8 Watch yourselves, that we don't lose the things which we have accomplished, but that we receive a full reward. 9 Whoever transgresses and doesn't remain in the teaching of Christ doesn't have God. He who remains in the teaching has both the Father and the Son.

**Responsorial Psalm:** Psalms 119: 1, 2, 10, 11, 17, 18

1 Blessed are those whose ways are blameless,
who walk according to Yahweh's law.
2 Blessed are those who keep his statutes,
who seek him with their whole heart.
10 With my whole heart I have sought you.
Don't let me wander from your commandments.
11 I have hidden your word in my heart,
that I might not sin against you.
17 Do good to your servant.
I will live and I will obey your word.
18 Open my eyes,
that I may see wondrous things out of your law.

**Gospel: Luke 17: 26-37**

26 As it was in the days of Noah, even so it will also be in the days of the Son of Man. 27 They ate, they drank, they married, and they were given in marriage until the day that Noah entered into the ship, and the flood came and destroyed them all. 28 Likewise, even as it was in the days of Lot: they ate, they drank, they bought, they sold, they planted, they built; 29 but in the day that Lot went out from Sodom, it rained fire and sulfur from the sky and destroyed them all. 30 It will be the same way in the day that the Son of Man is revealed. 31 In that day, he who will be on the housetop and his goods in the house, let him not go down to take them away. Let him who is in the field likewise not turn back. 32 Remember Lot's wife! 33 Whoever seeks to save his life loses it, but whoever loses his life preserves it. 34 I tell you, in that night there will be two people in one bed. One will be taken and the other will be left. 35 There will be two grinding grain together. One will be taken and the other will be left." 36

37 They, answering, asked him, "Where, Lord?"
He said to them, "Where the body is, there the vultures will also be gathered together."

---

---

## Saturday, November 16, 2024
### Saint Margaret of Scotland; Saint Gertrude, Virgin; BVM

**First Reading:** Third John 1: 5-8

5 Beloved, you do a faithful work in whatever you accomplish for those who are brothers and strangers. 6 They have testified about your love before the assembly. You will do well to send them forward on their journey in a way worthy of God, 7 because for the sake of the Name they went out, taking nothing from the Gentiles. 8 We therefore ought to receive such, that we may be fellow workers for the truth.

**Responsorial Psalm:** Psalms 112: 1-6

1 Praise Yah!†
Blessed is the man who fears Yahweh,
who delights greatly in his commandments.
2 His offspring will be mighty in the land.
The generation of the upright will be blessed.
3 Wealth and riches are in his house.
His righteousness endures forever.
4 Light dawns in the darkness for the upright,
gracious, merciful, and righteous.

5 It is well with the man who deals graciously and lends.
He will maintain his cause in judgment.
6 For he will never be shaken.
The righteous will be remembered forever.

**Gospel: Luke 18: 1-8**

1 He also spoke a parable to them that they must always pray and not give up, 2 saying, "There was a judge in a certain city who didn't fear God and didn't respect man. 3 A widow was in that city, and she often came to him, saying, 'Defend me from my adversary!' 4 He wouldn't for a while; but afterward he said to himself, 'Though I neither fear God nor respect man, 5 yet because this widow bothers me, I will defend her, or else she will wear me out by her continual coming.' "
6 The Lord said, "Listen to what the unrighteous judge says. 7 Won't God avenge his chosen ones who are crying out to him day and night, and yet he exercises patience with them? 8 I tell you that he will avenge them quickly. Nevertheless, when the Son of Man comes, will he find faith on the earth?"

1. Invite the Holy Spirit into this reading, asking the Author of Scripture to speak to you through His Word
2. Read today's passage as many times as you need, take your time
3. Write down (below) what the Lord is saying to you today
4. Live with this Word in your heart through the day

_____

_____

### Sunday, November 17, 2024
THIRTY-THIRD SUNDAY IN ORDINARY TIME'

**First Reading:** Daniel 12: 1-3

1 "At that time Michael will stand up, the great prince who stands for the children of your people; and there will be a time of trouble, such as never was since there was a nation even to that same time. At that time your people will be delivered, everyone who

is found written in the book. 2 Many of those who sleep in the dust of the earth will awake, some to everlasting life, and some to shame and everlasting contempt. 3 Those who are wise will shine as the brightness of the expanse. Those who turn many to righteousness will shine as the stars forever and ever.

**Responsorial Psalm:** Psalms 16: 5, 8- 11

5 Yahweh assigned my portion and my cup.
You made my lot secure.
8 I have set Yahweh always before me.
Because he is at my right hand, I shall not be moved.
9 Therefore my heart is glad, and my tongue rejoices.
My body shall also dwell in safety.
10 For you will not leave my soul in Sheol,†
neither will you allow your holy one to see corruption.
11 You will show me the path of life.
In your presence is fullness of joy.
In your right hand there are pleasures forever more.

**Second Reading:** Hebrews 10: 11-14, 18

11 Every priest indeed stands day by day serving and offering often the same sacrifices, which can never take away sins, 12 but he, when he had offered one sacrifice for sins forever, sat down on the right hand of God, 13 from that time waiting until his enemies are made the footstool of his feet. 14 For by one offering he has perfected forever those who are being sanctified.
18 Now where remission of these is, there is no more offering for sin.

**Gospel: Mark 13: 24-32**

24 But in those days, after that oppression, the sun will be darkened, the moon will not give its light, 25 the stars will be falling from the sky, and the powers that are in the heavens will be shaken.* 26 Then they will see the Son of Man coming in clouds with great power and glory. 27 Then he will send out his angels, and will gather together his chosen ones from the four winds, from the ends of the earth to the ends of the sky.
28 "Now from the fig tree, learn this parable. When the branch has now become tender and produces its leaves, you know that the summer is near; 29 even so you also, when

you see these things coming to pass, know that it is near, at the doors. 30 Most certainly I say to you, this generation‡ will not pass away until all these things happen. 31 Heaven and earth will pass away, but my words will not pass away.

32 "But of that day or that hour no one knows—not even the angels in heaven, nor the Son, but only the Father.

1. Invite the Holy Spirit into this reading, asking the Author of Scripture to speak to you through His Word
2. Read today's passage as many times as you need, take your time
3. Write down (below) what the Lord is saying to you today
4. Live with this Word in your heart through the day

_____

_____

## Monday, November 18, 2024
The Dedication of the Basilicas of Saints Peter and Paul, Apostles;
USA: Saint Rose Philippine Duchesne, Virgin

**First Reading:** Revelation 1: 1-4; 2: 1-5

1 This is the Revelation of Jesus Christ,† which God gave him to show to his servants the things which must happen soon, which he sent and made known by his angel‡ to his servant, John, 2 who testified to God's word and of the testimony of Jesus Christ, about everything that he saw.

3 Blessed is he who reads and those who hear the words of the prophecy, and keep the things that are written in it, for the time is near.

4 John, to the seven assemblies that are in Asia: Grace to you and peace from God, who is and who was and who is to come; and from the seven Spirits who are before his throne;

1 "To the angel of the assembly in Ephesus write:

"He who holds the seven stars in his right hand, he who walks among the seven golden lamp stands says these things:

2 "I know your works, and your toil and perseverance, and that you can't tolerate evil men, and have tested those who call themselves apostles, and they are not, and found

them false. 3 You have perseverance and have endured for my name's sake, and have † not grown weary. 4 But I have this against you, that you left your first love. 5 Remember therefore from where you have fallen, and repent and do the first works; or else I am coming to you swiftly, and will move your lamp stand out of its place, unless you repent.

**Responsorial Psalm:** Psalms 1: 1-4 and 6

1 Blessed is the man who doesn't walk in the counsel of the wicked,
nor stand on the path of sinners,
nor sit in the seat of scoffers;
2 but his delight is in Yahweh's† law.
On his law he meditates day and night.
3 He will be like a tree planted by the streams of water,
that produces its fruit in its season,
whose leaf also does not wither.
Whatever he does shall prosper.
4 The wicked are not so,
but are like the chaff which the wind drives away.
6 For Yahweh knows the way of the righteous,
but the way of the wicked shall perish.

**Gospel: Luke 18: 35-43**

35 As he came near Jericho, a certain blind man sat by the road, begging. 36 Hearing a multitude going by, he asked what this meant. 37 They told him that Jesus of Nazareth was passing by. 38 He cried out, "Jesus, you son of David, have mercy on me!" 39 Those who led the way rebuked him, that he should be quiet; but he cried out all the more, "You son of David, have mercy on me!"
40 Standing still, Jesus commanded him to be brought to him. When he had come near, he asked him, 41 "What do you want me to do?"
He said, "Lord, that I may see again."
42 Jesus said to him, "Receive your sight. Your faith has healed you."
43 Immediately he received his sight and followed him, glorifying God. All the people, when they saw it, praised God.

1. Invite the Holy Spirit into this reading, asking the Author of Scripture to speak to you through His Word
2. Read today's passage as many times as you need, take your time
3. Write down (below) what the Lord is saying to you today
4. Live with this Word in your heart through the day

_____

_____

## Tuesday, November 19, 2024

**First Reading:** Revelation 3: 1-6, 14-22

1 "And to the angel of the assembly in Sardis write:

"He who has the seven Spirits of God and the seven stars says these things:

"I know your works, that you have a reputation of being alive, but you are dead. 2 Wake up and strengthen the things that remain, which you were about to throw away,† for I have found no works of yours perfected before my God. 3 Remember therefore how you have received and heard. Keep it and repent. If therefore you won't watch, I will come as a thief, and you won't know what hour I will come upon you. 4 Nevertheless you have a few names in Sardis that didn't defile their garments. They will walk with me in white, for they are worthy. 5 He who overcomes will be arrayed in white garments, and I will in no way blot his name out of the book of life, and I will confess his name before my Father, and before his angels. 6 He who has an ear, let him hear what the Spirit says to the assemblies.

14 "To the angel of the assembly in Laodicea write:

"The Amen, the Faithful and True Witness, the Beginning‡ of God's creation, says these things:

15 "I know your works, that you are neither cold nor hot. I wish you were cold or hot. 16 So, because you are lukewarm, and neither hot nor cold, I will vomit you out of my mouth. 17 Because you say, 'I am rich, and have gotten riches, and have need of nothing,' and don't know that you are the wretched one, miserable, poor, blind, and naked; 18 I counsel you to buy from me gold refined by fire, that you may become rich; and white garments, that you may clothe yourself, and that the shame of your nakedness may not be revealed; and eye salve to anoint your eyes, that you may see. 19

As many as I love, I reprove and chasten. Be zealous therefore, and repent. 20 Behold, I stand at the door and knock. If anyone hears my voice and opens the door, then I will come in to him and will dine with him, and he with me. 21 He who overcomes, I will give to him to sit down with me on my throne, as I also overcame and sat down with my Father on his throne. 22 He who has an ear, let him hear what the Spirit says to the assemblies."

**Responsorial Psalm:** Psalms 15: 2-5

2 He who walks blamelessly and does what is right,
and speaks truth in his heart;
3 he who doesn't slander with his tongue,
nor does evil to his friend,
nor casts slurs against his fellow man;
4 in whose eyes a vile man is despised,
but who honors those who fear Yahweh;
he who keeps an oath even when it hurts, and doesn't change;
5 he who doesn't lend out his money for usury,
nor take a bribe against the innocent.

**Gospel: Luke 19: 1-10**

1 He entered and was passing through Jericho. 2 There was a man named Zacchaeus. He was a chief tax collector, and he was rich. 3 He was trying to see who Jesus was, and couldn't because of the crowd, because he was short. 4 He ran on ahead and climbed up into a sycamore tree to see him, for he was going to pass that way. 5 When Jesus came to the place, he looked up and saw him, and said to him, "Zacchaeus, hurry and come down, for today I must stay at your house." 6 He hurried, came down, and received him joyfully. 7 When they saw it, they all murmured, saying, "He has gone in to lodge with a man who is a sinner."
8 Zacchaeus stood and said to the Lord, "Behold, Lord, half of my goods I give to the poor. If I have wrongfully exacted anything of anyone, I restore four times as much."
9 Jesus said to him, "Today, salvation has come to this house, because he also is a son of Abraham. 10 For the Son of Man came to seek and to save that which was lost."

1. Invite the Holy Spirit into this reading, asking the Author of Scripture to speak to you through His Word
2. Read today's passage as many times as you need, take your time

3. Write down (below) what the Lord is saying to you today
4. Live with this Word in your heart through the day

_____

_____

## Wednesday, November 20, 2024

**First Reading:** Revelation 4: 1-11

1 After these things I looked and saw a door opened in heaven; and the first voice that I heard, like a trumpet speaking with me, was one saying, "Come up here, and I will show you the things which must happen after this."
2 Immediately I was in the Spirit. Behold, there was a throne set in heaven, and one sitting on the throne 3 that looked like a jasper stone and a sardius. There was a rainbow around the throne, like an emerald to look at. 4 Around the throne were twenty-four thrones. On the thrones were twenty-four elders sitting, dressed in white garments, with crowns of gold on their heads. 5 Out of the throne proceed lightnings, sounds, and thunders. There were seven lamps of fire burning before his throne, which are the seven Spirits of God. 6 Before the throne was something like a sea of glass, similar to crystal. In the middle of the throne, and around the throne were four living creatures full of eyes before and behind. 7 The first creature was like a lion, the second creature like a calf, the third creature had a face like a man, and the fourth was like a flying eagle. 8 The four living creatures, each one of them having six wings, are full of eyes around and within. They have no rest day and night, saying, "Holy, holy, holy† is the Lord God, the Almighty, who was and who is and who is to come!"
9 When the living creatures give glory, honor, and thanks to him who sits on the throne, to him who lives forever and ever, 10 the twenty-four elders fall down before him who sits on the throne and worship him who lives forever and ever, and throw their crowns before the throne, saying, 11 "Worthy are you, our Lord and God, the Holy One,‡ to receive the glory, the honor, and the power, for you created all things, and because of your desire they existed and were created!"

**Responsorial Psalm:** Psalms 150: 1b-6

1 Praise God in his sanctuary!

Praise him in his heavens for his acts of power!

2 Praise him for his mighty acts!

Praise him according to his excellent greatness!

3 Praise him with the sounding of the trumpet!

Praise him with harp and lyre!

4 Praise him with tambourine and dancing!

Praise him with stringed instruments and flute!

5 Praise him with loud cymbals!

Praise him with resounding cymbals!

6 Let everything that has breath praise Yah!

Praise Yah!

## Gospel: Luke 19: 11-28

11 As they heard these things, he went on and told a parable, because he was near Jerusalem, and they supposed that God's Kingdom would be revealed immediately. 12 He said therefore, "A certain nobleman went into a far country to receive for himself a kingdom and to return. 13 He called ten servants of his and gave them ten mina coins, † and told them, 'Conduct business until I come.' 14 But his citizens hated him, and sent an envoy after him, saying, 'We don't want this man to reign over us.'

15 "When he had come back again, having received the kingdom, he commanded these servants, to whom he had given the money, to be called to him, that he might know what they had gained by conducting business. 16 The first came before him, saying, 'Lord, your mina has made ten more minas.'

17 "He said to him, 'Well done, you good servant! Because you were found faithful with very little, you shall have authority over ten cities.'

18 "The second came, saying, 'Your mina, Lord, has made five minas.'

19 "So he said to him, 'And you are to be over five cities.'

20 Another came, saying, 'Lord, behold, your mina, which I kept laid away in a handkerchief, 21 for I feared you, because you are an exacting man. You take up that which you didn't lay down, and reap that which you didn't sow.'

22 "He said to him, 'Out of your own mouth I will judge you, you wicked servant! You knew that I am an exacting man, taking up that which I didn't lay down and reaping that which I didn't sow. 23 Then why didn't you deposit my money in the bank, and at my coming, I might have earned interest on it?' 24 He said to those who stood by, 'Take the mina away from him and give it to him who has the ten minas.'

25 "They said to him, 'Lord, he has ten minas!' 26 'For I tell you that to everyone who has, will more be given; but from him who doesn't have, even that which he has will be taken away from him. 27 But bring those enemies of mine who didn't want me to reign over them here, and kill them before me.' " 28 Having said these things, he went on ahead, going up to Jerusalem.

1. Invite the Holy Spirit into this reading, asking the Author of Scripture to speak to you through His Word
2. Read today's passage as many times as you need, take your time
3. Write down (below) what the Lord is saying to you today
4. Live with this Word in your heart through the day

_____

_____

### Thursday, November 21, 2024
The Presentation of the Blessed Virgin Mary

**First Reading:** Revelation 5: 1-10

1 I saw, in the right hand of him who sat on the throne, a book written inside and outside, sealed shut with seven seals. 2 I saw a mighty angel proclaiming with a loud voice, "Who is worthy to open the book, and to break its seals?" 3 No one in heaven above, or on the earth, or under the earth, was able to open the book or to look in it. 4 Then I wept much, because no one was found worthy to open the book or to look in it. 5 One of the elders said to me, "Don't weep. Behold, the Lion who is of the tribe of Judah, the Root of David, has overcome: he who opens the book and its seven seals."
6 I saw in the middle of the throne and of the four living creatures, and in the middle of the elders, a Lamb standing, as though it had been slain, having seven horns and seven eyes, which are the seven Spirits of God, sent out into all the earth. 7 Then he came, and he took it out of the right hand of him who sat on the throne. 8 Now when he had taken the book, the four living creatures and the twenty-four elders fell down before the Lamb, each one having a harp, and golden bowls full of incense, which are the prayers of the saints. 9 They sang a new song, saying,
"You are worthy to take the book
and to open its seals,

for you were killed,
and bought us for God with your blood
out of every tribe, language, people, and nation,
10 and made us kings and priests to our God;
and we will reign on the earth."

**Responsorial Psalm:** Psalms 149: 1b-6a and 9b

1 Sing to Yahweh a new song,
his praise in the assembly of the saints.
2 Let Israel rejoice in him who made them.
Let the children of Zion be joyful in their King.
3 Let them praise his name in the dance!
Let them sing praises to him with tambourine and harp!
4 For Yahweh takes pleasure in his people.
He crowns the humble with salvation.
5 Let the saints rejoice in honor.
Let them sing for joy on their beds.
6 May the high praises of God be in their mouths,
9b All his saints have this honor.
Praise Yah!

**Gospel: Luke 19: 41-44**

41 When he came near, he saw the city and wept over it, 42 saying, "If you, even you, had known today the things which belong to your peace! But now, they are hidden from your eyes. 43  For the days will come on you when your enemies will throw up a barricade against you, surround you, hem you in on every side, 44  and will dash you and your children within you to the ground. They will not leave in you one stone on another, because you didn't know the time of your visitation."

1. Invite the Holy Spirit into this reading, asking the Author of Scripture to speak to you through His Word
2. Read today's passage as many times as you need, take your time
3. Write down (below) what the Lord is saying to you today
4. Live with this Word in your heart through the day

## Friday, November 22, 2024
### Saint Cecilia, Virgin and Martyr

**First Reading:** Revelation 10: 8-11

8 The voice which I heard from heaven, again speaking with me, said, "Go, take the book which is open in the hand of the angel who stands on the sea and on the land."
9 I went to the angel, telling him to give me the little book.
He said to me, "Take it and eat it. It will make your stomach bitter, but in your mouth it will be as sweet as honey."
10 I took the little book out of the angel's hand, and ate it. It was as sweet as honey in my mouth. When I had eaten it, my stomach was made bitter. 11 They† told me, "You must prophesy again over many peoples, nations, languages, and kings."

**Responsorial Psalm:** Psalms 119: 14, 24, 72, 103, 111, 131

14 I have rejoiced in the way of your testimonies,
as much as in all riches.
24 Indeed your statutes are my delight,
and my counselors.
72 The law of your mouth is better to me than thousands of pieces of gold and silver.
103 How sweet are your promises to my taste,
more than honey to my mouth!
111 I have taken your testimonies as a heritage forever,
for they are the joy of my heart.
131 I opened my mouth wide and panted,
for I longed for your commandments.

**Gospel: Luke 19: 45-48**

45 He entered into the temple and began to drive out those who bought and sold in it, 46 saying to them, "It is written, 'My house is a house of prayer,' * but you have made it a 'den of robbers'!" *

47 He was teaching daily in the temple, but the chief priests, the scribes, and the leading men among the people sought to destroy him. 48 They couldn't find what they might do, for all the people hung on to every word that he said.

1. Invite the Holy Spirit into this reading, asking the Author of Scripture to speak to you through His Word
2. Read today's passage as many times as you need, take your time
3. Write down (below) what the Lord is saying to you today
4. Live with this Word in your heart through the day

---

---

## Saturday, November 23, 2024
Saint Clement I, Pope and Martyr; Saint Columban, Abbot;
USA: Blessed Miguel Agustín Pro, Priest and Martyr; BVM

**First Reading:** Revelation 11: 4-12

4 These are the two olive trees and the two lamp stands, standing before the Lord of the earth. 5 If anyone desires to harm them, fire proceeds out of their mouth and devours their enemies. If anyone desires to harm them, he must be killed in this way. 6 These have the power to shut up the sky, that it may not rain during the days of their prophecy. They have power over the waters, to turn them into blood, and to strike the earth with every plague, as often as they desire.

7 When they have finished their testimony, the beast that comes up out of the abyss will make war with them, and overcome them, and kill them. 8 Their dead bodies will be in the street of the great city, which spiritually is called Sodom and Egypt, where also their Lord was crucified. 9 From among the peoples, tribes, languages, and nations, people will look at their dead bodies for three and a half days, and will not allow their dead bodies to be laid in a tomb. 10 Those who dwell on the earth will rejoice

over them, and they will be glad. They will give gifts to one another, because these two prophets tormented those who dwell on the earth.

11 After the three and a half days, the breath of life from God entered into them, and they stood on their feet. Great fear fell on those who saw them. 12 I heard a loud voice from heaven saying to them, "Come up here!" They went up into heaven in a cloud, and their enemies saw them.

**Responsorial Psalm:** Psalms 144: 1, 2, 9-10

1 Blessed be Yahweh, my rock,
who trains my hands to war,
and my fingers to battle—
2 my loving kindness, my fortress,
my high tower, my deliverer,
my shield, and he in whom I take refuge,
who subdues my people under me.
9 I will sing a new song to you, God.
On a ten-stringed lyre, I will sing praises to you.
10 You are he who gives salvation to kings,
who rescues David, his servant, from the deadly sword.

**Gospel: Luke 20: 27-40**

27 Some of the Sadducees came to him, those who deny that there is a resurrection. 28 They asked him, "Teacher, Moses wrote to us that if a man's brother dies having a wife, and he is childless, his brother should take the wife and raise up children for his brother. 29 There were therefore seven brothers. The first took a wife, and died childless. 30 The second took her as wife, and he died childless. 31 The third took her, and likewise the seven all left no children, and died. 32 Afterward the woman also died. 33 Therefore in the resurrection whose wife of them will she be? For the seven had her as a wife."

34 Jesus said to them, "The children of this age marry and are given in marriage. 35 But those who are considered worthy to attain to that age and the resurrection from the dead neither marry nor are given in marriage. 36 For they can't die any more, for they are like the angels and are children of God, being children of the resurrection. 37 But that the dead are raised, even Moses showed at the bush, when he called the Lord 'The God of Abraham, the God of Isaac, and the God of Jacob.' * 38 Now he is not the God of the dead, but of the living, for all are alive to him."

39 Some of the scribes answered, "Teacher, you speak well." 40 They didn't dare to ask him any more questions.

1. Invite the Holy Spirit into this reading, asking the Author of Scripture to speak to you through His Word
2. Read today's passage as many times as you need, take your time
3. Write down (below) what the Lord is saying to you today
4. Live with this Word in your heart through the day

---

---

## Sunday, November 24, 2024
### OUR LORD JESUS CHRIST, KING OF THE UNIVERSE

**First Reading:** Daniel 7: 13-14

13 "I saw in the night visions, and behold, there came with the clouds of the sky one like a son of man, and he came even to the Ancient of Days, and they brought him near before him. 14 Dominion was given him, and glory, and a kingdom, that all the peoples, nations, and languages should serve him. His dominion is an everlasting dominion, which will not pass away, and his kingdom one that will not be destroyed.

**Responsorial Psalm:** Psalms 93: 1-2, 5

1 Yahweh reigns!
He is clothed with majesty!
Yahweh is armed with strength.
The world also is established.
It can't be moved.
2 Your throne is established from long ago.
You are from everlasting.
5 Your statutes stand firm.
Holiness adorns your house,
Yahweh, forever more.

**Second Reading:** Revelation 1: 5-8

5 and from Jesus Christ, the faithful witness, the firstborn of the dead, and the ruler of the kings of the earth. To him who loves us, and washed us from our sins by his blood—
6 and he made us to be a Kingdom, priests* to his God and Father—to him be the glory and the dominion forever and ever. Amen.
7 Behold,§ he is coming with the clouds, and every eye will see him, including those who pierced him. All the tribes of the earth will mourn over him. Even so, Amen.
8 "I am the Alpha and the Omega,†" says the Lord God,‡ "who is and who was and who is to come, the Almighty."

**Gospel: John 18: 33b-37**

33 Pilate therefore entered again into the Praetorium, called Jesus, and said to him, "Are you the King of the Jews?"
34 Jesus answered him, "Do you say this by yourself, or did others tell you about me?"
35 Pilate answered, "I'm not a Jew, am I? Your own nation and the chief priests delivered you to me. What have you done?"
36 Jesus answered, "My Kingdom is not of this world. If my Kingdom were of this world, then my servants would fight, that I wouldn't be delivered to the Jews. But now my Kingdom is not from here."
37 Pilate therefore said to him, "Are you a king then?"
Jesus answered, "You say that I am a king. For this reason I have been born, and for this reason I have come into the world, that I should testify to the truth. Everyone who is of the truth listens to my voice."

1. Invite the Holy Spirit into this reading, asking the Author of Scripture to speak to you through His Word
2. Read today's passage as many times as you need, take your time
3. Write down (below) what the Lord is saying to you today
4. Live with this Word in your heart through the day

_____

_____

# Monday, November 25, 2024
## Saint Catherine of Alexandria, Virgin and Martyr

**First Reading:** Revelation 14: 1-3, 4b-5

1 I saw, and behold, the Lamb standing on Mount Zion, and with him a number, one hundred forty-four thousand, having his name and the name of his Father written on their foreheads. 2 I heard a sound from heaven like the sound of many waters and like the sound of a great thunder. The sound which I heard was like that of harpists playing on their harps. 3 They sing a new song before the throne and before the four living creatures and the elders. No one could learn the song except the one hundred forty-four thousand, those who had been redeemed out of the earth. 4b These are those who follow the Lamb wherever he goes. These were redeemed by Jesus from among men, the first fruits to God and to the Lamb. 5 In their mouth was found no lie, for they are blameless.

**Responsorial Psalm:** Psalms 24: 1bc-6

1 The earth is Yahweh's, with its fullness;
the world, and those who dwell in it.
2 For he has founded it on the seas,
and established it on the floods.
3 Who may ascend to Yahweh's hill?
Who may stand in his holy place?
4 He who has clean hands and a pure heart;
who has not lifted up his soul to falsehood,
and has not sworn deceitfully.
5 He shall receive a blessing from Yahweh,
righteousness from the God of his salvation.
6 This is the generation of those who seek Him,
who seek your face—even Jacob.

**Gospel: Luke 21: 1-4**

1 He looked up and saw the rich people who were putting their gifts into the treasury. 2 He saw a certain poor widow casting in two small brass coins.† 3 He said, "Truly I tell

you, this poor widow put in more than all of them, 4 for all these put in gifts for God from their abundance, but she, out of her poverty, put in all that she had to live on."

1. Invite the Holy Spirit into this reading, asking the Author of Scripture to speak to you through His Word
2. Read today's passage as many times as you need, take your time
3. Write down (below) what the Lord is saying to you today
4. Live with this Word in your heart through the day

_____

_____

## Tuesday, November 26, 2024

**First Reading:** Revelation 14: 14-19

14 I looked, and saw a white cloud, and on the cloud one sitting like a son of man,* having on his head a golden crown, and in his hand a sharp sickle. 15 Another angel came out of the temple, crying with a loud voice to him who sat on the cloud, "Send your sickle and reap, for the hour to reap has come; for the harvest of the earth is ripe!" 16 He who sat on the cloud thrust his sickle on the earth, and the earth was reaped.
17 Another angel came out of the temple which is in heaven. He also had a sharp sickle. 18 Another angel came out from the altar, he who has power over fire, and he called with a great voice to him who had the sharp sickle, saying, "Send your sharp sickle and gather the clusters of the vine of the earth, for the earth's grapes are fully ripe!" 19 The angel thrust his sickle into the earth, and gathered the vintage of the earth and threw it into the great wine press of the wrath of God.

**Responsorial Psalm:** Psalms 96: 10-13

10 Say among the nations, "Yahweh reigns."
The world is also established.
It can't be moved.
He will judge the peoples with equity.

11 Let the heavens be glad, and let the earth rejoice.
Let the sea roar, and its fullness!
12 Let the field and all that is in it exult!
Then all the trees of the woods shall sing for joy
13 before Yahweh; for he comes,
for he comes to judge the earth.
He will judge the world with righteousness,
the peoples with his truth.

## Gospel: Luke 21: 5-11

5 As some were talking about the temple and how it was decorated with beautiful stones and gifts, he said, 6 "As for these things which you see, the days will come in which there will not be left here one stone on another that will not be thrown down."
7 They asked him, "Teacher, so when will these things be? What is the sign that these things are about to happen?"
8 He said, "Watch out that you don't get led astray, for many will come in my name, saying, 'I am he‡,' and, 'The time is at hand.' Therefore don't follow them. 9 When you hear of wars and disturbances, don't be terrified, for these things must happen first, but the end won't come immediately."
10 Then he said to them, "Nation will rise against nation, and kingdom against kingdom. 11 There will be great earthquakes, famines, and plagues in various places. There will be terrors and great signs from heaven.

1. Invite the Holy Spirit into this reading, asking the Author of Scripture to speak to you through His Word
2. Read today's passage as many times as you need, take your time
3. Write down (below) what the Lord is saying to you today
4. Live with this Word in your heart through the day

_____

_____

**Wednesday, November 27, 2024**

**First Reading:** Revelation 15: 1-4

1 I saw another great and marvelous sign in the sky: seven angels having the seven last plagues, for in them God's wrath is finished.

2 I saw something like a sea of glass mixed with fire, and those who overcame the beast, his image,† and the number of his name, standing on the sea of glass, having harps of God. 3 They sang the song of Moses, the servant of God, and the song of the Lamb, saying,

"Great and marvelous are your works, Lord God, the Almighty!

Righteous and true are your ways, you King of the nations.

4 Who wouldn't fear you, Lord,

and glorify your name?

For you only are holy.

For all the nations will come and worship before you.

For your righteous acts have been revealed."

**Responsorial Psalm:** Psalms 98: 1-3ab, 7-9

1 Sing to Yahweh a new song,

for he has done marvelous things!

His right hand and his holy arm have worked salvation for him.

2 Yahweh has made known his salvation.

He has openly shown his righteousness in the sight of the nations.

3 He has remembered his loving kindness and his faithfulness toward the house of Israel.

All the ends of the earth have seen the salvation of our God.

7 Let the sea roar with its fullness;

the world, and those who dwell therein.

8 Let the rivers clap their hands.

Let the mountains sing for joy together.

9 Let them sing before Yahweh,

for he comes to judge the earth.

He will judge the world with righteousness,

and the peoples with equity.

**Gospel: Luke 21: 12-19**

12 But before all these things, they will lay their hands on you and will persecute you, delivering you up to synagogues and prisons, bringing you before kings and governors

for my name's sake. 13  It will turn out as a testimony for you. 14  Settle it therefore in your hearts not to meditate beforehand how to answer, 15  for I will give you a mouth and wisdom which all your adversaries will not be able to withstand or to contradict. 16  You will be handed over even by parents, brothers, relatives, and friends. They will cause some of you to be put to death. 17  You will be hated by all men for my name's sake. 18  And not a hair of your head will perish.

19  "By your endurance you will win your lives.

1. Invite the Holy Spirit into this reading, asking the Author of Scripture to speak to you through His Word
2. Read today's passage as many times as you need, take your time
3. Write down (below) what the Lord is saying to you today
4. Live with this Word in your heart through the day

_____

_____

### Thursday, November 28, 2024
Thanksgiving Day
**First Reading:** Revelation 18: 1-2, 21-23; 19: 1-3, 9a

1 After these things, I saw another angel coming down out of the sky, having great authority. The earth was illuminated with his glory. 2 He cried with a mighty voice, saying, "Fallen, fallen is Babylon the great, and she has become a habitation of demons, a prison of every unclean spirit, and a prison of every unclean and hated bird!
21 A mighty angel took up a stone like a great millstone and cast it into the sea, saying, "Thus with violence will Babylon, the great city, be thrown down, and will be found no more at all. 22 The voice of harpists, minstrels, flute players, and trumpeters will be heard no more at all in you. No craftsman of whatever craft will be found any more at all in you. The sound of a mill will be heard no more at all in you. 23 The light of a lamp will shine no more at all in you. The voice of the bridegroom and of the bride will be heard no more at all in you, for your merchants were the princes of the earth; for with your sorcery all the nations were deceived.
1 After these things I heard something like a loud voice of a great multitude in heaven, saying, "Hallelujah! Salvation, power, and glory belong to our God; 2 for his judgments

are true and righteous. For he has judged the great prostitute who corrupted the earth with her sexual immorality, and he has avenged the blood of his servants at her hand."

3 A second said, "Hallelujah! Her smoke goes up forever and ever."

9a He said to me, "Write, 'Blessed are those who are invited to the wedding supper of the Lamb.'

**Responsorial Psalm:** Psalms 100: 2- 5

2 Serve Yahweh with gladness.
Come before his presence with singing.
3 Know that Yahweh, he is God.
It is he who has made us, and we are his.
We are his people, and the sheep of his pasture.
4 Enter into his gates with thanksgiving,
and into his courts with praise.
Give thanks to him, and bless his name.
5 For Yahweh is good.
His loving kindness endures forever,
his faithfulness to all generations.

**Gospel: Luke 21: 20-28**

20 "But when you see Jerusalem surrounded by armies, then know that its desolation is at hand. 21 Then let those who are in Judea flee to the mountains. Let those who are in the middle of her depart. Let those who are in the country not enter therein. 22 For these are days of vengeance, that all things which are written may be fulfilled. 23 Woe to those who are pregnant and to those who nurse infants in those days! For there will be great distress in the land and wrath to this people. 24 They will fall by the edge of the sword, and will be led captive into all the nations. Jerusalem will be trampled down by the Gentiles until the times of the Gentiles are fulfilled.

25 "There will be signs in the sun, moon, and stars; and on the earth anxiety of nations, in perplexity for the roaring of the sea and the waves; 26 men fainting for fear and for expectation of the things which are coming on the world, for the powers of the heavens will be shaken. 27 Then they will see the Son of Man coming in a cloud with power and great glory. 28 But when these things begin to happen, look up and lift up your heads, because your redemption is near."

1. Invite the Holy Spirit into this reading, asking the Author of Scripture to speak to you through His Word
2. Read today's passage as many times as you need, take your time
3. Write down (below) what the Lord is saying to you today
4. Live with this Word in your heart through the day

---

---

## Friday, November 29, 2024

**First Reading:** Revelation 20: 1-4, 11-21: 2

1 I saw an angel coming down out of heaven, having the key of the abyss and a great chain in his hand. 2 He seized the dragon, the old serpent, who is the devil and Satan, who deceives the whole inhabited earth,† and bound him for a thousand years, 3 and cast him into the abyss, and shut it and sealed it over him, that he should deceive the nations no more until the thousand years were finished. After this, he must be freed for a short time.

4 I saw thrones, and they sat on them, and judgment was given to them. I saw the souls of those who had been beheaded for the testimony of Jesus and for the word of God, and such as didn't worship the beast nor his image, and didn't receive the mark on their forehead and on their hand. They lived and reigned with Christ for a thousand years.

11 I saw a great white throne and him who sat on it, from whose face the earth and the heaven fled away. There was found no place for them. 12 I saw the dead, the great and the small, standing before the throne, and they opened books. Another book was opened, which is the book of life. The dead were judged out of the things which were written in the books, according to their works. 13 The sea gave up the dead who were in it. Death and Hades‡ gave up the dead who were in them. They were judged, each one according to his works. 14 Death and Hades§ were thrown into the lake of fire. This is the second death, the lake of fire. 15 If anyone was not found written in the book of life, he was cast into the lake of fire.

I saw a new heaven and a new earth, for the first heaven and the first earth have passed away, and the sea is no more. 2 I saw the holy city, New Jerusalem, coming down out of heaven from God, prepared like a bride adorned for her husband.

**Responsorial Psalm:** Psalms 84: 3-6a and 8a

3 Yes, the sparrow has found a home,
and the swallow a nest for herself, where she may have her young,
near your altars, Yahweh of Armies, my King, and my God.
4 Blessed are those who dwell in your house.
They are always praising you.
5 Blessed are those whose strength is in you,
who have set their hearts on a pilgrimage.
6 Passing through the valley of Weeping, they make it a place of springs.
8 Yahweh, God of Armies, hear my prayer.

**Gospel: Luke 21: 29-33**

29 He told them a parable. "See the fig tree and all the trees. 30 When they are already budding, you see it and know by your own selves that the summer is already near. 31 Even so you also, when you see these things happening, know that God's Kingdom is near. 32 Most certainly I tell you, this generation will not pass away until all things are accomplished. 33 Heaven and earth will pass away, but my words will by no means pass away.

1. Invite the Holy Spirit into this reading, asking the Author of Scripture to speak to you through His Word
2. Read today's passage as many times as you need, take your time
3. Write down (below) what the Lord is saying to you today
4. Live with this Word in your heart through the day

_____

_____

### Saturday, November 30, 2024
Saint Andrew, Apostle

**First Reading:** Romans 10: 9-18

9 that if you will confess with your mouth that Jesus is Lord and believe in your heart that God raised him from the dead, you will be saved. 10 For with the heart one believes resulting in righteousness; and with the mouth confession is made resulting in salvation. 11 For the Scripture says, "Whoever believes in him will not be disappointed."*

12 For there is no distinction between Jew and Greek; for the same Lord is Lord of all, and is rich to all who call on him. 13 For, "Whoever will call on the name of the Lord will be saved."* 14 How then will they call on him in whom they have not believed? How will they believe in him whom they have not heard? How will they hear without a preacher? 15 And how will they preach unless they are sent? As it is written:
"How beautiful are the feet of those who preach the Good News of peace,
who bring glad tidings of good things!"*

16 But they didn't all listen to the glad news. For Isaiah says, "Lord, who has believed our report?"* 17 So faith comes by hearing, and hearing by the word of God. 18 But I say, didn't they hear? Yes, most certainly,
"Their sound went out into all the earth,
their words to the ends of the world."

**Responsorial Psalm:** Psalms 19: 8- 11

8 Yahweh's precepts are right, rejoicing the heart.
Yahweh's commandment is pure, enlightening the eyes.
9 The fear of Yahweh is clean, enduring forever.
Yahweh's ordinances are true, and righteous altogether.
10 They are more to be desired than gold, yes, than much fine gold,
sweeter also than honey and the extract of the honeycomb.
11 Moreover your servant is warned by them.
In keeping them there is great reward.

**Gospel: Matthew 4: 18-22**

18 Walking by the sea of Galilee, he‡ saw two brothers: Simon, who is called Peter, and Andrew, his brother, casting a net into the sea; for they were fishermen. 19 He said to them, "Come after me, and I will make you fishers for men."

20 They immediately left their nets and followed him. 21 Going on from there, he saw two other brothers, James the son of Zebedee, and John his brother, in the boat with Zebedee their father, mending their nets. He called them. 22 They immediately left the boat and their father, and followed him.

1. Invite the Holy Spirit into this reading, asking the Author of Scripture to speak to you through His Word
2. Read today's passage as many times as you need, take your time
3. Write down (below) what the Lord is saying to you today
4. Live with this Word in your heart through the day

_____

_____

## Sunday, December 1, 2024
### FIRST SUNDAY OF ADVENT

**First Reading:** Jeremiah 33: 14-16

14 "Behold, the days come," says Yahweh, "that I will perform that good word which I have spoken concerning the house of Israel and concerning the house of Judah.
15 "In those days and at that time,
I will cause a Branch of righteousness to grow up to David.
He will execute justice and righteousness in the land.
16 In those days Judah will be saved,
and Jerusalem will dwell safely.
This is the name by which she will be called:
Yahweh our righteousness."

**Responsorial Psalm:** Psalms 25: 4-5, 8-10, 14

4 Show me your ways, Yahweh.
Teach me your paths.
5 Guide me in your truth, and teach me,
for you are the God of my salvation.
I wait for you all day long.
8 Good and upright is Yahweh,
therefore he will instruct sinners in the way.
9 He will guide the humble in justice.

He will teach the humble his way.
10 All the paths of Yahweh are loving kindness and truth
to such as keep his covenant and his testimonies.
14 The friendship of Yahweh is with those who fear him.
He will show them his covenant.

**Second Reading:** First Thessalonians 3: 12 – 4: 2

12 May the Lord make you to increase and abound in love toward one another and toward all men, even as we also do toward you, 13 to the end he may establish your hearts blameless in holiness before our God and Father at the coming of our Lord Jesus with all his saints.
1 Finally then, brothers, we beg and exhort you in the Lord Jesus, that as you received from us how you ought to walk and to please God, that you abound more and more. 2 For you know what instructions we gave you through the Lord Jesus.

**Gospel: Luke 21: 25-28, 34-36**

25 "There will be signs in the sun, moon, and stars; and on the earth anxiety of nations, in perplexity for the roaring of the sea and the waves; 26 men fainting for fear and for expectation of the things which are coming on the world, for the powers of the heavens will be shaken. 27 Then they will see the Son of Man coming in a cloud with power and great glory. 28 But when these things begin to happen, look up and lift up your heads, because your redemption is near."
34 "So be careful, or your hearts will be loaded down with carousing, drunkenness, and cares of this life, and that day will come on you suddenly. 35 For it will come like a snare on all those who dwell on the surface of all the earth. 36 Therefore be watchful all the time, praying that you may be counted worthy to escape all these things that will happen, and to stand before the Son of Man."

1. Invite the Holy Spirit into this reading, asking the Author of Scripture to speak to you through His Word
2. Read today's passage as many times as you need, take your time
3. Write down (below) what the Lord is saying to you today
4. Live with this Word in your heart through the day

_____

_____

**First Reading:** Isaiah 2: 1-5

1 This is what Isaiah the son of Amoz saw concerning Judah and Jerusalem.
2 It shall happen in the latter days, that the mountain of Yahweh's house shall be established on the top of the mountains,
and shall be raised above the hills;
and all nations shall flow to it.
3 Many peoples shall go and say,
"Come, let's go up to the mountain of Yahweh,
to the house of the God of Jacob;
and he will teach us of his ways,
and we will walk in his paths."
For the law shall go out of Zion,
and Yahweh's word from Jerusalem.
4 He will judge between the nations,
and will decide concerning many peoples.
They shall beat their swords into plowshares,
and their spears into pruning hooks.
Nation shall not lift up sword against nation,
neither shall they learn war any more.
5 House of Jacob, come, and let's walk in the light of Yahweh.

**Responsorial Psalm:** Psalms 122: 1-9

1 I was glad when they said to me,
"Let's go to Yahweh's house!"
2 Our feet are standing within your gates, Jerusalem!
3 Jerusalem is built as a city that is compact together,
4 where the tribes go up, even Yah's tribes,
according to an ordinance for Israel,
to give thanks to Yahweh's name.
5 For there are set thrones for judgment,
the thrones of David's house.
6 Pray for the peace of Jerusalem.
Those who love you will prosper.

7 Peace be within your walls,
and prosperity within your palaces.
8 For my brothers' and companions' sakes,
I will now say, "Peace be within you."
9 For the sake of the house of Yahweh our God,
I will seek your good.

**Gospel: Matthew 8: 5-11**

5 When he came into Capernaum, a centurion came to him, asking him for help, 6 saying, "Lord, my servant lies in the house paralyzed, grievously tormented."
7 Jesus said to him, "I will come and heal him."
8 The centurion answered, "Lord, I'm not worthy for you to come under my roof. Just say the word, and my servant will be healed. 9 For I am also a man under authority, having under myself soldiers. I tell this one, 'Go,' and he goes; and tell another, 'Come,' and he comes; and tell my servant, 'Do this,' and he does it."
10 When Jesus heard it, he marveled and said to those who followed, "Most certainly I tell you, I haven't found so great a faith, not even in Israel. 11 I tell you that many will come from the east and the west, and will sit down with Abraham, Isaac, and Jacob in the Kingdom of Heaven

1. Invite the Holy Spirit into this reading, asking the Author of Scripture to speak to you through His Word
2. Read today's passage as many times as you need, take your time
3. Write down (below) what the Lord is saying to you today
4. Live with this Word in your heart through the day

_____

_____

**Tuesday, December 3, 2024**
Saint Francis Xavier, Priest

**First Reading:** Isaiah 11: 1-10

1 A shoot will come out of the stock of Jesse,
and a branch out of his roots will bear fruit.
2 Yahweh's Spirit will rest on him:
the spirit of wisdom and understanding,
the spirit of counsel and might,
the spirit of knowledge and of the fear of Yahweh.
3 His delight will be in the fear of Yahweh.
He will not judge by the sight of his eyes,
neither decide by the hearing of his ears;
4 but he will judge the poor with righteousness,
and decide with equity for the humble of the earth.
He will strike the earth with the rod of his mouth;
and with the breath of his lips he will kill the wicked.
5 Righteousness will be the belt around his waist,
and faithfulness the belt around his waist.
6 The wolf will live with the lamb,
and the leopard will lie down with the young goat,
the calf, the young lion, and the fattened calf together;
and a little child will lead them.
7 The cow and the bear will graze.
Their young ones will lie down together.
The lion will eat straw like the ox.
8 The nursing child will play near a cobra's hole,
and the weaned child will put his hand on the viper's den.
9 They will not hurt nor destroy in all my holy mountain;
for the earth will be full of the knowledge of Yahweh,
as the waters cover the sea.
10 It will happen in that day that the nations will seek the root of Jesse, who stands as
a banner of the peoples; and his resting place will be glorious.

**Responsorial Psalm:** Psalms 72: 1-2, 7-8, 12-13, 17

1 God, give the king your justice;
your righteousness to the royal son.
2 He will judge your people with righteousness,
and your poor with justice.
7 In his days, the righteous shall flourish,
and abundance of peace, until the moon is no more.

8 He shall have dominion also from sea to sea,
from the River to the ends of the earth.
12 For he will deliver the needy when he cries;
the poor, who has no helper.
13 He will have pity on the poor and needy.
He will save the souls of the needy.
17 His name endures forever.
His name continues as long as the sun.
Men shall be blessed by him.
All nations will call him blessed.

### Gospel: Luke 10: 21-24

21 In that same hour, Jesus rejoiced in the Holy Spirit, and said, "I thank you, O Father, Lord of heaven and earth, that you have hidden these things from the wise and understanding, and revealed them to little children. Yes, Father, for so it was well-pleasing in your sight."
22 Turning to the disciples, he said, "All things have been delivered to me by my Father. No one knows who the Son is, except the Father, and who the Father is, except the Son, and he to whomever the Son desires to reveal him."
23 Turning to the disciples, he said privately, "Blessed are the eyes which see the things that you see, 24 for I tell you that many prophets and kings desired to see the things which you see, and didn't see them, and to hear the things which you hear, and didn't hear them."

1. Invite the Holy Spirit into this reading, asking the Author of Scripture to speak to you through His Word
2. Read today's passage as many times as you need, take your time
3. Write down (below) what the Lord is saying to you today
4. Live with this Word in your heart through the day

_____

_____

### Wednesday, December 4, 2024
Saint John Damascene, Priest and Doctor of the Church

**First Reading:** Isaiah 25: 6-10a

6 In this mountain, Yahweh of Armies will make all peoples a feast of choice meat,† a feast of choice wines, of choice meat full of marrow, of well refined choice wines. 7 He will destroy in this mountain the surface of the covering that covers all peoples, and the veil that is spread over all nations. 8 He has swallowed up death forever! The Lord Yahweh will wipe away tears from off all faces. He will take the reproach of his people away from off all the earth, for Yahweh has spoken it.
9 It shall be said in that day, "Behold, this is our God! We have waited for him, and he will save us! This is Yahweh! We have waited for him. We will be glad and rejoice in his salvation!" 10 For Yahweh's hand will rest in this mountain.

**Responsorial Psalm:** Psalms 23: 1-6

1 Yahweh is my shepherd;
I shall lack nothing.
2 He makes me lie down in green pastures.
He leads me beside still waters.
3 He restores my soul.
He guides me in the paths of righteousness for his name's sake.
4 Even though I walk through the valley of the shadow of death,
I will fear no evil, for you are with me.
Your rod and your staff,
they comfort me.
5 You prepare a table before me
in the presence of my enemies.
You anoint my head with oil.
My cup runs over.
6 Surely goodness and loving kindness shall follow me all the days of my life,
and I will dwell in Yahweh's house forever.

**Gospel: Matthew 15: 29-37**

29 Jesus departed from there and came near to the sea of Galilee; and he went up on the mountain and sat there. 30 Great multitudes came to him, having with them the lame, blind, mute, maimed, and many others, and they put them down at his feet. He

healed them, 31 so that the multitude wondered when they saw the mute speaking, the injured healed, the lame walking, and the blind seeing—and they glorified the God of Israel.

32 Jesus summoned his disciples and said, "I have compassion on the multitude, because they have continued with me now three days and have nothing to eat. I don't want to send them away fasting, or they might faint on the way."

33 The disciples said to him, "Where could we get so many loaves in a deserted place as to satisfy so great a multitude?"

34 Jesus said to them, "How many loaves do you have?"
They said, "Seven, and a few small fish."

35 He commanded the multitude to sit down on the ground; 36 and he took the seven loaves and the fish. He gave thanks and broke them, and gave to the disciples, and the disciples to the multitudes. 37 They all ate and were filled. They took up seven baskets full of the broken pieces that were left over.

1. Invite the Holy Spirit into this reading, asking the Author of Scripture to speak to you through His Word
2. Read today's passage as many times as you need, take your time
3. Write down (below) what the Lord is saying to you today
4. Live with this Word in your heart through the day

_____

_____

## Thursday, December 5, 2024

**First Reading:** Isaiah 26: 1-6

1 In that day, this song will be sung in the land of Judah:
"We have a strong city.
God appoints salvation for walls and bulwarks.
2 Open the gates, that the righteous nation may enter:
the one which keeps faith.
3 You will keep whoever's mind is steadfast in perfect peace,

because he trusts in you.
4 Trust in Yahweh forever;
for in Yah, Yahweh, is an everlasting Rock.
5 For he has brought down those who dwell on high, the lofty city.
He lays it low.
He lays it low even to the ground.
He brings it even to the dust.
6 The foot shall tread it down,
even the feet of the poor
and the steps of the needy."

**Responsorial Psalm:** Psalms 118: 1 and 8-9, 19-21, 25-27a

1 Give thanks to Yahweh, for he is good,
for his loving kindness endures forever.
8 It is better to take refuge in Yahweh,
than to put confidence in man.
9 It is better to take refuge in Yahweh,
than to put confidence in princes.
19 Open to me the gates of righteousness.
I will enter into them.
I will give thanks to Yah.
20 This is the gate of Yahweh;
the righteous will enter into it.
21 I will give thanks to you, for you have answered me,
and have become my salvation.
25 Save us now, we beg you, Yahweh!
Yahweh, we beg you, send prosperity now.
26 Blessed is he who comes in Yahweh's name!
We have blessed you out of Yahweh's house.
27 Yahweh is God, and he has given us light.

**Gospel: Matthew 7: 21, 24-27**

21 "Not everyone who says to me, 'Lord, Lord,' will enter into the Kingdom of Heaven,
but he who does the will of my Father who is in heaven.
24 "Everyone therefore who hears these words of mine and does them, I will liken him
to a wise man who built his house on a rock. 25 The rain came down, the floods came,

and the winds blew and beat on that house; and it didn't fall, for it was founded on the rock. 26 Everyone who hears these words of mine and doesn't do them will be like a foolish man who built his house on the sand. 27 The rain came down, the floods came, and the winds blew and beat on that house; and it fell—and its fall was great."

1. Invite the Holy Spirit into this reading, asking the Author of Scripture to speak to you through His Word
2. Read today's passage as many times as you need, take your time
3. Write down (below) what the Lord is saying to you today
4. Live with this Word in your heart through the day

---

---

### Friday, December 6, 2024
Saint Nicholas, Bishop

**First Reading:** Isaiah 29: 17-24

17 Isn't it yet a very little while, and Lebanon will be turned into a fruitful field, and the fruitful field will be regarded as a forest? 18 In that day, the deaf will hear the words of the book, and the eyes of the blind will see out of obscurity and out of darkness. 19 The humble also will increase their joy in Yahweh, and the poor among men will rejoice in the Holy One of Israel. 20 For the ruthless is brought to nothing, and the scoffer ceases, and all those who are alert to do evil are cut off— 21 who cause a person to be indicted by a word, and lay a snare for one who reproves in the gate, and who deprive the innocent of justice with false testimony.
22 Therefore Yahweh, who redeemed Abraham, says concerning the house of Jacob: "Jacob shall no longer be ashamed, neither shall his face grow pale. 23 But when he sees his children, the work of my hands, in the middle of him, they will sanctify my name. Yes, they will sanctify the Holy One of Jacob, and will stand in awe of the God of Israel. 24 They also who err in spirit will come to understanding, and those who grumble will receive instruction."

**Responsorial Psalm:** Psalms 27: 1, 4, 13-14

1 Yahweh is my light and my salvation.
Whom shall I fear?
Yahweh is the strength of my life.
Of whom shall I be afraid?
4 One thing I have asked of Yahweh, that I will seek after:
that I may dwell in Yahweh's house all the days of my life,
to see Yahweh's beauty,
and to inquire in his temple.
13 I am still confident of this:
I will see the goodness of Yahweh in the land of the living.
14 Wait for Yahweh.
Be strong, and let your heart take courage.
Yes, wait for Yahweh.

**Gospel: Matthew 9: 27-31**

27 As Jesus passed by from there, two blind men followed him, calling out and saying, "Have mercy on us, son of David!" 28 When he had come into the house, the blind men came to him. Jesus said to them, "Do you believe that I am able to do this?"
They told him, "Yes, Lord."
29 Then he touched their eyes, saying, "According to your faith be it done to you." 30 Then their eyes were opened. Jesus strictly commanded them, saying, "See that no one knows about this." 31 But they went out and spread abroad his fame in all that land.

1. Invite the Holy Spirit into this reading, asking the Author of Scripture to speak to you through His Word
2. Read today's passage as many times as you need, take your time
3. Write down (below) what the Lord is saying to you today
4. Live with this Word in your heart through the day

_____

_____

**Saturday, December 7, 2024**
Saint Ambrose, Bishop and Doctor of the Church

**First Reading:** Isaiah 30: 19-21, 23-26

19 For the people will dwell in Zion at Jerusalem. You will weep no more. He will surely be gracious to you at the voice of your cry. When he hears you, he will answer you. 20 Though the Lord may give you the bread of adversity and the water of affliction, yet your teachers won't be hidden any more, but your eyes will see your teachers; 21 and when you turn to the right hand, and when you turn to the left, your ears will hear a voice behind you, saying, "This is the way. Walk in it."
23 He will give the rain for your seed, with which you will sow the ground; and bread of the increase of the ground will be rich and plentiful. In that day, your livestock will feed in large pastures. 24 The oxen likewise and the young donkeys that till the ground will eat savory feed, which has been winnowed with the shovel and with the fork. 25 There will be brooks and streams of water on every lofty mountain and on every high hill in the day of the great slaughter, when the towers fall. 26 Moreover the light of the moon will be like the light of the sun, and the light of the sun will be seven times brighter, like the light of seven days, in the day that Yahweh binds up the fracture of his people, and heals the wound they were struck with.

**Responsorial Psalm:** Psalms 147: 1-6

1 Praise Yah,
for it is good to sing praises to our God;
for it is pleasant and fitting to praise him.
2 Yahweh builds up Jerusalem.
He gathers together the outcasts of Israel.
3 He heals the broken in heart,
and binds up their wounds.
4 He counts the number of the stars.
He calls them all by their names.
5 Great is our Lord, and mighty in power.
His understanding is infinite.
6 Yahweh upholds the humble.
He brings the wicked down to the ground.

**Gospel: Matthew 9: 35 – 10: 1, 5a, 6-8**

35 Jesus went about all the cities and the villages, teaching in their synagogues and preaching the Good News of the Kingdom, and healing every disease and every sickness

among the people. 36 But when he saw the multitudes, he was moved with compassion for them because they were harassed§ and scattered, like sheep without a shepherd. 37 Then he said to his disciples, "The harvest indeed is plentiful, but the laborers are few. 38  Pray therefore that the Lord of the harvest will send out laborers into his harvest." 1 He called to himself his twelve disciples, and gave them authority over unclean spirits, to cast them out, and to heal every disease and every sickness.

5 Jesus sent these twelve out and commanded them, saying, "Don't go among the Gentiles, and don't enter into any city of the Samaritans. 6  Rather, go to the lost sheep of the house of Israel. 7  As you go, preach, saying, 'The Kingdom of Heaven is at hand!' 8  Heal the sick, cleanse the lepers,‡ and cast out demons. Freely you received, so freely give.

1. Invite the Holy Spirit into this reading, asking the Author of Scripture to speak to you through His Word
2. Read today's passage as many times as you need, take your time
3. Write down (below) what the Lord is saying to you today
4. Live with this Word in your heart through the day

_____

_____

### Sunday, December 8, 2024
### SECOND SUNDAY OF ADVENT

**First Reading:** Baruch 5: 1-9

1 Take off the garment of your mourning and affliction, O Jerusalem, and put on forever the beauty of the glory from God. 2 Put on the robe of the righteousness from God. Set on your head a diadem of the glory of the Everlasting. 3 For God will show your splendor everywhere under heaven. 4 For your name will be called by God forever "Righteous Peace, Godly Glory".

5 Arise, O Jerusalem, and stand upon the height. Look around you toward the east and see your children gathered from the going down of the sun to its rising at the word of the Holy One, rejoicing that God has remembered them. 6 For they went from you on foot, being led away by their enemies, but God brings them in to you carried on high with glory, on a royal throne. 7 For God has appointed that every high mountain and

the everlasting hills should be made low, and the valleys filled up to make the ground level, that Israel may go safely in the glory of God. 8 Moreover the woods and every sweet smelling tree have shaded Israel by the commandment of God. 9 For God will lead Israel with joy in the light of his glory with the mercy and righteousness that come from him.

**Responsorial Psalm:** Psalms 126: 1-6

1 When Yahweh brought back those who returned to Zion,
we were like those who dream.
2 Then our mouth was filled with laughter,
and our tongue with singing.
Then they said among the nations,
"Yahweh has done great things for them."
3 Yahweh has done great things for us,
and we are glad.
4 Restore our fortunes again, Yahweh,
like the streams in the Negev.
5 Those who sow in tears will reap in joy.
6 He who goes out weeping, carrying seed for sowing,
will certainly come again with joy, carrying his sheaves.

**Second Reading:** Philippians 1: 4-6, 8-11

4 always in every request of mine on behalf of you all, making my requests with joy, 5 for your partnership† in furtherance of the Good News from the first day until now; 6 being confident of this very thing, that he who began a good work in you will complete it until the day of Jesus Christ.
8 For God is my witness, how I long after all of you in the tender mercies of Christ Jesus.
9 This I pray, that your love may abound yet more and more in knowledge and all discernment, 10 so that you may approve the things that are excellent, that you may be sincere and without offense to the day of Christ, 11 being filled with the fruits of righteousness which are through Jesus Christ, to the glory and praise of God.

**Gospel: Luke 3: 1-6**

1 Now in the fifteenth year of the reign of Tiberius Caesar, Pontius Pilate being governor of Judea, and Herod being tetrarch of Galilee, and his brother Philip tetrarch of the region of Ituraea and Trachonitis, and Lysanias tetrarch of Abilene, 2 during the high priesthood of Annas and Caiaphas, the word of God came to John, the son of Zacharias, in the wilderness. 3 He came into all the region around the Jordan, preaching the baptism of repentance for remission of sins. 4 As it is written in the book of the words of Isaiah the prophet,

"The voice of one crying in the wilderness,

'Make ready the way of the Lord.

Make his paths straight.

5 Every valley will be filled.

Every mountain and hill will be brought low.

The crooked will become straight,

and the rough ways smooth.

6 All flesh will see God's salvation.' "

1. Invite the Holy Spirit into this reading, asking the Author of Scripture to speak to you through His Word
2. Read today's passage as many times as you need, take your time
3. Write down (below) what the Lord is saying to you today
4. Live with this Word in your heart through the day

_____

_____

## Monday, December 9, 2024
### THE IMMACULATE CONCEPTION OF THE BLESSED VIRGIN MARY
(Patronal Feastday of the United States of America)

**First Reading:** Genesis 3: 9-15, 20

9 Yahweh God called to the man, and said to him, "Where are you?"
10 The man said, "I heard your voice in the garden, and I was afraid, because I was naked; so I hid myself."

11 God said, "Who told you that you were naked? Have you eaten from the tree that I commanded you not to eat from?"

12 The man said, "The woman whom you gave to be with me, she gave me fruit from the tree, and I ate it."

13 Yahweh God said to the woman, "What have you done?"

The woman said, "The serpent deceived me, and I ate."

14 Yahweh God said to the serpent,

"Because you have done this,

you are cursed above all livestock,

and above every animal of the field.

You shall go on your belly

and you shall eat dust all the days of your life.

15 I will put hostility between you and the woman,

and between your offspring and her offspring.

He will bruise your head,

and you will bruise his heel."

20 The man called his wife Eve because she would be the mother of all the living.

**Responsorial Psalm:** Psalms 98: 1-4

1 Sing to Yahweh a new song,

for he has done marvelous things!

His right hand and his holy arm have worked salvation for him.

2 Yahweh has made known his salvation.

He has openly shown his righteousness in the sight of the nations.

3 He has remembered his loving kindness and his faithfulness toward the house of Israel.

All the ends of the earth have seen the salvation of our God.

4 Make a joyful noise to Yahweh, all the earth!

Burst out and sing for joy, yes, sing praises!

**Second Reading:** Ephesians 1: 3-6, 11-12

3 Blessed be the God and Father of our Lord Jesus Christ, who has blessed us with every spiritual blessing in the heavenly places in Christ, 4 even as he chose us in him before the foundation of the world, that we would be holy and without defect before him in love, 5 having predestined us for adoption as children through Jesus Christ to

himself, according to the good pleasure of his desire, 6 to the praise of the glory of his grace, by which he freely gave us favor in the Beloved.

11 We were also assigned an inheritance in him, having been foreordained according to the purpose of him who does all things after the counsel of his will, 12 to the end that we should be to the praise of his glory, we who had before hoped in Christ.

## Gospel: Luke 1: 26-38

26 Now in the sixth month, the angel Gabriel was sent from God to a city of Galilee named Nazareth, 27 to a virgin pledged to be married to a man whose name was Joseph, of David's house. The virgin's name was Mary. 28 Having come in, the angel said to her, "Rejoice, you highly favored one! The Lord is with you. Blessed are you among women!"

29 But when she saw him, she was greatly troubled at the saying, and considered what kind of salutation this might be. 30 The angel said to her, "Don't be afraid, Mary, for you have found favor with God. 31 Behold, you will conceive in your womb and give birth to a son, and shall name him 'Jesus.' 32 He will be great and will be called the Son of the Most High. The Lord God will give him the throne of his father David, 33 and he will reign over the house of Jacob forever. There will be no end to his Kingdom."

34 Mary said to the angel, "How can this be, seeing I am a virgin?"

35 The angel answered her, "The Holy Spirit will come on you, and the power of the Most High will overshadow you. Therefore also the holy one who is born from you will be called the Son of God. 36 Behold, Elizabeth your relative also has conceived a son in her old age; and this is the sixth month with her who was called barren. 37 For nothing spoken by God is impossible."‡

38 Mary said, "Behold, the servant of the Lord; let it be done to me according to your word."

Then the angel departed from her.

1. Invite the Holy Spirit into this reading, asking the Author of Scripture to speak to you through His Word
2. Read today's passage as many times as you need, take your time
3. Write down (below) what the Lord is saying to you today
4. Live with this Word in your heart through the day

_____

_____

**First Reading:** Isaiah 40: 1-11

1 "Comfort, comfort my people," says your God. 2 "Speak comfortably to Jerusalem, and call out to her that her warfare is accomplished, that her iniquity is pardoned, that she has received of Yahweh's hand double for all her sins."
3 The voice of one who calls out,
"Prepare the way of Yahweh in the wilderness!
Make a level highway in the desert for our God.
4 Every valley shall be exalted,
and every mountain and hill shall be made low.
The uneven shall be made level,
and the rough places a plain.
5 Yahweh's glory shall be revealed,
and all flesh shall see it together;
for the mouth of Yahweh has spoken it."
6 The voice of one saying, "Cry out!"
One said, "What shall I cry?"
"All flesh is like grass,
and all its glory is like the flower of the field.
7 The grass withers,
the flower fades,
because Yahweh's breath blows on it.
Surely the people are like grass.
8 The grass withers,
the flower fades;
but the word of our God stands forever."
9 You who tell good news to Zion, go up on a high mountain.
You who tell good news to Jerusalem, lift up your voice with strength!
Lift it up! Don't be afraid!
Say to the cities of Judah, "Behold, your God!"
10 Behold, the Lord Yahweh will come as a mighty one,
and his arm will rule for him.
Behold, his reward is with him,
and his recompense before him.

11 He will feed his flock like a shepherd.
He will gather the lambs in his arm,
and carry them in his bosom.
He will gently lead those who have their young.

**Responsorial Psalm:** Psalms 96: 1-3 and 10-13

1 Sing to Yahweh a new song!
Sing to Yahweh, all the earth.
2 Sing to Yahweh!
Bless his name!
Proclaim his salvation from day to day!
3 Declare his glory among the nations,
his marvelous works among all the peoples.
10 Say among the nations, "Yahweh reigns."
The world is also established.
It can't be moved.
He will judge the peoples with equity.
11 Let the heavens be glad, and let the earth rejoice.
Let the sea roar, and its fullness!
12 Let the field and all that is in it exult!
Then all the trees of the woods shall sing for joy
13 before Yahweh; for he comes,
for he comes to judge the earth.
He will judge the world with righteousness,
the peoples with his truth.

**Gospel: Matthew 18: 12-14**

12 "What do you think? If a man has one hundred sheep, and one of them goes astray, doesn't he leave the ninety-nine, go to the mountains, and seek that which has gone astray? 13 If he finds it, most certainly I tell you, he rejoices over it more than over the ninety-nine which have not gone astray. 14 Even so it is not the will of your Father who is in heaven that one of these little ones should perish.

1. Invite the Holy Spirit into this reading, asking the Author of Scripture to speak to you through His Word
2. Read today's passage as many times as you need, take your time

3. Write down (below) what the Lord is saying to you today
4. Live with this Word in your heart through the day

---

---

**Wednesday, December 11, 2024**
Saint Damasus I, Pope

**First Reading:** Isaiah 40: 25-31

25 "To whom then will you liken me?
Who is my equal?" says the Holy One.
26 Lift up your eyes on high,
and see who has created these,
who brings out their army by number.
He calls them all by name.
By the greatness of his might,
and because he is strong in power,
not one is lacking.

27 Why do you say, Jacob,
and speak, Israel,
"My way is hidden from Yahweh,
and the justice due me is disregarded by my God"?
28 Haven't you known?
Haven't you heard?
The everlasting God, Yahweh,
the Creator of the ends of the earth, doesn't faint.
He isn't weary.
His understanding is unsearchable.
29 He gives power to the weak.
He increases the strength of him who has no might.
30 Even the youths faint and get weary,
and the young men utterly fall;

31 but those who wait for Yahweh will renew their strength.
They will mount up with wings like eagles.
They will run, and not be weary.
They will walk, and not faint.

**Responsorial Psalm:** Psalms 103: 1-4, 8 and 10

1 Praise Yahweh, my soul!
All that is within me, praise his holy name!
2 Praise Yahweh, my soul,
and don't forget all his benefits,
3 who forgives all your sins,
who heals all your diseases,
4 who redeems your life from destruction,
who crowns you with loving kindness and tender mercies,
8 Yahweh is merciful and gracious,
slow to anger, and abundant in loving kindness.
10 He has not dealt with us according to our sins,
nor repaid us for our iniquities.

**Gospel: Matthew 11: 28-30**

28 "Come to me, all you who labor and are heavily burdened, and I will give you rest.
29 Take my yoke upon you and learn from me, for I am gentle and humble in heart;
and you will find rest for your souls. 30 For my yoke is easy, and my burden is light."

1. Invite the Holy Spirit into this reading, asking the Author of Scripture to speak to you through His Word
2. Read today's passage as many times as you need, take your time
3. Write down (below) what the Lord is saying to you today
4. Live with this Word in your heart through the day

_____

_____

## Thursday, December 12, 2024
### Our Lady of Guadalupe

**First Reading:** Revelation 11: 19a; 12: 1-6a, 10ab

19a God's temple that is in heaven was opened, and the ark of the Lord's covenant was seen in his temple.

1 A great sign was seen in heaven: a woman clothed with the sun, and the moon under her feet, and on her head a crown of twelve stars. 2 She was with child. She cried out in pain, laboring to give birth.

3 Another sign was seen in heaven. Behold, a great red dragon, having seven heads and ten horns, and on his heads seven crowns. 4 His tail drew one third of the stars of the sky, and threw them to the earth. The dragon stood before the woman who was about to give birth, so that when she gave birth he might devour her child. 5 She gave birth to a son, a male child, who is to rule all the nations with a rod of iron. Her child was caught up to God and to his throne. 6a The woman fled into the wilderness, where she has a place prepared by God.

10ab I heard a loud voice in heaven, saying, "Now the salvation, the power, and the Kingdom of our God, and the authority of his Christ has come;

**Responsorial Psalm:** Judith 13: 18bcde, 19

18 Ozias said to her, "Blessed are you, daughter, in the sight of the Most High God, above all the women upon the earth; and blessed is the Lord God, who created the heavens and the earth, who directed you to cut off the head of the prince of our enemies. 19 For your hope will not depart from the heart of men that remember the strength of God forever.

**Gospel: Luke 1: 26-38**

26 Now in the sixth month, the angel Gabriel was sent from God to a city of Galilee named Nazareth, 27 to a virgin pledged to be married to a man whose name was Joseph, of David's house. The virgin's name was Mary. 28 Having come in, the angel said to her, "Rejoice, you highly favored one! The Lord is with you. Blessed are you among women!"

29 But when she saw him, she was greatly troubled at the saying, and considered what kind of salutation this might be. 30 The angel said to her, "Don't be afraid, Mary, for

you have found favor with God. 31 Behold, you will conceive in your womb and give birth to a son, and shall name him 'Jesus.' 32 He will be great and will be called the Son of the Most High. The Lord God will give him the throne of his father David, 33 and he will reign over the house of Jacob forever. There will be no end to his Kingdom." 34 Mary said to the angel, "How can this be, seeing I am a virgin?"

35 The angel answered her, "The Holy Spirit will come on you, and the power of the Most High will overshadow you. Therefore also the holy one who is born from you will be called the Son of God. 36 Behold, Elizabeth your relative also has conceived a son in her old age; and this is the sixth month with her who was called barren. 37 For nothing spoken by God is impossible."‡

38 Mary said, "Behold, the servant of the Lord; let it be done to me according to your word."

Then the angel departed from her.

1. Invite the Holy Spirit into this reading, asking the Author of Scripture to speak to you through His Word
2. Read today's passage as many times as you need, take your time
3. Write down (below) what the Lord is saying to you today
4. Live with this Word in your heart through the day

_____

_____

### Friday, December 13, 2024
Saint Lucy, Virgin and Martyr

**First Reading:** Isaiah 48: 17-19

17 Yahweh,
your Redeemer,
the Holy One of Israel, says:
"I am Yahweh your God,
who teaches you to profit,
who leads you by the way that you should go.
18 Oh that you had listened to my commandments!

Then your peace would have been like a river
and your righteousness like the waves of the sea.
19 Your offspring also would have been as the sand
and the descendants of your body like its grains.
His name would not be cut off nor destroyed from before me."

**Responsorial Psalm:** Psalms 1: 1-4 and 6

1 Blessed is the man who doesn't walk in the counsel of the wicked,
nor stand on the path of sinners,
nor sit in the seat of scoffers;
2 but his delight is in Yahweh's† law.
On his law he meditates day and night.
3 He will be like a tree planted by the streams of water,
that produces its fruit in its season,
whose leaf also does not wither.
Whatever he does shall prosper.
4 The wicked are not so,
but are like the chaff which the wind drives away.
6 For Yahweh knows the way of the righteous,
but the way of the wicked shall perish.

**Gospel: Matthew 11: 16-19**

16 "But to what shall I compare this generation? It is like children sitting in the marketplaces, who call to their companions 17 and say, 'We played the flute for you, and you didn't dance. We mourned for you, and you didn't lament.' 18 For John came neither eating nor drinking, and they say, 'He has a demon.' 19 The Son of Man came eating and drinking, and they say, 'Behold, a gluttonous man and a drunkard, a friend of tax collectors and sinners!' But wisdom is justified by her children."

1. Invite the Holy Spirit into this reading, asking the Author of Scripture to speak to you through His Word
2. Read today's passage as many times as you need, take your time
3. Write down (below) what the Lord is saying to you today
4. Live with this Word in your heart through the day

_____

_____

**Saturday, December 14, 2024**
Saint John of the Cross, Priest and Doctor of the Church

**First Reading:** Sirach 48: 1-4, 9-11

1 Then Elijah arose, the prophet like fire.
His word burned like a torch.
2 He brought a famine upon them,
and by his zeal made them few in number.
3 By the word of the Lord he shut up the heavens.
He brought down fire three times.
4 How you were glorified, O Elijah, in your wondrous deeds!
Whose glory is like yours?
9 You were taken up in a tempest of fire,
in a chariot of fiery horses.
10 You were recorded for reproofs in their seasons,
to pacify anger, before it broke out into wrath,
to turn the heart of the father to the son,
and to restore the tribes of Jacob.
11 Blessed are those who saw you,
and those who have been beautified with love;
for we also shall surely live.

**Responsorial Psalm:** Psalms 80: 2ac and 3b, 15-16, 18-19

2 Before Ephraim, Benjamin, and Manasseh, stir up your might!
Come to save us!
3 Turn us again, God.
Cause your face to shine,
and we will be saved.
15 the stock which your right hand planted,
the branch that you made strong for yourself.
16 It's burned with fire.
It's cut down.
They perish at your rebuke.
18 So we will not turn away from you.
Revive us, and we will call on your name.

19 Turn us again, Yahweh God of Armies.
Cause your face to shine, and we will be saved.

**Gospel: Matthew 17: 9a, 10-13**

9 As they were coming down from the mountain, Jesus commanded them, saying, "Don't tell anyone what you saw, until the Son of Man has risen from the dead."
10 His disciples asked him, saying, "Then why do the scribes say that Elijah must come first?"
11 Jesus answered them, "Elijah indeed comes first, and will restore all things; 12 but I tell you that Elijah has come already, and they didn't recognize him, but did to him whatever they wanted to. Even so the Son of Man will also suffer by them." 13 Then the disciples understood that he spoke to them of John the Baptizer.

1. Invite the Holy Spirit into this reading, asking the Author of Scripture to speak to you through His Word
2. Read today's passage as many times as you need, take your time
3. Write down (below) what the Lord is saying to you today
4. Live with this Word in your heart through the day

_____

_____

**Sunday, December 15, 2024**
THIRD SUNDAY OF ADVENT

**First Reading:** Zephaniah 3: 14-18a

14 Sing, daughter of Zion! Shout, Israel! Be glad and rejoice with all your heart, daughter of Jerusalem. 15 Yahweh has taken away your judgments. He has thrown out your enemy. The King of Israel, Yahweh, is among you. You will not be afraid of evil any more. 16 In that day, it will be said to Jerusalem, "Don't be afraid, Zion. Don't let your hands be weak." 17 Yahweh, your God, is among you, a mighty one who will save. He will rejoice over you with joy. He will calm you in his love. He will rejoice over you

with singing. 18 I will remove those who grieve about the appointed feasts from you. They are a burden and a reproach to you.

**Responsorial Psalm:** Isaiah 12: 2-6

2 Behold, God is my salvation. I will trust, and will not be afraid; for Yah, Yahweh, is my strength and song; and he has become my salvation." 3 Therefore with joy you will draw water out of the wells of salvation. 4 In that day you will say, "Give thanks to Yahweh! Call on his name! Declare his doings among the peoples! Proclaim that his name is exalted! 5 Sing to Yahweh, for he has done excellent things! Let this be known in all the earth! 6 Cry aloud and shout, you inhabitant of Zion, for the Holy One of Israel is great among you!"

**Second Reading:** Philippians 4: 4-7

4 Rejoice in the Lord always! Again I will say, "Rejoice!" 5 Let your gentleness be known to all men. The Lord is at hand. 6 In nothing be anxious, but in everything, by prayer and petition with thanksgiving, let your requests be made known to God. 7 And the peace of God, which surpasses all understanding, will guard your hearts and your thoughts in Christ Jesus.

**Gospel: Luke 3: 10-18**

10 The multitudes asked him, "What then must we do?"
11 He answered them, "He who has two coats, let him give to him who has none. He who has food, let him do likewise."
12 Tax collectors also came to be baptized, and they said to him, "Teacher, what must we do?"
13 He said to them, "Collect no more than that which is appointed to you."
14 Soldiers also asked him, saying, "What about us? What must we do?"
He said to them, "Extort from no one by violence, neither accuse anyone wrongfully. Be content with your wages."
15 As the people were in expectation, and all men reasoned in their hearts concerning John, whether perhaps he was the Christ, 16 John answered them all, "I indeed baptize you with water, but he comes who is mightier than I, the strap of whose sandals I am not worthy to loosen. He will baptize you in the Holy Spirit and fire. 17 His winnowing fan is in his hand, and he will thoroughly cleanse his threshing floor, and will gather the wheat into his barn; but he will burn up the chaff with unquenchable fire."

18 Then with many other exhortations he preached good news to the people

_____

_____

## Monday, December 16, 2024

**First Reading:** Numbers 24: 2-7, 15-17

2 Balaam lifted up his eyes, and he saw Israel dwelling according to their tribes; and the Spirit of God came on him. 3 He took up his parable, and said,
"Balaam the son of Beor says,
the man whose eyes are open says;
4 he says, who hears the words of God,
who sees the vision of the Almighty,
falling down, and having his eyes open:
5 How goodly are your tents, Jacob,
and your dwellings, Israel!
6 As valleys they are spread out,
as gardens by the riverside,
as aloes which Yahweh has planted,
as cedar trees beside the waters.
7 Water shall flow from his buckets.
His seed shall be in many waters.
His king shall be higher than Agag.
His kingdom shall be exalted.
15 He took up his parable, and said,
"Balaam the son of Beor says,
the man whose eyes are open says;
16 he says, who hears the words of God,

knows the knowledge of the Most High,
and who sees the vision of the Almighty,
falling down, and having his eyes open:
17 I see him, but not now.
I see him, but not near.
A star will come out of Jacob.
A scepter will rise out of Israel,
and shall strike through the corners of Moab,
and crush all the sons of Sheth.

**Responsorial Psalm:** Psalms 25: 4-9

4 Show me your ways, Yahweh.
Teach me your paths.
5 Guide me in your truth, and teach me,
for you are the God of my salvation.
I wait for you all day long.
6 Yahweh, remember your tender mercies and your loving kindness,
for they are from old times.
7 Don't remember the sins of my youth, nor my transgressions.
Remember me according to your loving kindness,
for your goodness' sake, Yahweh.
8 Good and upright is Yahweh,
therefore he will instruct sinners in the way.
9 He will guide the humble in justice.
He will teach the humble his way.

**Gospel: Matthew 21: 23-27**

23 When he had come into the temple, the chief priests and the elders of the people came to him as he was teaching, and said, "By what authority do you do these things? Who gave you this authority?"
24 Jesus answered them, "I also will ask you one question, which if you tell me, I likewise will tell you by what authority I do these things. 25 The baptism of John, where was it from? From heaven or from men?"
They reasoned with themselves, saying, "If we say, 'From heaven,' he will ask us, 'Why then did you not believe him?' 26 But if we say, 'From men,' we fear the multitude, for all hold John as a prophet." 27 They answered Jesus, and said, "We don't know."

He also said to them, "Neither will I tell you by what authority I do these things.

_____

_____

## Tuesday, December 17, 2024

**First Reading:** Genesis 49: 2, 8-10

2 Assemble yourselves, and hear, you sons of Jacob.
Listen to Israel, your father.
8 "Judah, your brothers will praise you.
Your hand will be on the neck of your enemies.
Your father's sons will bow down before you.
9 Judah is a lion's cub.
From the prey, my son, you have gone up.
He stooped down, he crouched as a lion,
as a lioness.
Who will rouse him up?
10 The scepter will not depart from Judah,
nor the ruler's staff from between his feet,
until he comes to whom it belongs.
The obedience of the peoples will be to him.

**Responsorial Psalm:** Psalms 72: 1-4ab, 7-8, 17

1 God, give the king your justice;
your righteousness to the royal son.
2 He will judge your people with righteousness,
and your poor with justice.

3 The mountains shall bring prosperity to the people.
The hills bring the fruit of righteousness.
4 He will judge the poor of the people.
He will save the children of the needy,
and will break the oppressor in pieces.
7 In his days, the righteous shall flourish,
and abundance of peace, until the moon is no more.
8 He shall have dominion also from sea to sea,
from the River to the ends of the earth.
17 His name endures forever.
His name continues as long as the sun.
Men shall be blessed by him.
All nations will call him blessed.

## Gospel: Matthew 1: 1-17

1 The book of the genealogy of Jesus Christ,† the son of David, the son of Abraham. 2 Abraham became the father of Isaac. Isaac became the father of Jacob. Jacob became the father of Judah and his brothers. 3 Judah became the father of Perez and Zerah by Tamar. Perez became the father of Hezron. Hezron became the father of Ram. 4 Ram became the father of Amminadab. Amminadab became the father of Nahshon. Nahshon became the father of Salmon. 5 Salmon became the father of Boaz by Rahab. Boaz became the father of Obed by Ruth. Obed became the father of Jesse. 6 Jesse became the father of King David. David the king‡ became the father of Solomon by her who had been Uriah's wife. 7 Solomon became the father of Rehoboam. Rehoboam became the father of Abijah. Abijah became the father of Asa. 8 Asa became the father of Jehoshaphat. Jehoshaphat became the father of Joram. Joram became the father of Uzziah. 9 Uzziah became the father of Jotham. Jotham became the father of Ahaz. Ahaz became the father of Hezekiah. 10 Hezekiah became the father of Manasseh. Manasseh became the father of Amon. Amon became the father of Josiah. 11 Josiah became the father of Jechoniah and his brothers at the time of the exile to Babylon.
12 After the exile to Babylon, Jechoniah became the father of Shealtiel. Shealtiel became the father of Zerubbabel. 13 Zerubbabel became the father of Abiud. Abiud became the father of Eliakim. Eliakim became the father of Azor. 14 Azor became the father of Zadok. Zadok became the father of Achim. Achim became the father of Eliud. 15 Eliud became the father of Eleazar. Eleazar became the father of Matthan. Matthan became the father of Jacob. 16 Jacob became the father of Joseph, the husband of Mary, from whom was born Jesus,§ who is called Christ.

17 So all the generations from Abraham to David are fourteen generations; from David to the exile to Babylon fourteen generations; and from the carrying away to Babylon to the Christ, fourteen generations.

1. Invite the Holy Spirit into this reading, asking the Author of Scripture to speak to you through His Word
2. Read today's passage as many times as you need, take your time
3. Write down (below) what the Lord is saying to you today
4. Live with this Word in your heart through the day

_____

_____

## Wednesday, December 18, 2024

**First Reading:** Jeremiah 23: 5-8

5 "Behold, the days come," says Yahweh,
"that I will raise to David a righteous Branch;
and he will reign as king and deal wisely,
and will execute justice and righteousness in the land.
6 In his days Judah will be saved,
and Israel will dwell safely.
This is his name by which he will be called:
Yahweh our righteousness.
7 "Therefore, behold, the days come," says Yahweh, "that they will no more say, 'As Yahweh lives, who brought up the children of Israel out of the land of Egypt;' 8 but, 'As Yahweh lives, who brought up and who led the offspring of the house of Israel out of the north country, and from all the countries where I had driven them.' Then they will dwell in their own land."

**Responsorial Psalm:** Psalms 72: 1-2, 12-13, 18-19

1 God, give the king your justice;
your righteousness to the royal son.

2 He will judge your people with righteousness,
and your poor with justice.
12 For he will deliver the needy when he cries;
the poor, who has no helper.
13 He will have pity on the poor and needy.
He will save the souls of the needy.
18 Praise be to Yahweh God, the God of Israel,
who alone does marvelous deeds.
19 Blessed be his glorious name forever!
Let the whole earth be filled with his glory!
Amen and amen.

## Gospel: Matthew 1: 18-25

18 Now the birth of Jesus Christ was like this: After his mother, Mary, was engaged to Joseph, before they came together, she was found pregnant by the Holy Spirit. 19 Joseph, her husband, being a righteous man, and not willing to make her a public example, intended to put her away secretly. 20 But when he thought about these things, behold,† an angel of the Lord appeared to him in a dream, saying, "Joseph, son of David, don't be afraid to take to yourself Mary as your wife, for that which is conceived in her is of the Holy Spirit. 21 She shall give birth to a son. You shall name him Jesus,‡ for it is he who shall save his people from their sins."
22 Now all this has happened that it might be fulfilled which was spoken by the Lord through the prophet, saying,
23 "Behold, the virgin shall be with child,
and shall give birth to a son.
They shall call his name Immanuel,"
which is, being interpreted, "God with us."*
24 Joseph arose from his sleep, and did as the angel of the Lord commanded him, and took his wife to himself; 25 and didn't know her sexually until she had given birth to her firstborn son. He named him Jesus.

1. Invite the Holy Spirit into this reading, asking the Author of Scripture to speak to you through His Word
2. Read today's passage as many times as you need, take your time
3. Write down (below) what the Lord is saying to you today
4. Live with this Word in your heart through the day

## Thursday, December 19, 2024

**First Reading:** Judges 13: 2-7, 24-25a

2 There was a certain man of Zorah, of the family of the Danites, whose name was Manoah; and his wife was barren, and childless. 3 Yahweh's angel appeared to the woman, and said to her, "See now, you are barren and childless; but you shall conceive and bear a son. 4 Now therefore please beware and drink no wine nor strong drink, and don't eat any unclean thing; 5 for, behold, you shall conceive and give birth to a son. No razor shall come on his head, for the child shall be a Nazirite to God from the womb. He shall begin to save Israel out of the hand of the Philistines."
6 Then the woman came and told her husband, saying, "A man of God came to me, and his face was like the face of the angel of God, very awesome. I didn't ask him where he was from, neither did he tell me his name; 7 but he said to me, 'Behold, you shall conceive and bear a son; and now drink no wine nor strong drink. Don't eat any unclean thing, for the child shall be a Nazirite to God from the womb to the day of his death.' "
24 The woman bore a son and named him Samson. The child grew, and Yahweh blessed him. 25 Yahweh's Spirit began to move him

**Responsorial Psalm:** Psalms 71: 3-6ab, 16-17

3 Be to me a rock of refuge to which I may always go.
Give the command to save me,
for you are my rock and my fortress.
4 Rescue me, my God, from the hand of the wicked,
from the hand of the unrighteous and cruel man.
5 For you are my hope, Lord Yahweh,
my confidence from my youth.
6 I have relied on you from the womb.
You are he who took me out of my mother's womb.
I will always praise you.
16 I will come with the mighty acts of the Lord Yahweh.

I will make mention of your righteousness, even of yours alone.

17 God, you have taught me from my youth.

Until now, I have declared your wondrous works.

## Gospel: Luke 1: 5-25

5 There was in the days of Herod, the king of Judea, a certain priest named Zacharias, of the priestly division of Abijah. He had a wife of the daughters of Aaron, and her name was Elizabeth. 6 They were both righteous before God, walking blamelessly in all the commandments and ordinances of the Lord. 7 But they had no child, because Elizabeth was barren, and they both were well advanced in years.

8 Now while he executed the priest's office before God in the order of his division 9 according to the custom of the priest's office, his lot was to enter into the temple of the Lord and burn incense. 10 The whole multitude of the people were praying outside at the hour of incense.

11 An angel of the Lord appeared to him, standing on the right side of the altar of incense. 12 Zacharias was troubled when he saw him, and fear fell upon him. 13 But the angel said to him, "Don't be afraid, Zacharias, because your request has been heard. Your wife, Elizabeth, will bear you a son, and you shall call his name John. 14 You will have joy and gladness, and many will rejoice at his birth. 15 For he will be great in the sight of the Lord, and he will drink no wine nor strong drink. He will be filled with the Holy Spirit, even from his mother's womb. 16 He will turn many of the children of Israel to the Lord their God. 17 He will go before him in the spirit and power of Elijah, 'to turn the hearts of the fathers to the children,'* and the disobedient to the wisdom of the just; to prepare a people prepared for the Lord."

18 Zacharias said to the angel, "How can I be sure of this? For I am an old man, and my wife is well advanced in years."

19 The angel answered him, "I am Gabriel, who stands in the presence of God. I was sent to speak to you and to bring you this good news. 20 Behold,† you will be silent and not able to speak until the day that these things will happen, because you didn't believe my words, which will be fulfilled in their proper time."

21 The people were waiting for Zacharias, and they marveled that he delayed in the temple. 22 When he came out, he could not speak to them. They perceived that he had seen a vision in the temple. He continued making signs to them, and remained mute. 23 When the days of his service were fulfilled, he departed to his house. 24 After these days Elizabeth his wife conceived, and she hid herself five months, saying, 25 "Thus has the Lord done to me in the days in which he looked at me, to take away my reproach among men."

1. Invite the Holy Spirit into this reading, asking the Author of Scripture to speak to you through His Word
2. Read today's passage as many times as you need, take your time
3. Write down (below) what the Lord is saying to you today
4. Live with this Word in your heart through the day

---

---

## Friday, December 20, 2024

**First Reading:** Isaiah 7: 10-14

10 Yahweh spoke again to Ahaz, saying, 11 "Ask a sign of Yahweh your God; ask it either in the depth, or in the height above."
12 But Ahaz said, "I won't ask. I won't tempt Yahweh."
13 He said, "Listen now, house of David. Is it not enough for you to try the patience of men, that you will try the patience of my God also? 14 Therefore the Lord himself will give you a sign. Behold, the virgin will conceive, and bear a son, and shall call his name Immanuel.

**Responsorial Psalm:** Psalms 24: 1-6

1 The earth is Yahweh's, with its fullness;
the world, and those who dwell in it.
2 For he has founded it on the seas,
and established it on the floods.
3 Who may ascend to Yahweh's hill?
Who may stand in his holy place?
4 He who has clean hands and a pure heart;
who has not lifted up his soul to falsehood,
and has not sworn deceitfully.
5 He shall receive a blessing from Yahweh,
righteousness from the God of his salvation.

6 This is the generation of those who seek Him,
who seek your face—even Jacob.

## Gospel: Luke 1: 26-38

26 Now in the sixth month, the angel Gabriel was sent from God to a city of Galilee named Nazareth, 27 to a virgin pledged to be married to a man whose name was Joseph, of David's house. The virgin's name was Mary. 28 Having come in, the angel said to her, "Rejoice, you highly favored one! The Lord is with you. Blessed are you among women!"

29 But when she saw him, she was greatly troubled at the saying, and considered what kind of salutation this might be. 30 The angel said to her, "Don't be afraid, Mary, for you have found favor with God. 31 Behold, you will conceive in your womb and give birth to a son, and shall name him 'Jesus.' 32 He will be great and will be called the Son of the Most High. The Lord God will give him the throne of his father David, 33 and he will reign over the house of Jacob forever. There will be no end to his Kingdom."

34 Mary said to the angel, "How can this be, seeing I am a virgin?"

35 The angel answered her, "The Holy Spirit will come on you, and the power of the Most High will overshadow you. Therefore also the holy one who is born from you will be called the Son of God. 36 Behold, Elizabeth your relative also has conceived a son in her old age; and this is the sixth month with her who was called barren. 37 For nothing spoken by God is impossible."‡

38 Mary said, "Behold, the servant of the Lord; let it be done to me according to your word."

Then the angel departed from her.

1. Invite the Holy Spirit into this reading, asking the Author of Scripture to speak to you through His Word
2. Read today's passage as many times as you need, take your time
3. Write down (below) what the Lord is saying to you today
4. Live with this Word in your heart through the day

_____

_____

## Saturday, December 21, 2024
### Saint Peter Canisius, Priest and Doctor of the Church

**First Reading:** Zephaniah 3: 14-18a

14 Sing, daughter of Zion! Shout, Israel! Be glad and rejoice with all your heart, daughter of Jerusalem. 15 Yahweh has taken away your judgments. He has thrown out your enemy. The King of Israel, Yahweh, is among you. You will not be afraid of evil any more. 16 In that day, it will be said to Jerusalem, "Don't be afraid, Zion. Don't let your hands be weak." 17 Yahweh, your God, is among you, a mighty one who will save. He will rejoice over you with joy. He will calm you in his love. He will rejoice over you with singing. 18a I will remove those who grieve about the appointed feasts from you.

**Responsorial Psalm:** Psalms 33: 2-3, 11-12, 20-21

2 Give thanks to Yahweh with the lyre.
Sing praises to him with the harp of ten strings.
3 Sing to him a new song.
Play skillfully with a shout of joy!
11 The counsel of Yahweh stands fast forever,
the thoughts of his heart to all generations.
12 Blessed is the nation whose God is Yahweh,
the people whom he has chosen for his own inheritance.
20 Our soul has waited for Yahweh.
He is our help and our shield.
21 For our heart rejoices in him,
because we have trusted in his holy name.

**Gospel: Luke 1: 39-45**

39 Mary arose in those days and went into the hill country with haste, into a city of Judah, 40 and entered into the house of Zacharias and greeted Elizabeth. 41 When Elizabeth heard Mary's greeting, the baby leaped in her womb; and Elizabeth was filled with the Holy Spirit. 42 She called out with a loud voice and said, "Blessed are you among women, and blessed is the fruit of your womb! 43 Why am I so favored, that the mother of my Lord should come to me? 44 For behold, when the voice of your greeting came into my ears, the baby leaped in my womb for joy! 45 Blessed is she who believed,

for there will be a fulfillment of the things which have been spoken to her from the Lord!"

1. Invite the Holy Spirit into this reading, asking the Author of Scripture to speak to you through His Word
2. Read today's passage as many times as you need, take your time
3. Write down (below) what the Lord is saying to you today
4. Live with this Word in your heart through the day

_____

_____

## Sunday, December 22, 2024
### FOURTH SUNDAY OF ADVENT

**First Reading:** Micah 5: 1-4a

1 Now you shall gather yourself in troops,
daughter of troops.
He has laid siege against us.
They will strike the judge of Israel with a rod on the cheek.
2 But you, Bethlehem Ephrathah,
being small among the clans of Judah,
out of you one will come out to me who is to be ruler in Israel;
whose goings out are from of old, from ancient times.
3 Therefore he will abandon them until the time that she who is in labor gives birth.
Then the rest of his brothers will return to the children of Israel.
4 He shall stand, and shall shepherd in the strength of Yahweh,
in the majesty of the name of Yahweh his God.
They will live, for then he will be great to the ends of the earth.

**Responsorial Psalm:** Psalms 80: 2-3, 15-16, 18-19

2 Before Ephraim, Benjamin, and Manasseh, stir up your might!
Come to save us!

3 Turn us again, God.
Cause your face to shine,
and we will be saved.
15 the stock which your right hand planted,
the branch that you made strong for yourself.
16 It's burned with fire.
It's cut down.
They perish at your rebuke.
18 So we will not turn away from you.
Revive us, and we will call on your name.
19 Turn us again, Yahweh God of Armies.
Cause your face to shine, and we will be saved.

**Second Reading:** Hebrews 10: 5-10

5 Therefore when he comes into the world, he says,
"You didn't desire sacrifice and offering,
but you prepared a body for me.
6 You had no pleasure in whole burnt offerings and sacrifices for sin.
7 Then I said, 'Behold, I have come (in the scroll of the book it is written of me)
to do your will, O God.' "*
8 Previously saying, "Sacrifices and offerings and whole burnt offerings and sacrifices for sin you didn't desire, neither had pleasure in them" (those which are offered according to the law), 9 then he has said, "Behold, I have come to do your will." He takes away the first, that he may establish the second, 10 by which will we have been sanctified through the offering of the body of Jesus Christ once for all.

**Gospel: Luke 1: 39-45**

39 Mary arose in those days and went into the hill country with haste, into a city of Judah, 40 and entered into the house of Zacharias and greeted Elizabeth. 41 When Elizabeth heard Mary's greeting, the baby leaped in her womb; and Elizabeth was filled with the Holy Spirit. 42 She called out with a loud voice and said, "Blessed are you among women, and blessed is the fruit of your womb! 43 Why am I so favored, that the mother of my Lord should come to me? 44 For behold, when the voice of your greeting came into my ears, the baby leaped in my womb for joy! 45 Blessed is she who believed, for there will be a fulfillment of the things which have been spoken to her from the Lord!"

1. Invite the Holy Spirit into this reading, asking the Author of Scripture to speak to you through His Word
2. Read today's passage as many times as you need, take your time
3. Write down (below) what the Lord is saying to you today
4. Live with this Word in your heart through the day

_____

_____

## Monday, December 23, 2024
### Saint John of Kanty, Priest

**First Reading:** Malachi 3: 1-4

1 "Behold, I send my messenger, and he will prepare the way before me! The Lord, whom you seek, will suddenly come to his temple. Behold, the messenger of the covenant, whom you desire, is coming!" says Yahweh of Armies. 2 "But who can endure the day of his coming? And who will stand when he appears? For he is like a refiner's fire, and like launderers' soap; 3 and he will sit as a refiner and purifier of silver, and he will purify the sons of Levi, and refine them as gold and silver; and they shall offer to Yahweh offerings in righteousness. 4 Then the offering of Judah and Jerusalem will be pleasant to Yahweh as in the days of old and as in ancient years.

**Responsorial Psalm:** Psalms 25: 4-5ab, 8-9, 10 and 14

4 Show me your ways, Yahweh.
Teach me your paths.
5 Guide me in your truth, and teach me,
for you are the God of my salvation.
I wait for you all day long.
8 Good and upright is Yahweh,
therefore he will instruct sinners in the way.
9 He will guide the humble in justice.
He will teach the humble his way.
10 All the paths of Yahweh are loving kindness and truth

to such as keep his covenant and his testimonies.
14 The friendship of Yahweh is with those who fear him.
He will show them his covenant.

**Gospel: Luke 1: 57-66**

57 Now the time that Elizabeth should give birth was fulfilled, and she gave birth to a son. 58 Her neighbors and her relatives heard that the Lord had magnified his mercy toward her, and they rejoiced with her. 59 On the eighth day, they came to circumcise the child; and they would have called him Zacharias, after the name of his father. 60 His mother answered, "Not so; but he will be called John."
61 They said to her, "There is no one among your relatives who is called by this name."
62 They made signs to his father, what he would have him called.
63 He asked for a writing tablet, and wrote, "His name is John."
They all marveled. 64 His mouth was opened immediately and his tongue freed, and he spoke, blessing God. 65 Fear came on all who lived around them, and all these sayings were talked about throughout all the hill country of Judea. 66 All who heard them laid them up in their heart, saying, "What then will this child be?" The hand of the Lord was with him.

1. Invite the Holy Spirit into this reading, asking the Author of Scripture to speak to you through His Word
2. Read today's passage as many times as you need, take your time
3. Write down (below) what the Lord is saying to you today
4. Live with this Word in your heart through the day

_____

_____

**Tuesday, December 24, 2024**

**First Reading:** Second Samuel 7: 1-5, 8b-12, 14a, 16

1 When the king lived in his house, and Yahweh had given him rest from all his enemies all around, 2 the king said to Nathan the prophet, "See now, I dwell in a house of cedar, but God's ark dwells within curtains."

3 Nathan said to the king, "Go, do all that is in your heart, for Yahweh is with you."

4 That same night, Yahweh's word came to Nathan, saying, 5 "Go and tell my servant David, 'Yahweh says, "Should you build me a house for me to dwell in?

8 Now therefore tell my servant David this: 'Yahweh of Armies says, "I took you from the sheep pen, from following the sheep, to be prince over my people, over Israel. 9 I have been with you wherever you went, and have cut off all your enemies from before you. I will make you a great name, like the name of the great ones who are in the earth. 10 I will appoint a place for my people Israel, and will plant them, that they may dwell in their own place and be moved no more. The children of wickedness will not afflict them any more, as at the first, 11 and as from the day that I commanded judges to be over my people Israel. I will cause you to rest from all your enemies. Moreover Yahweh tells you that Yahweh will make you a house. 12 When your days are fulfilled and you sleep with your fathers, I will set up your offspring after you, who will proceed out of your body, and I will establish his kingdom.

14a I will be his father, and he will be my son. 15 but my loving kindness will not depart from him, as I took it from Saul, whom I put away before you. 16 Your house and your kingdom will be made sure forever before you. Your throne will be established forever."
'

**Responsorial Psalm:** Psalms 89: 2-5, 27 and 29

2 I indeed declare, "Love stands firm forever.
You established the heavens.
Your faithfulness is in them."
3 "I have made a covenant with my chosen one,
I have sworn to David, my servant,
4 'I will establish your offspring forever,
and build up your throne to all generations.' "
5 The heavens will praise your wonders, Yahweh,
your faithfulness also in the assembly of the holy ones.
27 I will also appoint him my firstborn,
the highest of the kings of the earth.
29 I will also make his offspring endure forever,
and his throne as the days of heaven.

### Gospel: Luke 1: 67-79

67 His father Zacharias was filled with the Holy Spirit, and prophesied, saying,
68 "Blessed be the Lord, the God of Israel,
for he has visited and redeemed his people;
69 and has raised up a horn of salvation for us in the house of his servant David
70 (as he spoke by the mouth of his holy prophets who have been from of old),
71 salvation from our enemies and from the hand of all who hate us;
72 to show mercy toward our fathers,
to remember his holy covenant,
73 the oath which he swore to Abraham our father,
74 to grant to us that we, being delivered out of the hand of our enemies,
should serve him without fear,
75 in holiness and righteousness before him all the days of our life.
76 And you, child, will be called a prophet of the Most High;
for you will go before the face of the Lord to prepare his ways,
77 to give knowledge of salvation to his people by the remission of their sins,
78 because of the tender mercy of our God,
by which the dawn from on high will visit us,
79 to shine on those who sit in darkness and the shadow of death;
to guide our feet into the way of peace."

1. Invite the Holy Spirit into this reading, asking the Author of Scripture to speak to you through His Word
2. Read today's passage as many times as you need, take your time
3. Write down (below) what the Lord is saying to you today
4. Live with this Word in your heart through the day

_____

_____

### Wednesday, December 25, 2024
### THE NATIVITY OF THE LORD (Christmas)

**First Reading:** Isaiah 52: 7-10

7 How beautiful on the mountains are the feet of him who brings good news,
who publishes peace,
who brings good news,
who proclaims salvation,
who says to Zion, "Your God reigns!"
8 Your watchmen lift up their voice.
Together they sing;
for they shall see eye to eye when Yahweh returns to Zion.
9 Break out into joy!
Sing together, you waste places of Jerusalem;
for Yahweh has comforted his people.
He has redeemed Jerusalem.
10 Yahweh has made his holy arm bare in the eyes of all the nations.
All the ends of the earth have seen the salvation of our God.

**Responsorial Psalm:** Psalms 98: 1-6

1 Sing to Yahweh a new song,
for he has done marvelous things!
His right hand and his holy arm have worked salvation for him.
2 Yahweh has made known his salvation.
He has openly shown his righteousness in the sight of the nations.
3 He has remembered his loving kindness and his faithfulness toward the house of Israel.
All the ends of the earth have seen the salvation of our God.
4 Make a joyful noise to Yahweh, all the earth!
Burst out and sing for joy, yes, sing praises!
5 Sing praises to Yahweh with the harp,
with the harp and the voice of melody.
6 With trumpets and sound of the ram's horn,
make a joyful noise before the King, Yahweh.

**Second Reading:** Hebrews 1: 1-6

1 God, having in the past spoken to the fathers through the prophets at many times and in various ways, 2 has at the end of these days spoken to us by his Son, whom he appointed heir of all things, through whom also he made the worlds. 3 His Son is the radiance of his glory, the very image of his substance, and upholding all things by the

word of his power, who, when he had by himself purified us of our sins, sat down on the right hand of the Majesty on high, 4 having become as much better than the angels as the more excellent name he has inherited is better than theirs. 5 For to which of the angels did he say at any time,
"You are my Son.
Today I have become your father?"*
and again,
"I will be to him a Father,
and he will be to me a Son?"*
6 When he again brings in the firstborn into the world he says, "Let all the angels of God worship him."

## Gospel: John 1: 1-18

1 In the beginning was the Word, and the Word was with God, and the Word was God. 2 The same was in the beginning with God. 3 All things were made through him. Without him, nothing was made that has been made. 4 In him was life, and the life was the light of men. 5 The light shines in the darkness, and the darkness hasn't overcome† it.
6 There came a man sent from God, whose name was John. 7 The same came as a witness, that he might testify about the light, that all might believe through him. 8 He was not the light, but was sent that he might testify about the light. 9 The true light that enlightens everyone was coming into the world.
10 He was in the world, and the world was made through him, and the world didn't recognize him. 11 He came to his own, and those who were his own didn't receive him. 12 But as many as received him, to them he gave the right to become God's children, to those who believe in his name: 13 who were born, not of blood, nor of the will of the flesh, nor of the will of man, but of God.
14 The Word became flesh and lived among us. We saw his glory, such glory as of the only born‡ Son of the Father, full of grace and truth. 15 John testified about him. He cried out, saying, "This was he of whom I said, 'He who comes after me has surpassed me, for he was before me.' " 16 From his fullness we all received grace upon grace. 17 For the law was given through Moses. Grace and truth were realized through Jesus Christ.§ 18 No one has seen God at any time. The only born† Son,‡ who is in the bosom of the Father, has declared him.

1. Invite the Holy Spirit into this reading, asking the Author of Scripture to speak to you through His Word

2. Read today's passage as many times as you need, take your time
3. Write down (below) what the Lord is saying to you today
4. Live with this Word in your heart through the day

_____

_____

**Thursday, December 26, 2024**
Saint Stephen, The First Martyr

**First Reading:** Acts 6: 8-10; 7: 54-59

8 Stephen, full of faith and power, performed great wonders and signs among the people. 9 But some of those who were of the synagogue called "The Libertines", and of the Cyrenians, of the Alexandrians, and of those of Cilicia and Asia arose, disputing with Stephen. 10 They weren't able to withstand the wisdom and the Spirit by which he spoke.

54 Now when they heard these things, they were cut to the heart, and they gnashed at him with their teeth. 55 But he, being full of the Holy Spirit, looked up steadfastly into heaven and saw the glory of God, and Jesus standing on the right hand of God, 56 and said, "Behold, I see the heavens opened and the Son of Man standing at the right hand of God!"

57 But they cried out with a loud voice and stopped their ears, then rushed at him with one accord. 58 They threw him out of the city and stoned him. The witnesses placed their garments at the feet of a young man named Saul. 59 They stoned Stephen as he called out, saying, "Lord Jesus, receive my spirit!"

**Responsorial Psalm:** Psalms 31: 3cd-4, 6 and 8ab, 16bc and 17

3 For you are my rock and my fortress,
therefore for your name's sake lead me and guide me.
4 Pluck me out of the net that they have laid secretly for me,
for you are my stronghold.
6 I hate those who regard lying vanities,
but I trust in Yahweh.

8 You have not shut me up into the hand of the enemy.
You have set my feet in a large place.
16 Make your face to shine on your servant.
Save me in your loving kindness.
17 Let me not be disappointed, Yahweh, for I have called on you.
Let the wicked be disappointed.

## Gospel: Matthew 10: 17-22

17 But beware of men, for they will deliver you up to councils, and in their synagogues they will scourge you. 18 Yes, and you will be brought before governors and kings for my sake, for a testimony to them and to the nations. 19 But when they deliver you up, don't be anxious how or what you will say, for it will be given you in that hour what you will say. 20 For it is not you who speak, but the Spirit of your Father who speaks in you.
21 "Brother will deliver up brother to death, and the father his child. Children will rise up against parents and cause them to be put to death. 22 You will be hated by all men for my name's sake, but he who endures to the end will be saved.

1. Invite the Holy Spirit into this reading, asking the Author of Scripture to speak to you through His Word
2. Read today's passage as many times as you need, take your time
3. Write down (below) what the Lord is saying to you today
4. Live with this Word in your heart through the day

_____

_____

## Friday, December 27, 2024
Saint John, Apostle and Evangelist

**First Reading:** First John 1: 1-4

1 That which was from the beginning, that which we have heard, that which we have seen with our eyes, that which we saw, and our hands touched, concerning the Word

of life 2 (and the life was revealed, and we have seen, and testify, and declare to you the life, the eternal life, which was with the Father, and was revealed to us); 3 that which we have seen and heard we declare to you, that you also may have fellowship with us. Yes, and our fellowship is with the Father and with his Son, Jesus Christ.† 4 And we write these things to you, that our joy may be fulfilled.

**Responsorial Psalm:** Psalms 97: 1-2, 5-6, 11-12

1 Yahweh reigns!
Let the earth rejoice!
Let the multitude of islands be glad!
2 Clouds and darkness are around him.
Righteousness and justice are the foundation of his throne.
5 The mountains melt like wax at the presence of Yahweh,
at the presence of the Lord of the whole earth.
6 The heavens declare his righteousness.
All the peoples have seen his glory.
11 Light is sown for the righteous,
and gladness for the upright in heart.
12 Be glad in Yahweh, you righteous people!
Give thanks to his holy Name.

**Gospel: John 20: 1a and 2-8**

1 Now on the first day of the week, Mary Magdalene went early, while it was still dark, to the tomb, and saw that the stone had been taken away from the tomb. 2 Therefore she ran and came to Simon Peter and to the other disciple whom Jesus loved, and said to them, "They have taken away the Lord out of the tomb, and we don't know where they have laid him!"
3 Therefore Peter and the other disciple went out, and they went toward the tomb. 4 They both ran together. The other disciple outran Peter and came to the tomb first. 5 Stooping and looking in, he saw the linen cloths lying there; yet he didn't enter in. 6 Then Simon Peter came, following him, and entered into the tomb. He saw the linen cloths lying, 7 and the cloth that had been on his head, not lying with the linen cloths, but rolled up in a place by itself. 8 So then the other disciple who came first to the tomb also entered in, and he saw and believed.

1. Invite the Holy Spirit into this reading, asking the Author of Scripture to speak to you through His Word
2. Read today's passage as many times as you need, take your time
3. Write down (below) what the Lord is saying to you today
4. Live with this Word in your heart through the day

_____

_____

## Saturday, December 28, 2024
### The Holy Innocents, Martyrs

**First Reading:** First John 1: 5 – 2: 2

5 This is the message which we have heard from him and announce to you, that God is light, and in him is no darkness at all. 6 If we say that we have fellowship with him and walk in the darkness, we lie and don't tell the truth. 7 But if we walk in the light as he is in the light, we have fellowship with one another, and the blood of Jesus Christ his Son, cleanses us from all sin. 8 If we say that we have no sin, we deceive ourselves, and the truth is not in us. 9 If we confess our sins, he is faithful and righteous to forgive us the sins and to cleanse us from all unrighteousness. 10 If we say that we haven't sinned, we make him a liar, and his word is not in us.
1 My little children, I write these things to you so that you may not sin. If anyone sins, we have a Counselor† with the Father, Jesus Christ, the righteous. 2 And he is the atoning sacrifice‡ for our sins, and not for ours only, but also for the whole world.

**Responsorial Psalm:** Psalms 124: 2-5, 7b-8

2 if it had not been Yahweh who was on our side,
when men rose up against us,
3 then they would have swallowed us up alive,
when their wrath was kindled against us,
4 then the waters would have overwhelmed us,
the stream would have gone over our soul.
5 Then the proud waters would have gone over our soul.

7b The snare is broken, and we have escaped.
8 Our help is in Yahweh's name,
who made heaven and earth.

### Gospel: Matthew 2: 13-18

13 Now when they had departed, behold, an angel of the Lord appeared to Joseph in a dream, saying, "Arise and take the young child and his mother, and flee into Egypt, and stay there until I tell you, for Herod will seek the young child to destroy him."
14 He arose and took the young child and his mother by night and departed into Egypt, 15 and was there until the death of Herod, that it might be fulfilled which was spoken by the Lord through the prophet, saying, "Out of Egypt I called my son."*
16 Then Herod, when he saw that he was mocked by the wise men, was exceedingly angry, and sent out and killed all the male children who were in Bethlehem and in all the surrounding countryside, from two years old and under, according to the exact time which he had learned from the wise men. 17 Then that which was spoken by Jeremiah the prophet was fulfilled, saying,
18 "A voice was heard in Ramah,
lamentation, weeping and great mourning,
Rachel weeping for her children;
she wouldn't be comforted,
because they are no more."

1. Invite the Holy Spirit into this reading, asking the Author of Scripture to speak to you through His Word
2. Read today's passage as many times as you need, take your time
3. Write down (below) what the Lord is saying to you today
4. Live with this Word in your heart through the day

_____

_____

### Sunday, December 29, 2024
### THE HOLY FAMILY OF JESUS, MARY AND JOSEPH

**First Reading:** First Samuel 1: 20-22, 24-28

20 When the time had come, Hannah conceived, and bore a son; and she named him Samuel,§ saying, "Because I have asked him of Yahweh."
21 The man Elkanah, and all his house, went up to offer to Yahweh the yearly sacrifice and his vow. 22 But Hannah didn't go up, for she said to her husband, "Not until the child is weaned; then I will bring him, that he may appear before Yahweh, and stay there forever."
24 When she had weaned him, she took him up with her, with three bulls, and one ephah† of meal, and a container of wine, and brought him to Yahweh's house in Shiloh. The child was young. 25 They killed the bull, and brought the child to Eli. 26 She said, "Oh, my lord, as your soul lives, my lord, I am the woman who stood by you here, praying to Yahweh. 27 I prayed for this child, and Yahweh has given me my petition which I asked of him. 28 Therefore I have also given him to Yahweh. As long as he lives he is given to Yahweh." He worshiped Yahweh there.

**Responsorial Psalm:** Psalms 84: 2-3, 5-6, 9-10

2 My soul longs, and even faints for the courts of Yahweh.
My heart and my flesh cry out for the living God.
3 Yes, the sparrow has found a home,
and the swallow a nest for herself, where she may have her young,
near your altars, Yahweh of Armies, my King, and my God.
5 Blessed are those whose strength is in you,
who have set their hearts on a pilgrimage.
6 Passing through the valley of Weeping, they make it a place of springs.
Yes, the autumn rain covers it with blessings.
9 Behold, God our shield,
look at the face of your anointed.
10 For a day in your courts is better than a thousand.
I would rather be a doorkeeper in the house of my God,
than to dwell in the tents of wickedness.

**Second Reading:** First John 3: 1-2, 21-24

1 See how great a love the Father has given to us, that we should be called children of God! For this cause the world doesn't know us, because it didn't know him. 2 Beloved,

now we are children of God. It is not yet revealed what we will be; but we know that when he is revealed, we will be like him, for we will see him just as he is.

21 Beloved, if our hearts don't condemn us, we have boldness toward God; 22 so whatever we ask, we receive from him, because we keep his commandments and do the things that are pleasing in his sight. 23 This is his commandment, that we should believe in the name of his Son, Jesus Christ, and love one another, even as he commanded. 24 He who keeps his commandments remains in him, and he in him. By this we know that he remains in us, by the Spirit which he gave us.

## Gospel: Luke 2: 41-52

41 His parents went every year to Jerusalem at the feast of the Passover. 42 When he was twelve years old, they went up to Jerusalem according to the custom of the feast; 43 and when they had fulfilled the days, as they were returning, the boy Jesus stayed behind in Jerusalem. Joseph and his mother didn't know it, 44 but supposing him to be in the company, they went a day's journey; and they looked for him among their relatives and acquaintances. 45 When they didn't find him, they returned to Jerusalem, looking for him. 46 After three days they found him in the temple, sitting in the middle of the teachers, both listening to them and asking them questions. 47 All who heard him were amazed at his understanding and his answers. 48 When they saw him, they were astonished; and his mother said to him, "Son, why have you treated us this way? Behold, your father and I were anxiously looking for you."

49 He said to them, "Why were you looking for me? Didn't you know that I must be in my Father's house?" 50 They didn't understand the saying which he spoke to them. 51 And he went down with them and came to Nazareth. He was subject to them, and his mother kept all these sayings in her heart. 52 And Jesus increased in wisdom and stature, and in favor with God and men.

1. Invite the Holy Spirit into this reading, asking the Author of Scripture to speak to you through His Word
2. Read today's passage as many times as you need, take your time
3. Write down (below) what the Lord is saying to you today
4. Live with this Word in your heart through the day

_____

_____

**First Reading:** First John 2: 12-17

12 I write to you, little children, because your sins are forgiven you for his name's sake.
13 I write to you, fathers, because you know him who is from the beginning.
I write to you, young men, because you have overcome the evil one.
I write to you, little children, because you know the Father.
14 I have written to you, fathers, because you know him who is from the beginning.
I have written to you, young men, because you are strong, and the word of God remains in you, and you have overcome the evil one.
15 Don't love the world or the things that are in the world. If anyone loves the world, the Father's love isn't in him. 16 For all that is in the world—the lust of the flesh, the lust of the eyes, and the pride of life—isn't the Father's, but is the world's. 17 The world is passing away with its lusts, but he who does God's will remains forever.

**Responsorial Psalm:** Psalms 96: 7-10

7 Ascribe to Yahweh, you families of nations,
ascribe to Yahweh glory and strength.
8 Ascribe to Yahweh the glory due to his name.
Bring an offering, and come into his courts.
9 Worship Yahweh in holy array.
Tremble before him, all the earth.
10 Say among the nations, "Yahweh reigns."
The world is also established.
It can't be moved.
He will judge the peoples with equity.

**Gospel: Luke 2: 36-40**

36 There was one Anna, a prophetess, the daughter of Phanuel, of the tribe of Asher (she was of a great age, having lived with a husband seven years from her virginity, 37 and she had been a widow for about eighty-four years), who didn't depart from the temple, worshiping with fastings and petitions night and day. 38 Coming up at that

very hour, she gave thanks to the Lord, and spoke of him to all those who were looking for redemption in Jerusalem.

39 When they had accomplished all things that were according to the law of the Lord, they returned into Galilee, to their own city, Nazareth. 40 The child was growing, and was becoming strong in spirit, being filled with wisdom, and the grace of God was upon him.

1. Invite the Holy Spirit into this reading, asking the Author of Scripture to speak to you through His Word
2. Read today's passage as many times as you need, take your time
3. Write down (below) what the Lord is saying to you today
4. Live with this Word in your heart through the day

_____

_____

# Tuesday, December 31, 2024
## Seventh Day within the Octave of the Nativity of the Lord
### Saint Sylvester I, Pope

**First Reading:** First John 2: 18-21

18 Little children, these are the end times, and as you heard that the Antichrist is coming, even now many antichrists have arisen. By this we know that it is the final hour. 19 They went out from us, but they didn't belong to us; for if they had belonged to us, they would have continued with us. But they left, that they might be revealed that none of them belong to us. 20 You have an anointing from the Holy One, and you all have knowledge.§ 21 I have not written to you because you don't know the truth, but because you know it, and because no lie is of the truth.

**Responsorial Psalm:** Psalms 96: 1-2, 11-13

1 Sing to Yahweh a new song!
Sing to Yahweh, all the earth.

2 Sing to Yahweh!
Bless his name!
Proclaim his salvation from day to day!
11 Let the heavens be glad, and let the earth rejoice.
Let the sea roar, and its fullness!
12 Let the field and all that is in it exult!
Then all the trees of the woods shall sing for joy
13 before Yahweh; for he comes,
for he comes to judge the earth.
He will judge the world with righteousness,
the peoples with his truth.

### Gospel: John 1: 1-18

1 In the beginning was the Word, and the Word was with God, and the Word was God. 2 The same was in the beginning with God. 3 All things were made through him. Without him, nothing was made that has been made. 4 In him was life, and the life was the light of men. 5 The light shines in the darkness, and the darkness hasn't overcome† it.

6 There came a man sent from God, whose name was John. 7 The same came as a witness, that he might testify about the light, that all might believe through him. 8 He was not the light, but was sent that he might testify about the light. 9 The true light that enlightens everyone was coming into the world.

10 He was in the world, and the world was made through him, and the world didn't recognize him. 11 He came to his own, and those who were his own didn't receive him. 12 But as many as received him, to them he gave the right to become God's children, to those who believe in his name: 13 who were born, not of blood, nor of the will of the flesh, nor of the will of man, but of God.

14 The Word became flesh and lived among us. We saw his glory, such glory as of the only born‡ Son of the Father, full of grace and truth. 15 John testified about him. He cried out, saying, "This was he of whom I said, 'He who comes after me has surpassed me, for he was before me.' " 16 From his fullness we all received grace upon grace. 17 For the law was given through Moses. Grace and truth were realized through Jesus Christ.§ 18 No one has seen God at any time. The only born† Son,‡ who is in the bosom of the Father, has declared him.

1. Invite the Holy Spirit into this reading, asking the Author of Scripture to speak to you through His Word

2. Read today's passage as many times as you need, take your time
3. Write down (below) what the Lord is saying to you today
4. Live with this Word in your heart through the day

_____

_____

Made in the USA
Coppell, TX
29 September 2024